Shell Script
Pearls

Ron Peters

16
Ton

PRESS

Shell Script Pearls

ISBN: 978-0-6151-4105-3

Trademarks

All terms mentioned in this book that are known to be trademarks or service marks have been appropriately capitalized. Use of a term in this book should not be regarded as affecting the validity of any trademark or service mark. All other trademarks are the property of their respective owners.

Disclaimer

This book is designed to provide information about shell scripting. Every effort has been made to make this book as complete and as accurate as possible, but no warranty or fitness is implied.

The information is provided on an as-is basis. The author and 16 Ton Press shall have neither liability nor responsibility to any person or entity with respect to any loss or damages arising from the information contained in this book.

Composed in vim and Open Office Writer.

Acknowledgments

As with most things in this world, we are dependent on others. This book is no exception and since this is a project larger than most I have taken on, I could not have done this alone. I would firstly and most importantly like to thank my God for the free gift of life[1] as well as the skills and abilities that enabled me to write this book[2]. I would also like to thank my wife Kathleen and my two boys Austin and Grant for enduring the seemingly endless hours and evenings I've been spending with my laptop.

I want to express my gratitude to the two Brians: To Brian Grell for giving me ideas and discussing many topics that have now found their way into this book. And to Brian Culp for reviewing the whole book and keeping me focused on what I'm trying to say and asking the right questions so I can maintain clarity.

Finally, I want to thank all the other editors who have had a hand in helping me remove the Englilsh[3] from my writing.

---

1 Romans 6:23 New International Version (NIV)
2 Deuteronomy 8:17-18 New Inernational Version (NIV)
3 http://www.homestarrunner.com/sbemail64.swf

Contents

Preface

I learned the basics of programming when I was in school; I learned how to shell script by example.

I've met and worked with many system administrators and other *NIX folks, each of which have their own bag of tricks when it comes to managing a system, interacting with their environment or coding a script. It's always very useful to have conversations and interact with people like this because you invariably gain some tidbits that you can throw into your own collection of tricks. I decided that putting together a book that contained all the useful shell scripting and interaction techniques that I have gained through the years in one place would make a very beneficial reference guide. In fact, I have used this collection of notes during its initial writing. Since I haven't memorized everything in my book, I would periodically look up items when I was working on various tasks. I want this book to be the beginning of a higher level reference library that can be added upon and continually grow.

You might be aware of the large number of shell scripting books and on-line resources aiding in the mastery of shell scripting. Many are excellent and cover a wide range of topics. The main purpose of this book is to combine some of the more unique tools, snippets of code and scripts that go beyond the level of basic scripts. I wanted to create a cookbook of sorts somewhat less obvious recipes and more advanced algorithms that have proved useful to me in the past.

I have included scripts that can be used as is and sample scripts that illustrate a specific algorithm. Sometimes I just demonstrate a few complex commands that may be useful right there on the command line. I have tried to tailor the scripts to be useful at multiple levels. Most times, however, there is little or no error checking since that is not necessarily the point of a specific script. You need to be prepared to make modifications to fit your local environment.

How it Came About

My friend Brian Culp and I have worked together as UNIX system administrators for many years. Periodically, Brian or I will be working on some script and run into a problem. One of us will stop, walk over to the other and say something like: "do you have any code that does X?". The answer may be no, in which case we'll launch into a discussion on how we might tackle the problem or come up with a few different solutions. However, many times it might be something like: "hmm, yeah, I think I remember doing something like that in a script that does X on system Y. Let me look for a minute". A few carefully chosen `grep` commands and the solution is at hand.

Although finding the solution we want is great, it's not the most efficient use of our time. To go from having a place to store and organize all of our (and, of course, other programmers') gems, and having them in a heavily documented form, to writing a book on the subject was only a short step. Even though it is possible to search quickly for specific code from on-line references, there were many occasions when I just wanted to pull a physical book off my shelf. It's not always obvious what to search for when you have a specific itch that needs scratching and, thus, you're not sure what exactly to search for.

I also hoped that once the first edition of this book had been published, others in the user community would have additional ideas for subsequent editions. This book could become a community driven reference manual. This is to some extent an expression of my own limitations: my family and friends think I'm a computer guru, but rest assured, I know better. There are many programmers out there who are much more adept at shell coding than I am. I mainly intended to collect, order and explain code that I have found to be highly useful in my professional experience as a system administrator, and share them with others who may also put them to good use.

Who Should Read This Book

The book is meant for the intermediate shell coder up to the advanced shell code hacker, since I'm not explaining many basic programming structures. Those who would want that type of book should probably look to some of the other resources mentioned in Appendix C.

This is not to say that the beginner may not want to use this book, since it may actually be of some use as a supplementary reference to a more traditional shell scripting training guide. But there is a difference between learning English as a second language and learning how to apply sarcasm. The latter requires some experience with the former. In any case, learning how to code in a programming language is often helped by the use of many examples.

I've tried to go into great detail about how and why the scripts were written in their present form, but I also have some explanation of how to avoid some problems. Even though much of my learning came from sources heavy in obfuscation and light on clarity, I tried to be as explicit as possible and probably in some cases, I tried to explain too much rather than too little. You can think of many chapters I included as shell scripts with extremely detailed commentary.

What is Included

The book is roughly ordered into four main categories: Variables and General Scripting, User Input, Text Processing and System Administration. Many of the scripts and discussions could be moved to other sections as they illustrate more than just the points emphasized by the section headers. Most chapters have been written as stand alone discussions although they may refer to other chapters on some minor points.

The Variables and General Scripting section covers the more basic levels of scripting including debugging, library functions, variable usage techniques among others. The User Input section relates to script and shell interaction with an end user. The Text Processing section covers script based interaction with text files and other forms of text; Finally, the System Administration section covers tasks relating to computer system maintenance.

How it Was Written

Most of the code has been tested on a Gentoo Linux system. Much of the code has been run on other variations of Linux as well as some HP-UX and Solaris but the latter were not part of our present testing process.

The source text for this book was written using `vi` (actually `vim`) and then later processed in Open Office through many editing revisions. I wouldn't force the `vi` editor on anyone, but I really like `vi` as an editor and with practice have become quite proficient. I have no ill will toward you `emacs` folks out there, I'm sure you feel just as warm and fuzzy about your editor choice as I do.

Issues and Ideas

I have made every effort to test the code that is included in this book to validate that it works prior to inclusion. With a project of this size however, even with the number of eyes that have reviewed it, there may be mistakes. I would like to know about the mistakes as well as, and more importantly, any other ideas and scripts that could be used for future revisions of this book. Please drop me a note at rbpeters@peterro.com.

Chapter 1: Shell Script

Debugging

Even though this book isn't a '*how to script*' manual, there are a couple of issues that should be discussed. Debugging is one of them. Debugging code is a significant part of writing code. No matter how disciplined you are or how skilled you become at coding, you will have bugs in your code. These bugs will take the form of either syntax or logic errors. The syntactical problems tend to be more simple to resolve since many times they show up when the code throws an error when it is run. The logical bugs tend to be more difficult to track down since the code may run without error, but the resulting output does not match the design of the program. The more complex your code becomes as your skill increases, the more difficult these types of problems will be to detect.

Since writing bug free code is nearly an impossibility, you will need to have a few techniques up your sleeve that will help you finish, diagnose, repair, and clean up your code. Here are are a few ways to debug code that I have consistently used, which help me extract details from the inner workings of my scripts. These techniques validate that the code is living up to my expectations and demonstrate where the code needs more work to perform the task that was intended.

Shell Trace Options

The first technique is the simplest to implement and can give you great amounts of detail on how the logic is progressing and the values of variables internal to your script. It is the `set` tool. At least that's what I call it. It's really just the use of shell options to display verbose output when the script is running. One of the functions of the `set` command is to turn on and off the various options that are available in the shell. In this case, the option being set is -x or xtrace. This is where the running script will in addition to any normal output, display the expanded commands and variables of a given line of code before the code is run. With this increased output, you can easily view what is happening in the running script and possibly determine where your problem may lie.

When you put the instruction `set -x` into your script, each of the commands that execute after that `set` instruction will be displayed, together with any arguments that were supplied to the command, including variables and their values. each of these lines of output will be preceded by a '+' prompt to designate it as part of the trace output. Traced commands from the running shell that are being executed in a sub shell are denoted by a double '++' plus sign.

To demonstrate what the use of `set -x` can do for you, consider this script:

```
#!/bin/sh
#set -x
echo -n "Can you write device drivers? "
read answer
answer=`echo $answer | tr [a-z] [A-Z]`
if [ $answer = Y ]
then
  echo "Wow, you must be very skilled"
else
  echo "Neither can I, I'm just an example shell script"
fi
```

Note that the `set -x` line is currently commented out. When this script is entered in the file `example` and run, the behavior is as expected.

```
$ ./example
Can you write device drivers? y
Wow, you must be very skilled
```

Or:

```
$ ./example
Can you write device drivers? n
Neither can I, Im just an example shell script
```

This is the output when the `set -x` line is uncommented:

```
$ ./example
```

```
+ echo -n 'Can you write device drivers? '
Can you write device drivers? + read answer
y
++ tr '[a-z]' '[A-Z]'
++ echo y
+ answer=Y
+ '[' Y = Y ']'
+ echo Wow, you must be very skilled
Wow, you must be very skilled
```

Or:

```
$ ./example
+ echo -n 'Can you write device drivers? '
Can you write device drivers? + read answer
n
++ echo n
++ tr '[a-z]' '[A-Z]'
+ answer=N
+ '[' N = Y ']'
+ echo Neither can I, Im just an example shell script
Neither can I, Im just an example shell script
```

The output is a verbose trace of the execution of the script. Note that the lines without the '+' sign are the actual output of the script that are normally displayed. As you can see this type of trace is highly useful in determining the value that variables contain during the execution of a script as well as the route that the code took based on the conditions satisfied.

There is another shell option that is a slight variation of this output that can also be used for troubleshooting. The -v option to the shell is verbose mode and will display its input to standard error as it is read. In the case of a shell script, each line of code that is encountered during execution is output to standard error along with any other output from the script. This is the output from the same script when the set -v line is implemented:

```
$ ./example
echo -n "Can you write device drivers? "
Can you write device drivers? read answer
y
```

```
answer=`echo $answer | tr [a-z] [A-Z]`

echo $answer | tr [a-z] [A-Z]if [ $answer = Y ]
then
   echo "Wow, you must be very skilled"
else
   echo "Neither can I; I'm just an example shell script"
fi
Wow, you must be very skilled
```

Or:

```
$ ./example
echo -n "Can you write device drivers? "
Can you write device drivers? read answer
n
answer=`echo $answer | tr [a-z] [A-Z]`

echo $answer | tr [a-z] [A-Z]if [ $answer = Y ]
then
   echo "Wow, you must be very skilled"
else
   echo "Neither can I; I'm just an example shell script"
fi
Neither can I; I'm just an example shell script
```

The verbose (-v) option to the shell is more useful if you simply want to see the running code of the script that you're working with as opposed to the expanded values of variables to make sure the code is working as designed with the xtrace (-x) option. Both options can be used together by using set -xv and you'll see both types of output at the same time although it may be difficult to wade through.

Both of these options are valuable in their on way for troubleshooting both logical and syntactical problems. As with all options to the shell, they can be turned on and off. The syntax is the opposite of turning an option on. Instead of using a - sign such as -x, you would replace it with a + sign as in +x. This will disable the option from that point on. This is very useful if you only want to debug a small portion of the script. You would enable the option just prior to the problem area of code and disable it just after so you aren't inundated with irrelevant output.

Simple Output Statements

The next form of debugging output is also very simple, but it is used frequently to gather specific variable values from a running script as opposed to displaying potentially large amounts of data using the `set -x` option. This is the use of `echo` or `print` statements in the code. These commands are typically used for simple output of a script to some type of display or file. In this case however, These will be used as somewhat of a checkpoint in the code to validate variable assignments.

There are at least a couple of ways that these additional output instructions are typically used. The first is to output the value of a specific variable at a specific time. Sometimes variables get changed when you aren't expecting them to be, and adding a simple output line will show this. The main advantage of this type of output compared to `set -x` is that you have the ability to format your output for ease of reading. While `set -x` has a valid use and is valuable in tracing through the running of a script, it can be somewhat cumbersome to dissect the exact piece of data that you're looking for. With an `echo` or `print` statement, you can display a single line of output with multiple variables that include some headings for easy reading. The following line is an example of what you might use:

```
echo Var1: $var1 Var2: $var2 Var3: $var3
```

The output doesn't need to be polished since it is simply for your validation and troubleshooting but you will want it to be meaningful. This way, you can see the exact data at the exact spot in the code that you're looking for.

The second way is to output a debugging line to verify that the logic is correct for known input data. If you are running a script which should have known results but does not, it may contain a logical error where what you've designed and what you've coded don't quite match. These can be difficult to find. Adding some `echo` statements in key positions can reveal the flow of control through the script as it executes and so validate whether you are performing the right logical steps.

I've slightly modified the script to add a couple of `echo` statements at two key positions where only one of the two statements will be executed because of the if statement. The value here is that with this you not only see the output of the statement itself, but you know which condition of the if statement the code executed. In this very simple example code, you already see this because there is an `echo` statement as part of the original code. In the event where there may be many conditions and comparisons without output, these types of statements are very valuable in determining if your logic is correct.

```
#!/bin/sh
```

```
echo -n "Can you write device drivers? "
read answer
answer=`echo $answer | tr [a-z] [A-Z]`

if [ $answer = Y ]
then
  echo Wow, you must be very skilled
echo this is answer: $answer
else
  echo Neither can I, Im just an example shell script
echo this is answer: $answer
fi
```

One other aspect of these type of output statements that I want to mention is that I tend not to format these debugging `echo` statements with the traditional indentation. The reason for this is that they are usually temporary additions while I'm troubleshooting and indenting them with the normal code makes them more difficult to find when I want them removed.

Debug Level

The problem with using `echo` statements as described previously is that you have to comment or remove them when you don't want their output displayed. This is fine if your program is working to perfection and will not need further modification. However, if you're constantly making changes to a script that is actually being used, the need to add back or uncomment `echo` statements each time you debug can be tiresome. This next debugging technique improves upon the basic `echo` statement by adding a debugging level that can be turned on or off. After you've prepped your script once, enabling or disabling debugging output is as simple as changing a single variable.

The technique is to set a debug variable near the beginning of the script. This variable will then be tested during script execution and the debug statements are either displayed or suppressed based on its value.

Our original code has once again been modified for this technique:

```
#!/bin/sh
debug=1
test $debug -gt 0 && echo "Debug is on"
```

```
echo -n "Can you write device drivers? "
read answer
test $debug -gt 0 && echo "The answer is $answer"
answer=`echo $answer | tr [a-z] [A-Z]`

if [ $answer = Y ]
then
   echo Wow, you must be very skilled
   test $debug -gt 0 && echo "The answer is $answer"
else
   echo Neither can I, Im just an example shell script
   test $debug -gt 0 && echo "The answer is $answer"
fi
```

This idea can be expanded to include many debug statements in the code providing output of varying levels of detail during execution. By varying the value to which $debug is compared in the test (e.g., $debug -gt 2), you can in principle have an unlimited number of levels of debug output, with 1 being the most simple and the highest-numbered level of your choosing being the most complex. You can of course create any debug level logic you wish. In the example here, I am checking if the debug variable is greater than some specified value. If it is, the debug output is displayed. With this model, if you have various debug output levels and your debug variable is assigned a value higher than the highest debug level, all levels below that one will be displayed. Here are a few lines of code that may illustrate this better:

```
debug=2
test $debug -gt 0 && echo "A little data"
test $debug -gt 1 && echo "Some more data"
test $debug -gt 2 && echo "Even some more data"
```

If these three lines were executed in a script, only the output from the first two would be displayed. By changing the logic of the test from 'greater than' (-gt) to 'equal to' (-eq), only the output of the last debug statement would be displayed.

My mind works best when things are simple. For simple scripts I usually only set the debug value to either on or off. Multilevel debugging becomes more valuable as the script becomes larger, since the code can then become quite complex and difficult to track. Using multiple debug levels in a complex script allows you to follow the logic of the code as it executes, selecting the level of detail desired.

A further improvement to this technique is to design the script to accept a debug switch when the script is called. You can then use the switch to specify whatever value of debug level you desire for the information you're looking for, without having to modify the code every time you would like to view debugging output. See Chapter 5 for more information on how to process command line switches passed to a script.

Alert Function

The last debugging approach demonstrated here is an error checking technique. Instead of simply checking the values of variables and debug statements as previously noted, this method is more proactive in nature. You evaluate the final condition of an executed command and output a notification if the command was unsuccessful for some reason.

The code is a very simple function that I include in a standard function library that I use. More information on function libraries can be found in Chapter 2. This function makes use of the $? variable to check the return code of the previous command and alerts of its success or failure. The return code of a command is a numeric value that defines the exit status of the most recently executed command. Traditionally, a successful completion of a command will yield a value of 0 for $?. Error checking is an important part of all types of coding. Not only do you need to get the commands, logic, and functionality of the program correct along the desired path of execution, you should also check for problem conditions along the way. Anticipating potential problems will make your code more robust and resilient.

The function that is included here is called 'alert' since it notifies you of any issues. A function is something like a mini-program within the main code and it can be called like any other regular command. A good use for a function is to reduce duplication of code if you're going to perform a given task many times throughout the script. This function, like all others, needs to be included in the code (defined) prior to it being called by the script. Once the alert function has been defined, it should be called following any critical commands. By "critical", I mean those commands that are most important to the success of the script. For instance, if you had a script that does some file manipulation (such as finding files matching certain criteria, and moving them around or modifying them), there will be plenty of lines of code, but the key commands might be find, mv, sed, and a few others. These are the commands that are performing real action and I would consider critical.

When you identify a line of code that you want to check, you should call the alert function directly following the execution of that command because that is when you can first retrieve the value of the $? shell variable and this determine the effect of the executed command.

The explanation of the alert function's code is simple. The alert function is called with $? as its first argument and a string describing what is being reported as its second argument. If the value of $? is 0, the function echoes that the operation succeeded, and otherwise it echoes that it didn't.

```
alert () {
# usage: alert <$?> <object>
    if [ "$1" -ne 0 ]
    then
       echo "WARNING: $2 did not complete successfully." >&2
       exit $1
    else
       echo "INFO: $2 completed successfully" >&2
    fi
}
```

Here is an example of a command followed by a call to the alert function. The command simply mails the contents of a log file, specified in the environment variable LOG, to a predefined recipient, specified in the variable TO.

```
cat $LOG | mail -s "$FROM attempting to get $FILE" $TO
alert $? "Mail of $LOG to $TO"
```

Depending on the success or failure of the cat and mail commands, the output of the call to alert() would look like this:

```
INFO: Mail of $LOG to $TO completed successfully
```

Or like this:

```
INFO: Mail of $LOG to $TO did not complete successfully
```

with the LOG and TO variables expanded to their values, but this is for demonstration purposes only.

The following code is a more advanced form of the previous function. It is simpler to call and has a couple of additional features. First it has been combined with a global DEBUG variable so that it will only report issues if that variable is set. It has also been combined with a global STEP_THROUGH variable. When that variable is set to 1, the code pauses for input on any error it encounters. If the STEP_THROUGH variable is set to 2, the function will pause every time it has been called.

```
alert () {
  local RET_CODE=$?
  if [ -z "$DEBUG" ] || [ "$DEBUG" -eq 0 ] ; then
    return
  fi
```

The first tasks are to set the RET_CODE variable to the return code of the last command and then determine if the DEBUG variable is either undefined or set to 0. The -z test determines if a variable has a zero length. If either of these are true, return back to the main code that called this function.

```
  if [ "$RET_CODE" -ne 0 ] ; then
    echo "Warn: $* failed with a return code of $RET_CODE." >&2
    [ "$DEBUG" -gt 9 ] && exit "$RET_CODE"
```

The next step is to determine if the return code of the command was non-zero which implies a failure of some kind. If that is the case, echo out a warning that states what the command was attempting to do and the return code that it received. The $* variable holds all the positional parameters that were passed to the function itself. If it was called with something like: 'alert creating the archive of last months records' and there was a problem, the output would look like: Warn: creating the archive of last months records failed with a return code of 1. In a real case, the return code value itself will vary.

The last line here determines if the DEBUG variable is greater than 9. If this is the case, the script will exit with the return code of the most recent failure.

```
    [ "$STEP_THROUGH" = 1 ] && {
      echo "Press [Enter] to continue" >&2; read x
    }
  fi
  [ "$STEP_THROUGH" = 2 ] && {
    echo "Press [Enter] to continue" >&2; read x
  }
}
```

This last bit of code is where the function allows you to pause at only non-zero return codes or any time the alert function was called. This function could still be improved by sending output to an optional log file for later review.

Manual Stepping

My final comments on debugging code come from an interaction I had recently with a friend who was trying to debug an issue with her script. The code attempted to move around some files on the local disk as well as on an NFS-mounted file system. It was receiving a puzzling "permission denied" error. Looking at the code, there didn't seem to be anything obviously wrong, and the permissions on the directories seemed correct as well. It wasn't until we started manually performing the steps in the script that we found the problem. A file move was attempting to overwrite a preexisting file in the destination directory with read-only permissions and obviously (hindsight, you know) this was what gave the "permission denied" errors. When we had initially looked at the code and the directories involved, we were focusing on the directory permissions and user that needed to write to this directory. We failed to notice the permissions on the files in the directory.

Now I'm not suggesting that all problems are this easy to find. Debugging code can take hours, days, or even longer when the code becomes complex, but there are a few lessons that can be learned from this simple example.

First, before you start writing a program, attempt to perform the steps that the code will be using manually where appropriate. There will likely be times when this may not be feasible but for the times that it is, you may be able to weed out some trouble spots before they are mixed in with all the other tasks of the script.

Second, try out the code with sample input and try to follow it through by performing the loops and conditionals as they are written. It is not an easy task, but attempt to look at the code as objectively as possible without making assumptions and ask the too-obvious-to-ask questions about what is happening.

Lastly, another set of eyes is an excellent way of finding problems, especially when you've been working on the same issue for a long time. Sometimes a peer with a fresh viewpoint is able to solve it right away. This scenario is a good source for that feeling of "Duh, I should have known that." Sometimes your brain can get in the way of seeing what is in front of you.

Chapter 2: Standard Function

Library

After writing many scripts, I realized that there were several functions and routines that I was repeatedly using. Sometimes I would write the code for these duplicated functions again, other times I would copy and paste the code from an earlier script. But the best coding practice is to keep a file around that contains all of these already tested and working functions. This creates a scriptwriter's toolbox, or in programming speak, a library. With a library in place, many of the tools that you need often are then close at hand, and you don't have to code up the functions anew each time you need them. This chapter shows you how to set up a standard function library and how to utilize the library in your scripts.

The Library File

The library itself is simply a collection of functions held in a single file. When the library is brought into your scripts environment, you can call any of the library functions as if it were in your original code. More on the details of that a bit later. You could create a single library that contains all of your functions or if you have a large and varied number of them, create a set of libraries where each one is specific to a category of coding.

These libraries are not only handy to have around, they eliminate redundant coding as well as giving a common environment for all programmers involved to work from. Function libraries not only reduce redundant code and speed up the development process, they can reduce debugging and code hardening time. If there are bugs in any of the functions, fixes will positively impact all scripts that rely on those bits of code. Function libraries can also level the programming field when working with many and varied system types by adding a layer of abstraction between system differences and the programmer writing the code.

The following example library is very simple and contains only a single function. To keep things organized, especially when these files can get quite large, the functions should be written with good indenting form as well as comments about what the code does. Keeping a header in the file that lists all the functions and gives a brief description of each along with any variables that get defined will make using the library more simple. Included with the header could be a list of revisions and owners. This is especially useful when working in a team where other members may be making changes.

```
#!/bin/echo Warning: this library should be sourced!
# ostype(): Define OSTYPE variable to current operating system
ostype()
{
    osname=`uname -s`
    # Assume we do not know what this is
    OSTYPE=UNKNOWN
    case $osname in
      "FreeBSD") OSTYPE="FREEBSD"
              ;;
      "SunOS") OSTYPE="SOLARIS"
              ;;
      "Linux") OSTYPE="LINUX"
              ;;
    esac
      return 0
}
```

The first line of the library is an excellent method of ensuring that the library is sourced and not executed as a regular script. With this line, error output will be generated if someone attempts to run the library instead of sourcing it into the environment. The output would look like this:

```
Warning: this library should be sourced! /path_to_library
```

Another method to avoid execution of libraries would be to make them non-executable.

The first function, ostype(), determines the operating system of the computer on which the library is running. Because there are subtle differences between operating systems, knowing what OS your script is running on will help you take the differences into account. There are of course many more operating systems than we are able to list here.

Some Useful Functions

The code in this section comes from a few utility functions that I find very useful. You will probably come up with many more which are specifically geared toward the systems you work with. An excellent example of a library of shell functions can be found in Gentoo Linux: If you're running this Linux distribution, you can find the library under the filename /etc/init.d/functions.sh. Even if you're not a Gentoo user, you should be able to get a copy of this library and make use of it by performing a search for Gentoo and functions.sh, making sure that you follow the applicable usage guidelines.

Here are a few functions that I've found particularly useful to include in my standard library. The first function is fairly straightforward, but it contains a cool trick. Pass this function any number and it will determine whether the number is even or odd. This function was originally used in a moderately large environment where various tasks needed to be load balanced. We chose a simple method of splitting the environment in half based on the numeric value of the system name. The cool trick is the use of the sed command to determine the last character of a string. Once the last digit is found, the function returns a true value of 1 if the digit is an even number and a false of 0 if it is not. I will discuss this command and others like it in Chapter 24.

```
evenodd()
{
  # determine odd/even status by last digit
  LAST_DIGIT=`echo $1 | sed 's/\(.*\)\(.\)$/\2/'`
  case $LAST_DIGIT in
  0|2|4|6|8 )
    return 1
    ;;
  *)
    return 0
    ;;
  esac
}
```

This second function is one that I have used many times. It determines whether a remote system is running and connected to the network. It works by `ping`ing the specified machine three times and sending the output to `/dev/null`. Success is based on the value of `$?` that is returned following the ping command. If the value of `$?` is 0, then the machine is alive. The usage of the `ping` command is encapsulated in the `setupenv()` function which comes next. The switches and usage of this command varies among operating systems. This usage will work on Linux systems. HP-UX machines would use the command `ping $NODE 3` for the same functionality.

```
isalive()
{
  NODE=$1
  $PING -c 3 $NODE >/dev/null 2>&1

  if [ $? -eq 0 ]
  then
    return 1
  else
    return 0
  fi
}
```

This final function is one you'll find useful if you need to run your scripts on multiple hosts, some of which you don't know the exact configuration of. It sets the path to an executable based on the operating system type, in this case `ping`, and stores its value as a variable. Your scripts can then call this variable when they need to utilize the executable without you needing to hand code the exact path for each unique host. You can use this function as a template for storing the location of other executables.

You can see how this script uses the `ostype()` function covered earlier to determine your OS and thus executable path.

```
setupenv()
{
    if [ "$OSTYPE" = "" ]
    then
      ostype
    fi

    NAME=`uname -n`
```

```
case $OSTYPE in
  "LINUX" )
        PING=/usr/sbin/ping
        ;;
  "FREEBSD" )
        PING=/sbin/ping
        ;;
  "SOLARIS" )
        PING=/usr/sbin/ping
        ;;
    *)
        ;;
  esac
}
```

Using Your Library

Once a library has been included in your shell scripting environment, all functions it contains become available to your scripts. There are several ways in which it could be incorporated into the environment.

You can make the library available by entering the `source` command at the shell prompt, as shown here. This command evaluates the commands in a file, which in the case of our library places its resources inside the current shell environment.

```
source std_lib
```

Another way of sourcing a library file is with the dot syntax. This is a shorthand way of performing the same task as the `source` command by replacing the command with a dot (.). This is a built-in function included in both `ksh` and `bash`.

```
. std_lib
```

If you work with a large number of networked systems, keeping a copy of your library on every machine promotes consistency. It is very important to be able to count on the environment you are working to be the same on all machines. An excellent method for this is to store your libraries on a central NFS server that all machines in the environment have access to. This also gives you the benefit of being able to make library changes in one place that will update the whole environment. A somewhat less desirable method would be to keep the source copies of your libraries in one place for editing and propagate any changes to the remote machines through some utility such as `rsync`. The worse case would be to manually copy the libraries out to each machine when changes are made. This is only viable if you have a small environment with only a few systems.

If you have a heterogeneous environment, you will always have to cope with minor differences from OS to OS or even between different versions of the same OS. A standard library is a good way of dealing with those differences and keeping your scripts portable.

Chapter 3: Date and Time Manipulation

On occasion, the need for date math arises, such as when you find yourself trying to calculate a time interval between events. On the face of it, the calculations seem easy enough, because there are precise numbers of seconds, minutes, and hours in a day. It gets tricky when you realize that you need to consider the fact that values have to roll over when, for example, Monday turns into Tuesday or June becomes July.

For example, calculating the difference in minutes between 6:53 AM and 7:04 AM is easy enough: you can multiply the hours (6 and 7) by 60 for each value, add the minutes that do not make up the next full hour, then subtract to find the difference. But what if you want the difference in minutes between 11:57 PM and 1:13 AM? This calculation is more complex because it involves a change in day. And the complexity only increases when the date interval spans months or years.

Date in Days

The following script shows one way to make date and time calculations much easier. Since UNIX and Linux calculate time based on a starting point of January 1, 1970, the script measures time in seconds since that date.

Although the use of seconds may seem a bit cumbersome, the math is simple as you'll see in the optional bit of code below. You reduce the date and time values to numbers of seconds elapsed since the base date, then manipulate these values. All of the issues that arise when spanning across calendar increments, such as days or months, simply disappear.

You might use this type of calculation when determining the age of a users password. The third field of an account entry in a system /etc/shadow file contains the day value on which the password was changed for a particular account, as counted from 1/1/1970 (epoch). This number can be used, for example, to determine when passwords are about to expire so as to facilitate user notifications. You can find an example of this in Chapter 36 in connection with password aging.

Converting all temporal quantities to elapsed time also reduces the complexity of making time comparisons. Suppose, for example, that you would like to monitor time synchronization between multiple network nodes. When you convert the time on a system to seconds elapsed since the beginning of the UNIX epoch, the calculation becomes a simple subtraction.

Yes, the Network Time Protocol (NTP) keeps system clocks in sync. However, not all systems run NTP implementations. Also, clocks on some aging hardware keep such poor time that even NTP can't keep them in sync. NTP implementations can generally keep system clocks synchronized, but if a particular clock drifts beyond the panic threshold, NTP will not update the clock. Too, even where NTP is ubiquitous, systems can fail.

The following script calculates the number of days between two dates. The valid dates for this equation (taken from the Gregorian calendar) range from the October 15th 1582 to December 31st 9999. Dates outside this range (or dates from different calendars) will require a different equation. This script is a fairly long hand way of getting these values, but the benefit is that it will run on most any system using ksh or bash. The other alternatives may not.

The script is based on this formula with a couple of adjustments where a year, month and day are used as input and the output is the integer where that date lands on a number line. When the program is run, it calculates and displays the number of days that have elapsed since January 1st 1970 by determining the number for 1/1/1970 and subtracting that from the number for the current date.

```
(Year*365)+(Year/4)-(Year/100)+(Year/400)+(Month*306001/10000)+(Day)
```

There are a couple of caveats that have to be accounted for before using this formula to return the correct values. Before the calculation is done, the values of Month and Year need to be altered: For the months of January (1) and February (2), one must add 13 to Month and subtract 1 from Year; otherwise one just adds 1 to Month.. The Day value to be used is always the day of the month. Thus, the equation applied to January 1, 1970, is this:

```
(1969*365)+(1969/4)-(1969/100)+(1969/400)+(1*306001/10000)+1
```

Days Since Epoch

```sh
#!/bin/sh
epoch_days=719591
second=`date +'%S'`
minute=`date +'%M'`
hour=`date +'%k'`
day=`date +'%d'`
month=`date +'%m' | sed 's/0*//'`
year=`date +'%Y'`
```

The start of the script sets the variables for the current time and date. Since the epoch (1/1/1970) is fixed, its value can be calculated once and the constant 719591 used in its place, thus saving some CPU cycles.

You could improve the performance of the script although it reduces the readability. Instead of performing a date call in order to set each *time* and *date* variable, you could make one date call, output space delimited values, which place those values into an array.

To initialize the array in ksh, use

```
set -A DATE `date +"%S %M %k %d %m %Y"`
```

In bash, use

```
declare -a DATE=( `date +"%S %M %k %d %m %Y"` )
```

For example, to access, the third array element in either bash or ksh, use something like

```
echo ${DATE[2]}
```

where 2 is the third element in the DATE array. The first element in an array is accessed with a subscript of 0.

```
if [ $month -gt 2 ]
then
  month=$(($month+1))
else
  month=$(($month+13))
  year=$(($year-1))
fi
```

This code makes the initial changes to the month and year variables needed by the equation. From the original formula, if the month is not January or February (greater than values 1 or 2), you have to add 1 to the month. Otherwise, you have to add 13 to the month and subtract 1 from the year.

```
today_days=$((($year*365)+($year/4)-\
($year/100)+($year/400)+($month*306001/10000)+$day))
days_since_epoch=$(($today_days-$epoch_days))
echo $days_since_epoch
```

This code calculates the day value for today. Once we know this, we subtract the epoch value from it to get the number of days since the start of the epoch. The script then outputs that value. This output is left unformatted in case we want to use the number as input for another command or process.

You may find it useful to have two versions of this script: one that outputs the elapsed time in days and the other that outputs it in seconds.

```
seconds_since_epoch=`echo "($days_since_epoch*86400)+\
($hour*3600)+($minute*60)+$second" | bc`
```

The calculation to convert from days to seconds is fairly trivial. It may also be useful to turn the code for the calculations into functions and put them in your central library as discussed in Chapter 2. You then would only need to source this library into your current environment and call the function whenever needed.

Date in Seconds Alternatives

There are two other ways to calculate the number of seconds since the epoch. Both of them are much simpler than the script above, but they require system utilities that you may not have installed such as Perl and the latest GNU utilities. You may, as I have, worked on older systems that don't have these capabilities and still need a solution. Most administrators would probably install whatever is needed to get the job done, but there are controlled production environments where this is not that simple. Many requirements and testing must be performed before any changes are made to a system. In those cases, it is simpler to come up with a solution with existing resources.

The first alternative is provided with the GNU version of the date command. If you have this version, you can produce output that is almost identical to that of the script discussed in section Days Since Epoch above except that, because the number of seconds since epoch in that script is calculated based on GMT, it may well be out of sync with your local time zone. In that case, you may want to add the appropriate number of seconds for your local time zone. This may not be necessary if you're using these values to simply calculate the difference between two arbitrary dates/times in which the local time zone information is irrelevant.

```
gnu_seconds_since_epoch=`date +%s`
```

There is also a Perl function for performing the same task. You can access it like this:

```
perl_seconds_since_epoch=`perl -e 'print time'`
```

Evaluating for the Current Day and Time

Say you want to schedule a job, such as a system monitor, to run at particular times or on certain days. You want to know whether there are issues on the system, but you don't necessarily want to be jarred awake by your pager simply to learn that the message is non-critical; you'd like to get those routine notices by page during the day and by email at other times.

The following script should help. It will determine whether the current day and hour are within a certain time frame that you set. This code would be called from another script that actually performs the notification.

The script takes two sets of day and hour parameters (for a total of four) that are passed to the script when it is called. These parameters specify a range of days (Sunday through Monday) and a range of hours during those days when pages may be sent. The script returns a 0 () if the current day and hour are within those parameters and gives the user a message stating the same. If the current day and hour values do not lie within the given range, a different message is output and the function returns a −1 (representing failure).

```
#!/bin/sh
if [ $# -ne 4 ]
then
   echo Usage: $0 {day begin} {day end} {hour begin} {hour end}
   echo "        Days are 0-6 where 0 is Sunday."
   echo "        Hours are 0-23."
   exit
fi
```

The script starts by determining how many parameters have been sent to the script. (Recall that four is the expected number.) If that isn't the case, such as if the script calling this one was coded incorrectly, you should output a usage message containing some explanation of how the script should be invoked. The usage explanation here shows that the four parameters that should be passed are: day being, day end, hour begin and hour end. All of these values are integers in which the day values range from 0-6 where Sunday is 0 and the hours range from 0-23.

```
DAY_BEGIN=$1
DAY_END=$2
HOUR_BEGIN=$3
HOUR_END=$4
```

If the parameter count is correct, the code assigns the parameters to variables with more meaningful names such as DAY_BEGIN and DAY_END instead of 1 and 2. Making this change helps the readability and it is easier to see what is happening.

```
DAY=`date +%w`
HOUR=`date +%H`
```

Next, the variables for the current day and hour need to be set.

```
if [ $DAY -ge $DAY_BEGIN -a $DAY -le $DAY_END -a $HOUR -ge $HOUR_BEGIN
-a $HOUR -le $HOUR_END ]
then
   echo "It is time to notify"
   return 0
else
   echo "It is not time to notify"
   return 1
fi
```

The code here is the main check to determine whether it is time to notify the administrator. The large if statement above is comparing the current DAY and HOUR values with the values that were passed to the script.

Note: the valid day and hour ranges include the endpoints specified by the parameters.

That is, if the script was invoked with day *values of 1 and 5, the test should succeed on*

Monday, Friday, and on the days in between.

You should probably replace the `echo` lines with code for performing some type of actual notification such as a call to a paging utility such as QuickPage[1].

As mentioned earlier, we are assuming for simplicity that the actual notification is handled by the code that calls this script. That script might be an exhaustive monitoring utility that performs many types of monitoring tasks. Each monitor could call this script with different parameters based on the specific criticality. The calling script would then evaluate the return code by accessing the `$?` variable to determine whether or not to send the notification.

To simplify this script you could hard-code the `DAY_BEGIN`/`DAY_END` and `HOUR_BEGIN`/`HOUR_END` ranges instead of assigning them the values of the passed parameters. You would then remove the validation check for the number of parameters passed.

---

1 QuickPage is an application that allows you to send messages to an alphanumeric pager. More information can be found at http://www.qpage.org

Chapter 4: Comparisons and Tests

O ne of the fundamental types of operations in any programming language is the comparison or test. They are the building blocks of conditional statements (if/then and case) and iteration statements (while). They give you the ability to examine relationships between data items, such as files, variables, strings, numeric values, and take action based on the result. You can also carry out actions based on the attributes of a particular item, such as a file's type, whether a variable has been assigned a value, and the return code of a command.

The following examples represent various ways to compare items or to check their properties, and use the results. I have used all of these techniques throughout this book, although some are used more frequently than others. Here I want to present a diverse set of examples that demonstrate the many uses of the test shell programming structure.

In UNIX shell scripting there are both internal operators that allow you to test attributes or to compare values, and a /usr/bin/test system call. You might want to refer to Appendix B for more specific information.

```
if [ "$string" = "some_string" ];then...
if [ $integer -eq 15 ];then...
```

These first two comparison examples are among the most common forms you would use. The first example represents a string comparison and the second an integer test. The quotation marks are only required for an explicit string. Quote marks around the name of a string variable are not required. It is wise, however, to always quote your string variables, in order to gracefully handle the case that the variable is undefined or if there is white space within the string. A comparison involving an unquoted, undefined string variable in the bash shell will return an '*unary operator expected*' error, while ksh will return an '*argument expected*' message. A comparison involving an unquoted string containing white space will result in a '*too many arguments*' error in bash and '*unknown operator*' in ksh. All of these errors are related to the test command finding that there are too few or too many arguments in the comparison. Too few because an unquoted null variable is skipped over in the comparison and too many because an unquoted string containing white space will be viewed as more than one argument instead of a single string.

The spaces between the values being compared and the square brackets are required syntax, but the spaces between the values being compared and the comparison operator are optional.

One item to note is that the operators for string and numeric comparison are opposite of what you might intuitively assume. To my mind, the equality symbol '=' implies a numeric comparison, while the -eq operator suggests a string operation, but this is not the case. The other conditional operators besides this one mirror this distinction. The operators =, !=, >, and < used for string comparisons are direct counterparts to the numeric comparison operators -eq, -ne, -gt, and -lt. There are other operators as well that can be found in both the test man page and the man pages for specific shells.

```
if test $string = "some_string" ;then...
```

The square brackets in the previous example contain the enclosed expressions to create a statement representing the logical result (true or false) of the test described by the enclosed expressions. To be more accurate, the '[' bracket is a command both internal to the shell and a system command (/usr/bin/ [) that can be thought of the same as the test command. The '[' command has specific syntax that must be followed and the return code of this command is what determines if the comparison is true or not. In this example, the square brackets have been replaced with the test command to illustrate another method of forming a comparison statement. The square brackets can be used interchangeably with the test command.

```
test $debug -eq 1 && echo some_debug_output
```

All examples so far have used the if/then structure for comparing values. Usually, if the expression given to the test command or enclosed in the square brackets evaluates to TRUE, then we perform some task. The syntax of this example is slightly different. In this code pattern, the test on the left of the && operator is performed as before, and based on the result (true or false), the code on the right is executed or skipped. Here, if the debug variable is set to 1, the left-hand expression evaluates to true and the echo command will be run. The line of code can also be read as follows: "test the condition AND execute the additional code if the test evaluates as true."

```
test $debug -eq 1 || echo some_debug_output
```

The alternative is also available. If the logical AND (&&) is replaced with a logical OR (||), the additional code is executed only if the test returns false. This example can be read as "test the condition OR execute the additional code (if the test evaluates as false)." Both the logical AND (&&) and logical OR (||) sequences are simply shortcut versions of the more verbose syntax.

```
test $debug -eq 1 && {
    echo some_debug_output
    echo some_more_debug_output
}
```

In both of the previous examples, the additional code to be run was a single command. Compound commands can be formed by surrounding the individual commands with curly braces. Such groupings can contain any amount of code including output statements, control structures, assignments, or all of the above.

```
[ $debug -eq 1 ] && {
    echo some_debug_output
    echo some_more_debug_output
}
```

As we've seen before, the `test` command can be replaced with square brackets; the two forms of syntax are equivalent. This segment of code evaluates the expression within the square brackets AND runs the compound statement if the expression evaluates as true. I have not noticed any significant performance differences between these two syntax types.

```
[ "$txt" ] && [ "$txt" != "$txt2" ] && some_text="$txt $txt2"
```

Conditional logic can become quite complex. This example demonstrates two `test` expressions that must each evaluate as true before the additional code will be run. In this case, the logical AND (&&) characters are used to perform two separate functions. The first instance of && is used to require both the first AND second expressions to be true. The second instance is used to indicate the additional code that should be run if they both evaluate as true. The use of a logical OR (||) in both places is also valid, and specifies that both of the tests would need to be false to execute the additional code.

```
if [ "$txt" != "$txt2" -a $num -eq $num2 ] || [ $num2 -eq 100 ];then...
```

This example adds another layer of complexity to the previous example. Not only are there two expressions to evaluate, but the first expression of the two contains two

29

additional expressions of its own. Note that the two main expressions are surrounded by square brackets and are separated by a logical OR (||). The use of the OR indicates that the entire test evaluates as true whenever either one of the two expressions is true. You can see the -a operator inside the first expression, which is also a logical AND. You can string multiple expressions together with the -a or the logical OR (-o) operator, as you can with the && and || syntax. When such expressions become very complex, it is easy to make logic mistakes which can be difficult to track down.

```
if [ -n $string ];then...
if [ $any_variable ];then...
```

In these examples, the complexity has been toned down. These can be used to determine whether variables have been defined. The first of the two applies to string variables, since the -n operation evaluates to true if the length of the supplied string variable is non-zero. However, this method also works for determining whether a numeric variable has been defined, as its value is then treated as a string.

The second example simply tests a variable. Once the variable has been assigned a value, the expression will evaluate to true. thus, both expressions determine if a variable has been assigned a value.

```
if [ -z $string ];then...
if [ ! $any_variable ];then...
```

These are expressions similar to the previous ones, that will determine if a variable is undefined. These conditions are simply the negations of the corresponding expressions in the previous examples (-z tests whether a string has zero length, and ! is the logical not symbol).

```
if [ "`grep nodename /etc/hosts`" ];then...
```

This example uses a couple of features, one of which we have already seen. The test here evaluates to true if the quoted expression is not null. We saw one example of this earlier, in connection with quoted string variables. In this case, however, we are not looking at the value of a variable, but rather running an external command and capturing its output to be tested within the square brackets as if it were a string. An expression enclosed in reverse single quotes (`) is evaluated by the shell and substituted with the resulting output. Here, if the grep command returns a match from /etc/hosts, then there is output and the test evaluates as true because the quoted expression is non-null. If the grep returns nothing, the quoted expression would then be null and the test would evaluate as false.

```
if ping -c 3 node.mydomain.com > /dev/null 2>&1;then
```

A test can be performed on more than just a variable or a value, such as a number or a string. In this example, the test examines the return code of a command. As I mentioned earlier, all of these comparisons are really commands having their return code evaluated. If the command returns a `0` code (indicating successful termination), its execution, in the context of a test, evaluates as true. We can take advantage of this with the `ping` command, as shown here, because we don't need to know the actual output of the command to determine whether a system is responsive or not which is why all the output is being redirected to `/dev/null`. The return code will tell us that. If a system is unresponsive to a `ping`, the return code will be nonzero. This is a much simpler method than retrieving and analyzing the output of the command.

```
/usr/bin/test -l "hello" -gt 4 && echo some_message
```

This last example uses the `-l` switch to the `test` system command. Here, you are testing if the length of the string `'hello'` is greater than 4 . If this is true, `echo` a message. The reason I have included this example is that the syntax for this switch is not intuitively obvious from the `test` man page. There is a brief comment about the `-l` switch and no example. Also, I wanted to point out that there is both an internal shell `test` command and a system `test` command. The internal `test` is called unless the system command is specified using the fully qualified filename of the executable (including the path). If you don't specify the full path to the system `test`, as shown here, the shell's internal `test` will return a '*unary operator expected*' error if you run `bash`. An '*unknown operator*' error will appear from `ksh`. Neither shell's internal `test` command uses the `-l` switch to specify a length comparison.

31

Chapter 5: Accepting

Command Line Options,

Switches, and Parameters

There are times when you may want to pass optional parameters to your script allowing its behavior to be controlled more precisely. One example of a command that uses option parameters is the `tar` utility. It creates archives and restores directory and file trees, but it can do it in different ways. The GNU version of `tar` has roughly 80 different options that can be used in various combinations to tailor the ways in which the utility will perform. The major benefits of this technique is that you can write a single program and have it perform multiple tasks based on the command line input. Another benefit is of a single program is that you're not duplicating code by writing smaller more specific scripts tailored to each individual task.

You are unlikely to use this code in its current form, as it is designed to demonstrate processing of command line options within a framework of a specific task for a specific application environment. This might be a good basic set of simple utilities that could be given to first-level support staff for basic initial troubleshooting. They would then not have to remember all the paths and commands, which could be especially helpful if they are not very proficient from the command line. A possible way to modify this code for more general use could be to have the code view the `/var/log/messages` file with one switch, perform a `df -k` with another switch, and perform a `netstat -a` with yet another. This is much like creating a set of command line aliases that can be a time saver by reducing keystrokes for commonly used commands and utilities.

Most of the scripts I have written generally don't use many options because they are fairly specific in their purpose. If a single option is needed, you can easily have the user supply it as a command-line parameter and check the value of $1 to see if an option was in fact passed to the script. The complexity of this technique increases dramatically when you have multiple options that can be used in combination independently of each other and the method becomes unwieldy. Add to this the additional difficulty of accounting for the foibles of users and the ways in which they may, possibly erroneously, specify the options.

This can be seen with the `tar` command. A typical command might be `tar -xvf file.tar`. This could also be entered as `tar -x -v -f file.tar`. Attempting to account for all possible combinations of user-specified options using shell script code that works with positional variables, would be very problematic.

This brings us to the `getopts` utility, which handles command line switches much more elegantly. All you have to concern yourself with is how the script will function based on the supplied parameters—not how to actually read the parameters and account for their potential variability.

The example code here does not represent a full script. It is mainly a single function that would get sourced into your environment either through a login script such as `/etc/profile` or through a standard library of functions (see Chapter 2). This function is used by typing its name (`jkl` in this case) at the command line and passing various parameters to it to perform specific tasks.

The code was used in an environment where there were multiple machines, each of which had one or more versions of the same set of applications installed. Troubleshooting problems with the currently active application became tedious and time consuming because you had to first determine which installed version was active. The one constant that could be relied on was a single configuration file residing in a known location that held the currently active version of the installed software. This code allows users to immediately switch to the correct configuration or log directory among other tasks for quick troubleshooting.

```
APPHOME=/usr/local/apphome
if [ ! -f $APPHOME/myapp.sh ]
then
   echo "Myapp is not installed on this system so jkl is not functional"
   return 1
fi
```

First, we define a variable containing the top of the directory subtree where the installed applications live; then we determine if the main configuration file exists. If it does not exist, the script should exit and provide a notification. Next comes the `jkl()` function itself.

```
jkl () {
  Usage="Usage: \n \
  \tjkl [-lbmcdxh] [-f filename]\n \
  \t\t[-h] \tThis usage text.\n \
  \t\t[-f filename] \t cat the specified file. \n \
  \t\t[-l] \tGo to application log directory with ls. \n \
  \t\t[-b] \tGo to application bin directory. \n \
  \t\t[-c] \tGo to application config directory.\n \
  \t\t[-m] \tGo to application log directory and more log file.\n \
  \t\t[-d] \tTurn on debug information.\n \
  \t\t[-x] \tTurn off debug information.\n"
  APPLOG=myapp_log
  UNAME=`uname -n`
  DATE=`date '+%y%m'`
  MYAPP_ID=$APPHOME/myapp.sh
```

The start of the function sets up a number of variables, the most interesting of which is Usage. It manually formats the output of the usage statement with tabs and carriage returns. For more information on these character combinations and definitions, consult the man page for echo on your system. Here is a more readable output of the usage statement that demonstrates the formatting that is being done:

Usage:

jkl [-lf:bmcdxh]

[-h]   This usage text.

[-f]   cat specified file.

[-l]   Go to application log directory with ls.

[-b]   Go to application bin directory.

[-c]   Go to application config directory.

[-m]   Go to application log directory and more
log file.

[-d]   Turn on debug information.

[-x]   Turn off debug information.

```
major=`egrep "^MAJOR_VER=" $MYAPP_ID | cut -d"=" -f2`
minor=`egrep "^MINOR_VER=" $MYAPP_ID | cut -d"=" -f2`
dot=`egrep "^DOT_VER=" $MYAPP_ID | cut -d"=" -f2`
```

Then we define the software version numbers based on the information found in the application configuration file. This file isn't shown in this example, but you can assume that these values are found in that file, and I will include it in the down-loadable script package.

```
APPDIR=$APPHOME/myapp.$major.$minor.$dot
LOGDIR=$APPHOME/myapp.$major.$minor.$dot/log
CFGDIR=$APPHOME/myapp.$major.$minor.$dot/config
BINDIR=$APPHOME/myapp.$major.$minor.$dot/bin
```

The names of the various application directories are formed from the combination of application names and version number variables. Here we assign the directory variables their values.

```
if [ "$#" -lt 1 ]
then
        echo -e $Usage
fi
```

Then we check to see if there are any command line switches that have been used when the function was called. If none are found, the usage statement should be displayed. Note that the echo command uses the -e switch, which enables the use of the escape sequences found in the Usage variable. If the script did not use the -e switch, it would not format the output properly, printing the escape sequences along with the usage information.

```
OPTIND=1
```

User-supplied options are accessed through an argument vector. The getopts utility uses the OPTIND environment variable to index this array. Each time this function is invoked, the variable needs to be reset to 1 before option processing starts in order to point at the beginning of the options that have been passed. As the upcoming while loop iterates through the passed options, this value is incremented by the getopts utility while it is processing through any parameters that were passed.

This `while` loop is the core of the script. It is where the passed parameters are processed and appropriate actions are taken.

```
while getopts lf:bmcdxh ARGS
do
  case $ARGS in
    l) if [ -d $LOGDIR ] ; then
         cd $LOGDIR
         /bin/ls
       fi
    ;;
    f) FILE=$OPTARG
       if [ -f $FILE ]
       then
         cat $FILE
       else
         echo $FILE not found. Please try again.
       fi
    ;;
    b) if [ -d $BINDIR ] ; then
         cd $BINDIR
       fi
    ;;
    m) if [ -d $LOGDIR ] ; then
         cd $LOGDIR
         /bin/more $APPLOG
       fi
    ;;
    c) if [ -d $CFGDIR ] ; then
         cd $CFGDIR
       fi
    ;;
    d) set -x
    ;;
    x) set +x
    ;;
```

```
    h)  echo -e $Usage
    ;;
    *)  echo -e $Usage
    ;;
    esac
  done
}
```

The `getopts` command is invoked with a list of the valid switches, which it parses to determine which switches need arguments. Each time `getopts` is invoked, it checks whether there are still switches to be processed. If so, it retrieves the next switch (and updates the value of `OPTIND`), stores it in the specified environment variable (here, `ARGS`), and returns true. Otherwise, it returns false. In this way, the `while` loop iterates through the options vector. Each time the shell executes the loop body, the `case` statement applies the actions that the current option requires.

In this case, most of the options take you to an application-specific directory. The three most interesting cases here are the `-d`, `-x`, and `-f` switches. The `-d` option turns on command expansion and the `-x` option turns it off. This is very useful and an easy method for debugging scripts.

The `-f` switch is different from the rest. Note that it has a colon ':' following the 'f' in the `getopts` switch list. If a switch is followed by a colon, this means that an argument should follow it when it is used. In our example, the `-f` switch is used to list the contents of a file and requires the filename to follow. The case branch for `-f` sets the `FILE` variable to `$OPTARG`. This is another special environment variable that is set by `getopts` to assign the argument that is passed to the switch. If the file exists, it will be displayed, and if not, an error message will be given.

The last two switches cause the usage statement to be displayed. A more advanced example of the `getopts` construct can be found in Chapter 17. I have also included another script in the download package for this chapter that may be a bit more useful in its original form. It performs some basic administrative tasks, including turning on and off the `set -x` value.

Chapter 6: Testing Variables

and Assigning Defaults

Many scripts require a minimum set of input parameters or defined variables in order for them to run correctly. For example, they may contain customizable values used for configuration purposes, which are initially set to default values. In this chapter, we'll look at various methods of testing variables and setting default values. The differences between many of these syntactical variants are subtle, but each is useful for working with undefined variables, setting variable defaults, and debugging.

All of these methods check the state of a given variable and assign or substitute a value based on that assessment. The point here is to give a variety of ways to perform these types of tasks. While some are simple and will be used often, others are more specific in nature and will only be used in fairly specific situations.

For example, assume that you've written a script to change a machine's network name. At the very least, the script's input parameters would probably include the old and new machine names and the machine's IP address and perhaps the machine's domain or subnet mask.

While you may want the subnet mask and domain name to be set from the command line, it is likely that these values won't be changing often and you'll simply want to set default values for your local site and not have to worry about passing these parameters. The techniques in this chapter will give you the tools to easily set default values when a variable either has a null value or is otherwise undefined.

The code samples below demonstrate several ways that could be used to set and manage variables with default values. While these examples all perform the same task, they do it in slightly different ways. The first example is probably the easiest to read from a human perspective, but is likely the most verbose from the perspective of coding efficiency. The option you choose will depend on your motives. Many times I have used this first type of code because scripts I've written need to be simple to read and support by others with varying levels of shell scripting skill. I may want to use the more terse examples if supportability is less of a concern and efficiency is more important.

```
if [ -z "$VAR" ]
then
   VAR="some default"
fi
```

This code above first checks to see if a variable (VAR) has been set. The -z (zero) test checks to see if the length of the string variable is zero. If it is, the code resets the value of the variable to the default value.

The next example performs the same task as the one above, but it is a bit more elegant because it is contained within a single line of code instead of spread out over four. The same test is performed against the variable, but the && (logical 'and') syntax executes the code that follows if the test evaluates as true.

```
[ -z "$VAR" ] && VAR="some default"
```

Here we have streamlined the code again (by one character). The test syntax contained within the square brackets can determine if the variable is set without performing the -z, or zero length, test. The test used in this example determines whether the variable has been set by using the logical *not* modifier (!). If the variable being tested does not have a value, the use of the test ["$VAR"] will evaluate as false since there was no value to be found. With the addition of the *not* (!) modifier, the test will evaluate to true because of the combination of two negatives ("!" and an unassigned variable) yielding a positive outcome. The extra code, assigning the default value to the VAR variable, following the *and* operator && is then executed as before.

```
[ ! "$VAR" ] && VAR="some default"
```

Now we simplify the code one final time. If the variable is set, the simpler test evaluates as true, and we want to perform the extra code only in the opposite case. Remember that when we use the logical *or* syntax (||), the extra code is only run if the test is false. So we can streamline the code even more by using the simpler test and the *or* operation.

```
[ "$VAR" ] || VAR="some default"
```

Variable Substitution

Variable substitution is closely related to setting default variables, at least conceptually. In our previous examples, we set default values by testing a particular variable to see if it had been defined and then assigning it a value if not. The following syntax uses a type of parameter expansion to perform the same type of task.

Parameter expansion is where the parameter such as a variable is replaced with the value of that parameter. An example of this would be calling a simple variable in the form of echo $VAR, however there are more features that can be accessed. Included in this syntax are some characters that won't be expanded and have meaning of their own, the first of which performs the default variable assignment. In the case where these characters are used, braces are required to surround the whole expression.

```
: ${VAR:="some default"}
```

The single colon character that starts this line is a valid shell command that performs no active task. In this syntax it simply expands any arguments that may follow it on the line. In this case we simply want to expand the value contained within the braces.

The argument given to : is the interesting part of this line; it's a parameter expansion that surrounds some logic with curly brackets {}. The := syntax indicates that a test is to be performed on the VAR variable in comparison to the "some default" string.

In this expression, if the variable is unset, it is then assigned the value of the expression that follows the equal sign, which can be a number, string, or another variable.

```
: ${VAR:="some default"} ${VAR2:=42} ${VAR3:=$LOGNAME}
```

Your scripts may have more than one variable that you want to ensure has a default value. Instead of coding a list of variable substitutions, you can set multiple variable defaults on a single line which makes the code more compact and readable. This example shows various types of substitutions that you may want to perform. The first involves an explicit string, the second, an explicit integer, and finally, an already-defined variable.

There are several variable substitution types that are similar to the := syntax in the previous example. Because the syntax for the different substitution types is almost identical and their meanings are so subtly different, they can be easily confused. Most of these substitutions would be used for *substituting* values of another variable into the code at the location of the substitution syntax, rather than for *setting* variables. The definitions for all of the following syntax types can be found in your shell man pages but I have found that those explanations, while accurate, are inadequate in making their meaning clear. Below you will find each of the substitution types with their syntax, some example code to set up the scenario and an explanation of how the syntax works when making its comparison within the braces.

:= Syntax

```
username=""
echo "${username:=$LOGNAME}"
```

Here we use the same `:=` syntax that we used when we set a default variable in the previous example. When the `:=` comparison is encountered, the `username` variable is defined, but its value is null. As a result, this command uses the value of the `LOGNAME` variable for the `echo` command, and it will also set the value of `username` to the value of `LOGNAME`.

With this particular syntax, the only time the variable `username` would not be set to the value of `LOGNAME` is when the `username` variable is defined and has an actual, non null value.

The main difference between this and the previous example where a default variable was set is the use of an active command (`echo`) instead of the passive colon. When the active command is used, the default assignment is still performed and the resulting variable is then used to output to the display.

= Syntax

```
username=""
echo "${username=$LOGNAME}"
```

This statement looks very similar to the previous `:=` syntax, but the colon has been removed. As before, the variable has been defined but its value is null. With this syntax the command will `echo` the statement, but there will be no output other than a carriage return because the `username` variable was defined even though it was null. Only if the `username` variable was totally undefined would the variable be set to the value of `LOGNAME`.

This syntax could be useful in a login or cron script where you need to rely on certain variables being defined for the script to function. If a specific environment variable hasn't been defined, you can then assign it a the value that your script requires.

:- Syntax

```
username=""
echo "${username:-$LOGNAME}"
```

In this command, the value of the `LOGNAME` variable will be used for the `echo` statement because `username` is null even though it is defined. The value of the `username` variable remains unchanged. The difference between this command and the one that uses the = syntax is that the values are only *substituted* for the ${} syntax in the code before it executes. In other words, the echo command will output the value of the LOGNAME variable but that value will not be assigned to the username variable.

- Syntax

```
username=""
echo "${username-$LOGNAME}"
```

When the colon is removed from the previous :- statement, the output will be null because the username variable is defined. If it were undefined, the value of LOGNAME would have been used. Again, as in the :- syntax, the username variable is unchanged.

Both the :- and – syntax could be used when a script evaluates its environment where it is running. These two checks are essentially opposite from each other in that they will substitute the default value or not depending on whether or not the username variable is defined. If you have a list of variables that need to be defined and ones that shouldn't be defined, the combination of the two could make sure everything is set correctly before the script performs its tasks.

:? Syntax

```
username=""
echo "${username:?$LOGNAME}"
```

When using the :? syntax, if the username variable is defined and it has a non-null value, the value of the username variable is used in the echo command. If the username variable is defined but does not have a "real" value (i.e., it is null), or it is undefined, the value of LOGNAME is used in the echo command, and the script then exits.

Changing the argument that follows the question mark to some type of error string will make this statement very useful in debugging and finding undefined variables in your code. The code will not only output the string, but it will also display the line in the script that the code came from.

? Syntax

```
username=""
echo "${username?$LOGNAME}"
```

Removing the colon from the :? syntax removes the requirement that the username variable have a nonnull value in order for it to be used. If that variable is only set to a null value, then that value is used. If, however, the username variable is undefined, the script will exit and display the variable, the line of code where it exited, and its LOGNAME substitution, as with the :? syntax.

Both the :? and ? syntax are excellent for script debugging when variables need to be defined or have a real non null value. The big advantage to this code is that the script will exit at the line in the script where the problem was found and the line number will be displayed. Changing the value of the text that is to be displayed to something like "is undefined" or "has a null value" will easily point you to the problem in the script.

:+ Syntax

```
username="mars"
echo "${username:+$LOGNAME}"
```

This syntax has the opposite effect from the previous examples, because the alternative value will be substituted for the ${} expression if the variable is *defined* instead of undefined. Here, if the username variable is defined and not null, the value of LOGNAME will be used instead of username. If username is undefined, or defined but null, then a null value is used. In any event, the value of the username variable will not be changed.

+ Syntax

```
username=""
echo "${username+$LOGNAME}"
```

When the colon is removed from the previous example, the value of LOGNAME is used in place of the ${} expression whenever the username variable is defined; the username variable is not required to have an actual (non null) value for this substitution to take place. If the username variable is undefined, a null value is substituted.

The :+ and + syntax could be used in much the same way as the :- and − syntax is used. The main difference is that the :+ and + examples are checking for a defined value instead of undefined. This is much like addition and subtraction being opposite sides of the same coin. You can add negatives or subtract positives.

Experiment with each technique to gain a clear understanding of how they work and when they are most useful. You should also refer to your shell's man page which discusses each of these forms. In the bash shell, you can find these defined in the section on pattern expansion. In the ksh man page, they can be found in the parameter expansion section.

Chapter 7: Indirect Reference

Variables

It is possible to set a normal (direct) variable in a number of ways: a) directly, by assigning it a value, b) by storing the output of a command, or c) by storing the results of some type of calculation. In all of these cases, although you might not know the value of a variable in advance of any given point, you do know the name of the variable that is to receive the value.

For example, AGE=36 is a direct variable assignment. The value of 36 might change at a later stage; it may also have some calculation applied to it, but the variable *name* AGE will not change.

In some cases, however, you may need to have the ability to generate variable *names* on the fly. You may not know the number or names of variables you are going to need at the time of execution. These could be referred to as 'variable variables', or 'variable variable names'

The following script shows an example of how to create and use such indirect variables. It monitors log files and notifies the user when specified string values show up in the file. The script is designed to run continuously while keeping track of where it last left off in the file; thus, it knows where to start the next time it looks. The configuration value at the beginning of the script points to the log files it needs to watch and the string values to be tracked.

This configuration value can consist of many entries, each specifying strings which the script needs to watch for in all the tracked files. There may be several entries specifying different strings for the same log file. Our example script is configured in this way.

```
#!/bin/sh
#set -x
debug=0
DELAY=120
LOGCHKS="/var/log/messages:authentication%20failure:\
  rbpeters:warn /var/log/messages:recv%20failure::error"
```

This `LOGCHKS` variable configures which log files will be monitored. You could create a separate configuration file to hold this information, but to keep things straightforward, I've included the configuration variables as part of the script.

Each entry consists of four fields separated by ':'. These are the meanings of the four fields:

First: The full path to the log file being watched: nothing special here.

Second: The string or strings to watch for. Multiple strings can be specified in this field by separating each by '|'. Because the entries in the configuration string are themselves separated by spaces, you can't have a space within the watch string. If you want to watch for a phrase that includes spaces, they need to be replaced with '%20', as shown in the `LOGCHKS` variable assignment.

Third: Exception strings that are to be ignored. In our example, the script will watch for any *authentication failure* messages in the `/var/log/messages` file, with the *exception* of those containing the string *rbpeters*. The subfields of this field, like those of the second, are '|' separated, and any spaces should be replaced with '%20'.

Fourth: Notification level. The two values here are either *warn* or *error*. If the notification is not an *error*, the script defaults to *warn*. The notification strings are left undefined as they will be determined by the user implementing them.

```
while :
do
  entry_count=0
  for LOGCHK in `echo $LOGCHKS`
  do
```

First, start the infinite loop in which the script will be running is started. Then we can start looking at each configuration entry.

```
    logfile=`echo $LOGCHK | cut -d: -f1`
    strings="`echo $LOGCHK | cut -d: -f2`"
    strings="`echo $strings | sed -e \"s/%20/ /g\"`"
```

```
exceptions=`echo $LOGCHK | cut -d: -f3`
exceptions="`echo $exceptions | \
    sed -e \"s/%20/ /g\"`"
notify=`echo $LOGCHK | cut -d: -f4`
```

Now all values of the configured entry have to be parsed and then assigned to a (direct) variable. The script also replaces '%20' characters with real spaces.

```
entry_count=`expr $entry_count + 1`
```

entry_count represents the number assigned to the specific *entry* in the configuration string. If there are two log files that are configured to be watched, their entry_count values will be 1 and 2, respectively. This variable will be used later to create a new variable on the fly.

```
suffix=`echo $logfile | sed -e s/\\\//_/g`
suffix=`echo $suffix | sed -e s/\\\./_/g`
```

The suffix is nothing more than the name of the log file. Slashes (/'s) and dots (.'s) are replaced with underscores (_'s). The *suffix* value is also used later to build indirect variable names. The combination of this suffix and the entry_count will allow us to create unique variable names specific to the log files that the script is working with.

Next comes the first reference to an indirect variable. A normal line of code within a script is evaluated by the shell so that any variables are replaced with their values before any comparisons or calculations are performed.

The eval command is used when you want the shell to perform an *additional* evaluation prior to the normal evaluation. This is what will allow you to construct names for new variables using the values of existing variables.

In this case, the line in the script is this:

```
if [ "`eval echo '$COUNT'${suffix}_$entry_count`" = "" ]
```

After the first explicit evaluation (in the embedded eval), to the shell, the line would look like this:

```
if [ "$COUNT_var_log_messages_1" = "" ]
```

Then, when the shell evaluates the line normally, it just sees a direct variable, although we know that the direct variable has been conjured up by a prior evaluation.

```
if [ "`eval echo '$COUNT'${suffix}_$entry_count`" = "" ]
```

```
then
    eval BASE${suffix}_$entry_count=`wc -l $logfile \
      | awk '{ print $1 }'`
fi
```

Now back to the code logic: The code then checks whether the base line count of the file is null. The only time the base line count of the log file can be null is the first time the line count is tested. If this is the case, the base line count is set to the current file length (in number of lines).

Resetting the value of the line count the first time the loop is executed is a safe way of *not* having the monitor find any previous string entries being watched for in the log file. We don't want to see strings that were there prior to the monitor ever running.

```
eval COUNT${suffix}_$entry_count=`wc -l $logfile \
    | awk '{ print $1 }'`
```

Now the line count of the log file is set. The line count is different from the base count. Let us assume the script starts up to find 10 lines in the log file. The base value of the log is then set to 10. It then sets the line count of the file to 10, sees there is no difference between the two, and completes running this script segment.

The script then sleeps for the number of seconds specified at the beginning of the script and wakes up again. Suppose that it now finds 13 lines in the file. The difference between the line count of the file and the *base value* is what is used to detect new log entries.

```
if [ `eval echo '$COUNT'${suffix}_$entry_count` -gt \
    `eval echo '$BASE'${suffix}_$entry_count` ]
then
    LINES=`eval expr '$COUNT'${suffix}_$entry_count - \
      '$BASE'${suffix}_$entry_count`
    eval \ BASE${suffix}_$entry_count='$COUNT'${suffix}_$entry_count
    if [ "$exceptions" != "" ]
    then
      MSGS=`tail -$LINES $logfile | egrep -i \
          "\"$strings\"" | egrep -iv "$exceptions"`
      test $debug -gt 0 && echo "MSGS is $MSGS"
    else
      MSGS=`tail -$LINES $logfile | \
```

```
        egrep -i "$strings"`
    test $debug -gt 0 && echo "MSGS is $MSGS"
fi
```

This is the code that checks to see whether the log file has grown. If it has grown, we use the `tail` command to check the newly added lines inside the log file for the desired strings. The script then resets the *base value* of the file to whatever the current *count* happens to be so we don't look at lines that have already been checked.

```
if [ ! -z "$MSGS" ]
then
  if [ "$notify" != "error" ]
  then
     echo Send a warning notification...
  else
     echo Send an error notification...
  fi
fi
```

If there are any messages found in the log file that match what you're looking for, the script should send a notification. As mentioned earlier, there are two possible forms of notification: a warning and an error. In the environments I've worked with, both notification methods would normally result in an email with a warning status message, or in an alphanumeric page if it were a more critical message. You will want to decide how to configure the notifications, so the code here just echoes a message depending on the notification type.

```
elif [ `eval echo '$COUNT'${suffix}_$entry_count` \
    -lt `eval echo '$BASE'${suffix}_$entry_count` ]
then
  # This resets the tracked size of the
  # log if the log size gets smaller
  eval BASE${suffix}_$entry_count='$COUNT'${suffix}_$entry_count
  if [ "$exceptions" != "" ]
  then
    MSGS=`cat $logfile | egrep -i "\"$strings\"" | \
        egrep -iv "$exceptions"`
    test $debug -gt 0 && echo "MSGS is $MSGS"
```

```
    else
      MSGS=`cat $logfile | egrep -i "$strings"`
      test $debug -gt 0 && echo "MSGS is $MSGS"
    fi
    if [ ! -z "$MSGS" ]
    then
      if [ "$notify" != "error" ]
      then
        echo Send a warning notification...
      else
        echo Send an error notification...
      fi
    fi
```

If the line count of the file is less than the base value (the value from the previous loop through the code), you need to reset the base value. A likely scenario for this occurrence is when the log file is trimmed to a preset size in order to save disk space such as with the logrotate utility. If this is the case, we want to check the whole file for the strings we're looking for. If we don't, we might miss something.

```
    else
        test $debug -gt 0 && echo "No change in size of $logfile"
    fi
  done
  sleep $DELAY
done
```

If there is no change in the file size, there is nothing that needs to be done. We just complete the loop, and go back and repeat the same operations for all the other log files in the configuration string. Finally, the script should sleep for the specified amount of time before starting over again.

Chapter 8: Shell Process Tree

The process tree script presented in this chapter does exactly what its name suggests: It prints out the names of some or all of the currently running processes that are present in the process table, displaying the parent/child relationships that exist among them in the form of a visual tree. There is an implementation of this functionality on some versions of Solaris (`ptree`) and on all flavors of Linux (`pstree`). These have proved very valuable to me for finding the root of a process group quickly, especially when that part of the process tree needs to be shut down.

There are some UNIX-based operating systems that don't have this functionality, such as HP-UX, hence the reason for this script. Along the way, this script also demonstrates several interesting shell programming techniques.

This script was originally a shell wrapper for an `awk` script[1] whose code I decided to rewrite for this book using a shell scripting language. All of the versions of this script listed here use the same algorithm. The difference between them is that the first version stores data within arrays, and the second version uses indirect variables. The last version is one that will run in the Bourne shell if that is all you have. Although the array version provides a good demonstration of arrays, it is not ideal since it requires `bash`. While `bash` may be installed on many systems , there is no guarantee that you will find it on non-Linux systems. The indirect variable method is more useful as it can be run in either `ksh` or `bash` with only minor modifications. You can find a more in-depth explanation of the indirect variable technique in Chapter 7.

Here is some sample output from the script. It contains only some of the process tree of a running system, but it gives a good impression of the full output.

| \

---

1   Based on an `awk` script that was written by Mark Gemmell and posted to the `comp.unix.sco.misc` Usenet newsgroup in 1996.

```
|  2887 /usr/sbin/klogd -c 3 -2
|\
|  3362 /bin/sh /usr/bin/mysqld_safe
|   \
|     3425 /usr/sbin/mysqld --basedir=/usr
|      \
|        3542 /usr/sbin/mysqld --basedir=/usr
|       |\
|       |   3543 /usr/sbin/mysqld --basedir=/usr
|        \
|           3547 /usr/sbin/mysqld --basedir=/usr
 \
     3552 /usr/sbin/sshd
```

Process Tree Implemented Using Arrays

The concept of the script is simple enough: It can be run with no arguments, and its output is then the complete tree representation of all current entries in the process table. A process id can also be passed to the script, and then it will generate a tree displaying that process and its descendants.

```
#!/bin/bash
if [ "$1" = "" ]
then
  proc=1
else
  proc=$1
fi
```

By default, the root of the process tree output will be the init process, which has the process id 1. The first part of the code sets the process id to 1 if no process number has been passed to the script.

```
main () {
PSOUT=`ps -ef | grep -v "^UID" | sort -n -k2`
```

As its name suggests, the main() function contains the main code to be executed. A main() function is something that you may not often see in shell scripts, as it is not required. I have defined a `main()` function here because I wanted to explain this code first. Functions need to be defined before they can be called, and I would normally define functions near the beginning of a script and place the main script code that calls these functions after the function definitions. Here I have used a `main()` function, which is invoked at the bottom of the script, and put its definition at the top of the script, because it is easier to describe the main logic of the code before dealing with that of the helper function. Having a `main()` function is not required in shell scripts, however, (as it is in, say, C programs) and the script can easily be organized either way.

First, the script creates a variable containing the current process table information. The switches passed to the `ps` command here (`-ef`) are typical but depending on the OS you're running, different switches (-aux) may be more appropriate. You may also need to modify the variable assignments to properly reflect these variations. The command usage in Linux systems is somewhat of a combination of these types, and `ps` under Linux will accept both option sets.

```
while read line
do
```

Here is the start of the loop that goes through the whole process table and grabs the needed information for each process. My first inclination here would be to perform the `ps` command to generate the process table; then I would pipe the table to the `while` loop. That way we would not need to generate a temporary output file, which would be more efficient.

While the intention would be noble, it wouldn't work in `pdksh` or `bash`. It does, however, work in `ksh`. When the output from `ps` is piped to the loop in `pdksh` or `bash`, the loop is spawned in a sub-shell and so any variables defined there are not available to the parent shell after the loop completes. Instead of piping the output of `ps` to the `while` loop, the variable containing the process table output is redirected into an input file handle from the other end, and we get to keep our variable definitions. This technique is discussed further in Chapter 10.

This loop processes each line of the redirected file one by one and gathers information about each running system and user process.

```
line=`echo "$line" | sed -e s/\>/\\\\\\>/g`
```

Some entries in the process table may have the `'>'` character in the output displaying the command being executed. Occurrences of this character (which means redirection to the shell) must be escaped, or else they may cause the script to act inappropriately. The `sed` command here replaces the `'>'` character with `'\>'`. There are other characters, such as the pipe `'|'`, that may occur in the `ps` output and present the same issue. In these cases, which are not accounted for here, additional lines similar to this one would be needed.

```
declare -a process=( $line )
```

Next we need to define an array, here called `process[]`, to hold the elements of the `ps` output line being read. I chose the `bash` shell to run this version of the script because its array structure does not enforce an upper bound on the number of array elements or on the subscripts used to access them. The `pdksh` shell limits the size of arrays to 1024 elements, and `ksh93` will allow up to 4095 array elements. Both shells also require the subscripts that index the array elements to be integers starting from 0. This latter restriction isn't a problem when setting up the array that contains a single line from the `ps` output. However, the process id will be used later as an index into other arrays, and then this limitation does become a problem. Process ids are commonly integers greater than 1024, and it happens quite frequently that their values reach five-digit numbers.

A possible modification would be to use translation tables, that is, arrays associating smaller subscript values with the actual process id numbers. The tree structure would then be created using these values, and then it would be possible to print out the original process ids using the translation tables. Even with this modification, you would still be limited on the number of processes that could be handled. This script doesn't have that limitation. Later in this chapter we give a version of this script that uses indirect variables and `eval` to implement pseudo-arrays that allow very large sets of data items to be individually accessed using arbitrary indexes.

```
pid=${process[1]}
```

Here's where the arrays containing process information are populated. These arrays are indexed by process id. First we get the process id (pid) of the process whose line of information is being read.

```
owner[$pid]=${process[0]}
ppid[$pid]=${process[2]}
command[$pid]="`echo $line | awk '{for(i=8;i<=NF;i++) \
  {printf "%s ",$i}}'`"
```

We use an `owner[]` array to hold strings specifying the owner of each process. First we store the name of the current process's owner in the appropriate array location.

Next we assign the appropriate element of the `ppid[]` array (for *parent pid*) the process id of the parent of the current process.

Then we do the same for the `command[]` array, which holds the commands being executed by each running process. The difference here is that the command being run isn't necessarily a simple value. The command could be just one word, or it could be quite long. The array assignment statement pipes the `line` variable's current value to an `awk` script which outputs the fields of the `ps` output line for this process, starting from the eighth field. This is done using a loop controlled by NF (number of fields), since it cannot be known in advance how many whitespace-separated fields the command will occupy. What is known is that the elements of the command string start at the eighth field of the ps output. Keep in mind that if you change the switches given to the ps command that generates this output, you may need to modify this awk statement to reflect the new output format.

```
children[${ppid[$pid]}]="${children[${ppid[$pid]}]} $pid"
```

The last assignment is a bit tricky. The children[] array is indexed by pid and each of its elements contains a list of the pids of the corresponding process's children. This assignment adds the pid of the current process to the list of children of its parent process. An example may make the logic of this step more clear. Consider a process tree consisting entirely of two processes, process 1 and process 2, where process 2 is the child of process 1. Suppose that at this point in the script, the line variable contains the information for process 2. Then the array assignment adds the current pid (2) to the list stored in the element of the children[] array for the process with id 1. In this way, when the array has been populated and you want to know the children of a process with a particular pid you can access the children[] array using that pid as the subscript.

The assignment appends the current pid to the children[] array entry because any given process may have multiple children. For example, take the process with pid 1 on any running system. This is the original system startup process and will have many direct children. Note also, it is not necessary to explicitly track grandchildren (or further descendants), as they will be the direct children of other processes and appear elsewhere in the children[] array already.

```
Done <<EOF
$PSOUT
EOF
```

This completes the loop. As discussed above, the process table file handle is redirected into the loop from the back end. This is a very efficient algorithm, since it takes in the whole process table and appropriately categorizes all the data in it using only one iteration through the table.

```
print_tree $proc ""
}
```

Now that all the data has been read, we can call the function that prints it out in tree form, which completes the main() function.

```
print_tree () {
```

```
id=$1
```

The `print_tree()` function is called with two parameters. The first is the pid of the process that should be at the root of the tree. The second is a string that will be pre-pended to the information about a process to form a line of displayed output. This string contains the characters that depict the tree branch structure leading up to a tree leaf. The first time the function is called (from the `main()` function above) the second argument is set to null because the root of the process tree has no branches leading into it.

This function is used recursively to process the tree level by level. As can be seen by examining the sample output shown earlier, the ASCII characters needed to print out a particular node is determined by its level in the tree and whether or not it is the last child of its parent. When we recursively descend one level in the tree to the next child, this adds one more straight branch symbol and an appropriate slanted branch (or space) leading into the child.

```
echo "$2$id" ${owner[$id]} ${command[$id]}
```

This is where the output of the process id, owner and command are printed. You can add more information like parent pid or cpu time, but you would have to modify the main function.

```
if [ "${children[$id]}" = "" ]
then
   return
```

If the process has no children, the function will stop and return to the caller in order to process the next tree branch.

```
else
   for child in ${children[$id]}
   do
```

If the process does have child processes associated with it, we loop through the list of its children so that those branches of the tree can be printed.

```
    if [ "$child" = "`echo ${children[${ppid[$child]}]} |\
      awk '{print $NF}'`" ]
    then
      echo "$2 \\"
      temp="$2    "
    else
```

```
    echo "$2|\\"
    temp="$2|    "
  fi
```

Now we determine if the current child process is the last one in the `children` array. If it is, print a terminating branch character `'\'` to the screen. If it isn't, print a split branch `'|\'` which will allow for this child process and its direct descendants on the tree.

When this function is called, it is assumed that the ASCII characters depicting the tree structure have already been set for the current process being displayed. The responsibility of the function is to then determine what the branch structure will be for the next process to be displayed so the branches will line up appropriately.

```
  print_tree $child "$temp"
```

Now we recursively call the function with the current child process id and the new prefix string. This is a natural way to write a `print_tree()` function, because a tree is a recursive data structure. Each branch off the main trunk will either branch again or terminate. This continues on until all branches terminate. In the case of the processes running on a system, the `init` process will have child processes, which will in turn have children or be terminal (childless) processes.

```
  done
fi
}
main
```

This completes the loop and the function and the main code of the script itself, which as discussed earlier, just calls the `main()` function.

Process Tree Implemented Using Indirect Variables

The process tree script is interesting in its design, but it isn't that useful as a script because not all systems can run it, and those that can (mainly standard Linux systems using `bash`) already have a command that performs the same task. The following version of the script is more portable and it can be run using either `bash` or `ksh`. There will be very limited commentary on the code, as it is essentially the same as that of the previous script.

```
#!/bin/ksh
if [ "$1" = "" ]
```

```
then
  proc=1
else
  proc=$1
fi

main () {
PSOUT=`ps -ef | grep -v "^UID" | sort -n -k2`
while read line
do
  line=`echo "$line" | sed -e s/\>/\\\\\\\>/g`
  #declare -a process=( $line )
  set -A process $line
```

This array definition is the main line in this script that would need to be changed depending on the shell under which this script will be running. If you are using ksh, you should use set -A. If you are using bash, you should use the declare -a command. Since this script is written for ksh, the declare line has been commented out. The remainder of the script will work under either shell without modification.

```
  pid=${process[1]}
  eval owner$pid=${process[0]}
  eval ppid$pid=${process[2]}
  eval command$pid="\"`echo $line | awk '{for(i=8;i<=NF;i++) \
    {printf \"%s \",$i}}'`\""
  eval parent='$ppid'$pid
  eval children$parent=\"'$children'$parent $pid\"
done <<EOF
$PSOUT
EOF
print_tree $proc ""
}

print_tree () {
id=$1
echo -n "$2$id"
eval echo \"'$owner'$id '$command'$id\"
```

```
if eval [ \"'$children'$id\" = \"""\" ]
then
  return
else
  for child in `eval echo '$children'$id`
  do
  eval parent='$ppid'$child
    if [ "$child" = "`eval echo '$children'$parent |\
      awk '{print $NF}'`" ]
    then
      echo "$2 \\"
      temp="$2   "
    else
      echo "$2|\\"
      temp="$2|   "
    fi
    print_tree $child "$temp"
  done
fi
}
main
```

Bourne Shell Implementation of Process Tree

The last version of the script will run under the Bourne shell. The main difference from the other two is that the ps output stored in a temporary file is manually iterated through, one line at a time. This eliminates the issue of undefined variables, which we discuss in detail in Chapter 10. While not quite as elegant or speedy as the earlier versions, it does get the job done. It once again uses the same algorithm as the original and, like the second version, relies on indirect variables. I will limit the commentary to the differences from the previous versions.

```
#!/bin/sh
if [ "$1" = "" ]
then
  proc=1
else
```

```
  proc=$1
fi

main () {
PSFILE=/tmp/duh
ps -ef | sort -n +1 | tail +2 > $PSFILE
pscount=`wc -l $PSFILE`
count=0
```

Since I have written a manual counter loop, I have to initialize the counter. Then I have to determine the number of lines in the file through which we will iterate .

```
while [ $count -le $pscount ]
do
  line=`tail +$count $PSFILE | head -1`
```

The `while` loop continues until the counter is equal to the number of lines in the input file. The assignment of the `line` variable is the key here. It uses the `tail` utility to start its output at the appropriate line number and then pipes that to the `head` utility to capture only the first line.

```
  line=`echo "$line" | sed -e s/\>/\\\\\\>/g`
  pid=`echo $line | awk '{print $2}'`
  eval owner$pid=\"`echo $line | awk '{print $1}'`\"
  eval ppid$pid=\"`echo $line | awk '{print $3}'`\"
  eval command$pid="\"`echo $line | awk '{for(i=8;i<=NF;i++) \
    {printf \"%s \",$i}}'`\""
  eval parent='$ppid'$pid
  eval children$parent=\"'$children'$parent $pid\"
count=`echo $count+1 | bc`
done
print_tree $proc ""
}

print_tree () {
id=$1
echo "$2$id \c"
eval echo \"'$owner'$id '$command'$id\"
```

The last two lines here, which were combined in the earlier versions of this script, wouldn't play well together under the Bourne shell, so I split them up. The '\c' instructs the first echo command not to perform a carriage return after the output. The output of the subsequent echo of the owner and command variables completes the output.

```
if eval [ \"'$children'$id\" = "\"\"" ]
then
  return
else
  for child in `eval echo '$children'$id`
  do
    eval parent='$ppid'$child
    if [ "$child" = "`eval echo '$children'$parent | \
      awk '{print $NF}'`"]
    then
      echo "$2 \\"
      temp="$2   "
    else
      echo "$2|\\"
      temp="$2|   "
    fi
    print_tree $child "$temp"
  done
fi
}
main
```

Chapter 9: Data Redirection

Output redirection seems to be a common point of confusion among users. I have seen problems with its usage arise most often when a user wants to set up a `cron` job that sends all its output to `/dev/null`, such as in the following `crontab` entry.

```
10 5 * * * /run/some/script > /dev/null 2>&1
```

In this example, all of the output will be sent to `/dev/null`, whether it is standard output generated by the script or error output generated by the shell or the commands in the script. This kind of `cron` job is usually created because a simple `cron` entry without any redirection will cause an email containing all the output, both standard output and error output, to be sent to the owner of the job. Many users don't want this type of annoying email, but instead of modifying the script code to only output information when useful, they set up the `cron` job to throw all of it out. In general this is a bad habit to develop. I have seen jobs like this run for years under the assumption that it was performing the desired task, when all the while it did nothing because it was broken and the error output was never sent to alert the user of the problem.

```
10 5 * * * /run/some/script 2>&1 > /dev/null
```

As in the previous `cron` example, users will sometimes attempt to remove the output with syntax like this. Even assuming that we do want to suppress all output, this syntax is wrong for the intended purpose. You'll notice that the `> /dev/null` and `2>&1` pieces of the entry are reversed. In its current form, `stderr` output from the job will continue to be mailed to the user.

```
10 5 * * * /run/some/script > /dev/null
```

Other times something like this is attempted. While this will remove any normal output (output to stdout), it won't redirect error messages that the script might generate, and those will still be emailed to the user.

All of these problems seem to stem from a misunderstanding of the types of output that a process can generate. The file descriptors for the usual output streams are 1 for the standard output stream (also known as stdout), 2 for the standard error stream (also known as stderr), and 0 for the standard input stream (also known as stdin). You can think of these as separate communication channels between the script and its environment. For output, there is a channel for messages coming from a program such as echo or grep or a statement of the script code, which is stdout. There is also a separate channel for messages that are generated from failures of a command, such as when an attempt is made to open a nonexistent file. In this case, the "No such file or directory" error message will be sent to the stderr stream.

When the > or < characters are used without a specific file descriptor, stdout and stdin are assumed, respectively. I think of the characters as arrows showing the direction in which the data will travel for further processing. In the common cases, a command is run and its output is > pointed toward a destination file. When the reverse pointer < is used, the content of the file is being redirected into the initiating command or code sequence through its input stream.

Common Redirection

These are some of the most commonly used redirection arguments and their meaning. There are others as well, and more detailed explanations are specified in the bash and ksh man pages.

---

expression < *file*

Redirect the contents of *file* into the *expression*. An example of this usage is the command mail -s "/etc/hosts" you@domain.com < /etc/hosts, in which the /etc/hosts file will be used as the body of the mail message being sent.

---

expression > *file*

Redirect the output of *expression* to the specified *file*. If the file does not exist, it is created. If the file already exists, it is overwritten unless the noclobber option to set is applied. An example is grep 192.168 /etc/hosts > /tmp/outfile, where /tmp/outfile will contain the results of the grep command after the line finishes executing.

---

expression >| *file*

Redirect the output of *expression* to the specified *file*. This is similar to the previous example, except that it overrides the `noclobber` option of the shell. When the `noclobber` option is set, the file won't be overwritten when the `>` redirector is used. This syntax forces that overwrite.

expression `>>` *file*

Redirect the output of *expression* to the specified *file* in append mode. If the command in the earlier example above is followed by the command `grep 172.16 /etc/hosts >> /tmp/outfile`, then the output of this `grep` command will be appended to the end of the file containing the output of the `grep` command in the previous example.

expression `2> /dev/null > ` *file*

Redirect `stderr` output from the *expression* to `/dev/null` while redirecting `stdout` output to the specified *file*.

expression `> /dev/null 2> ` *file*

Redirect `stdout` from the *expression* to `/dev/null` while redirecting `stderr` to the *file*. This is the converse of the previous example.

expression `> ` *file* `2>&1`

Redirect both `stdout` and `stderr` output from *expression* to the specified *file*. This syntax specifies that `stderr` (2) output is assigned to `stdout` (1) and both are redirected to the specified *file*.

expression `&> ` *file*

Redirect both `stdout` and `stderr` output from the *expression* to the *file*. This is a shorthand version of the previous syntax that is available from the `bash` shell.

expression `2> ` *file*

Redirect `stderr` output from the *expression* to the *file*. An example of this is `find /home -type f -exec grep -l "some_string" {} \; 2> /dev/null`. This command will output all the file names returned by the `find` command containing the string *some_string,* but redirect any *'permission denied'* errors to `/dev/null`.

```
{
  cat file1
```

```
  cat file2
  cat file3
} > file.output
```

```
cat nodelist | while read line ; do
  echo $node
  rsh $node uptime
done >> uptime.report
```

```
while read line
do
  count=$((count+1))
  echo -n Field 2 of line $count is:
  echo $line | awk '{print $2}'
done < /input/file
```

```
count=0
while [ $count -lt 10 ]
do
  echo $count
  count=$((count+1))
done > count.output
```

Redirection can be used not only for simple commands and script invocations, but also with if, for, while, until, and case structures, as well as pipes and batched commands. The code above gives a few samples of how you might use redirection of complex statements in your scripts.

```
count=0
while read line
do
  count=$((count+1))
  echo $count: $line
done < /etc/hosts > lined.hosts
```

Multiple redirections can also be used. In this short example the code takes the contents of the /etc/hosts file as input to the while loop. The loop adds line numbers to the file and the final output is then redirected to the lined.hosts file.

Access to User-Specified File Handles

In most programming languages, you can open a file descriptor for reading, writing, or both, and then read or make modifications to the data and then close the file. Shell scripting languages are no exception. Up to now, I have only discussed redirection of output to a given file or to one of the standard input or output file streams. Now we'll discuss the method of opening a file handle for a specific type of operation (read/write/both), but instead of opening the file each time you want to access it, you instead create a file handle with a user-defined file descriptor that can then be accessed in various modes, using the same syntax as the standard input/output descriptors. Creating a handle for a specified file is done with the exec command. When opening the file, you give it a single-digit file descriptor in the range of 3–9 in order to not conflict with the standard stream descriptors of 0–2.

Any combination of these exec commands can be used in your code to open a file and assign it a single-digit file descriptor:

```
exec 3> file_1
```

This will open file_1 for output in overwrite mode, accessed with file descriptor 3.

```
exec 4< file_2
```

This will open file_2 for input in read mode, accessed with file descriptor 4.

```
exec 5>> file_3
```

This will open file_3 for output in append mode, accessed with file descriptor 5.

```
exec 6<> file_4
```

This will open file_4 for both reading and writing, accessed with file descriptor 6. Unlike the other examples, where you must access the files in the same way that the descriptors were opened, for either reading or writing, this type of descriptor can be accessed in both ways.

Once the file descriptors are open, you can access them with various input or output statements. To access a specific open file descriptor, complete an *expression* with the syntax >&*fd*, where *fd* denotes the single-digit descriptor.

```
echo "The quick brown fox jumped over the lazy dog" >&3
grep 172.16 /etc/hosts >&5
read line <&4
```

Here are a few examples of reading and writing to open files. I have matched the file descriptor numerals (relating to input and output) with the `exec` commands above that originally opened them.

```
If [ -n "$DEBUG" ]
then
   exec 5>&1
else
   exec 5> $LOGFILE
fi
echo "Some Text" >&5
```

Using the `exec` syntax you can also specify your output at runtime instead of hard coding it. This example demonstrates the technique. Based on the value of the DEBUG variable, the code sends output from file descriptor 5 either to `stdout` or to a log file.

When file access is complete, you should close the open file with the `exec` command as shown here:

```
exec 3>&-
```

This keeps your code clean. In both `bash` and `ksh` you will receive a 'Bad file descriptor' error if you attempt to access a file descriptor that hasn't been opened. There is no trouble with closing a file descriptor that is not already open.

Descriptor Access from the Shell

One other method of reading from and writing to an open file descriptor is to use the shell's built-in `print` and `read` commands. Only `ksh` has the `print` command, but both `ksh` and `bash` have `read`. Both of these built-in commands take the `-u` switch, which gives you the ability to specify the file descriptor that you want to access. Once the file is open, you can then output directly to or read directly from that specific descriptor using these built-in commands.

```
print "all your base are belong to us" >&3[1]
```

---

[1] http://wikipedia.org/wiki/All_your_base_are_belong_to_us

```
print -u3 "Now is the time"
```

There are two methods that can be used with the `print` command in `ksh`. The first of the two examples here is the redirection to a specific file descriptor already discussed. The second uses the -u switch with a single-digit file descriptor. These are equivalent commands and are only available in `ksh`.

```
echo "all your base are belong to us" >&3
```

For `bash`, the available command is very similar. You only have access to the redirection syntax, however, as the -u switch isn't supported. You also need to replace the `print` command with `echo`.

```
read line <&3
read -u3 line
```

As with the built-in `print` command, the `read` command can be used in two ways. The first of these examples specifies redirection to a file descriptor. The second uses the -u switch, like the `print` command in `ksh`. The main difference here is that both `bash` and `ksh` have this capability.

All of these examples assume the file has been opened for reading or writing as appropriate. When you try to access a file descriptor that has not been opened, you will receive an '*invalid file descriptor: Bad file descriptor*' error in `bash` and a '*bad file unit number [Bad file descriptor]*' error in `ksh`.

Chapter 10: Piping Input to

read

In this chapter we are going to deal with a gotcha that I came across while porting a script from ksh to bash. It was only a gotcha because at the time I wasn't aware of a fairly crucial difference in the behavior of the two shells. In both pdksh and bash, the last command of a pipeline is performed in a sub shell. This means that a variable assigned within the sub shell is not available to the parent shell. In ksh, the last commands of a pipeline is executed in the same shell.

This isn't an issue when using the pipe to set a variable, but if the result of a pipe is sent to a loop structure which then populates variables that you will use later, that is more of a problem. Once the loop completes, the variables that you were going to rely on don't exist. Included here are a few of examples of code that a less experienced user would expect to work, but actually don't. I also include some usable workarounds that will perform the intended task.

This is the part of the code that had problems when ported. It was used to process a file of extended output one line at a time. To perform this task in ksh, I would use the following.

```
cat somefile | while read line
do
  # Process the $line variable in some form.
  if [ "`echo $line | awk '{print $3}'`" = "somevalue" ]
  then
    $all="$all $line"
  fi
```

```
done
```

If everything within the loop is self-contained and nothing in it is outside the loop, this will work fine. However, the `bash` code parsed each line in the output of the piped command, and populated some variables based on that output. Once the loop completed, I wanted to access those values ($all in this example) for other purposes and found that they were undefined.

Below is the first workaround that I found to overcome the problem. Unfortunately it isn't quite as elegant or intuitive as the original code because it uses a temporary file. As a general rule, I try to avoid using temporary files in order to keep the code clean, but this was a case where I had no choice but to create and use a temporary file.

```
while read line
do
   # Process the $line variable in some form.
   if [ "`echo $line | awk '{print $3}'`" = "somevalue" ]
   then
     $all="$all $line"
   fi
done < somefile
```

First, the data originally piped to the `while read` loop is now sent to a temporary file. The file is then redirected into the back end of the loop. This functions the same way as the original code, but allows the variables populated within the loop to remain usable once the loop completes. Another example of this technique can be found in Chapter 8. This is the modified form of our initial example.

```
THE_INPUT=`ps -ef`
while read line
do
   # Process the $line variable in some form.
   if [ "`echo $line | awk '{print $3}'`" = "somevalue" ]
   then
     $all="$all $line"
   fi
done <<EOF
$THE_INPUT
EOF
```

This slight modification of prior example eliminates the need for a temporary file. Instead of redirecting a file into the back of the loop, we start what is called a here-document and feed it the data we want to process through the loop. A here-document is where the shell reads input from the current source until it reaches the matching tag alone on a single line, in this case EOF. This solution works in the same way as a real file with both bash and pdksh.

The following sections show four methods for reading input one line at a time. With each method, I'll explain what variables are available at the various points within the code for each of the four shells (bash, ksh, pdksh, and Bourne sh).

Line by Line Option 1

The original method of piping input to a read loop looks like this:

```
ps -ef | while read firstvar
do
  echo firstvar within the loop: $firstvar
  secondvar=$firstvar
  echo secondvar within the loop: $secondvar
done
echo firstvar outside the loop: $firstvar
echo secondvar outside the loop: $secondvar
```

ksh

Both firstvar and secondvar are available within the loop. Only secondvar is available outside the loop. This is useful because even though you can't use the original read variable, you can assign it to some other variable which is then available when the loop completes.

bash

Both firstvar and secondvar are available within the loop. Neither firstvar nor secondvar are available after the loop completes.

pdksh

Both firstvar and secondvar are available within the loop. Neither firstvar nor secondvar are available after the loop completes.

Bourne

Both firstvar and secondvar are available within the loop. Neither firstvar nor secondvar are available after the loop completes.

Line by Line Option 2

This is the workaround option we originally discussed. The input will be sent to a temporary file and then redirected to the back of the loop.

```
ps -ef > /tmp/testfile
while read firstvar
do
  echo firstvar within the loop: $firstvar
  secondvar=$firstvar
  echo secondvar within the loop: $secondvar
done < /tmp/testfile
echo firstvar outside the loop: $firstvar
echo secondvar outside the loop: $secondvar
```

ksh

Both `firstvar` and `secondvar` are available within the loop. Only `secondvar` is available outside the loop.

bash

Both `firstvar` and `secondvar` are available within the loop. Only `secondvar` is available outside the loop. This version now performs in the same manner as the `ksh` version.

pdksh

Both `firstvar` and `secondvar` are available within the loop. Only `secondvar` is available outside the loop.

Bourne

Both `firstvar` and `secondvar` are available within the loop. Neither variable is available outside the loop.

Line by Line Option 3

This is the here-document workaround option where we remove the need for a temporary file. This functions in the same way as option 2. A here-document is where the shell reads input from the current source until it reaches the end tag alone on a single line, in this case EOF

```
the_input=`ps -ef`
```

```
while read firstvar
do
  echo firstvar within the loop: $firstvar
  secondvar=$firstvar
  echo secondvar within the loop: $secondvar
done <<EOF
$the_input
EOF
echo firstvar outside the loop: $firstvar
echo secondvar outside the loop: $secondvar
```

ksh

Both firstvar and secondvar are available within the loop. Only secondvar is available outside the loop.

bash

Both firstvar and secondvar are available within the loop. Only secondvar is available outside the loop. This version now performs in the same manner as the ksh version.

pdksh

Both firstvar and secondvar are available within the loop. Only secondvar is available outside the loop.

Bourne

Both firstvar and secondvar are available within the loop. Neither variable is available outside the loop.

Line by Line Option 4

This last option removes the pipe '|' from the loop and processes an input file manually. If you have only the Bourne shell at your disposal, this would be your only option, and the script will be somewhat slower. With this option, all set variables from both inside and outside the loop will be available following loop completion. This is valid for all shells we mentioned.

```
ps -ef > /tmp/testfile
filecount=`wc -l /tmp/testfile`
count=0
```

```
while [ $count -le $filecount ]
do
    firstvar=`tail +$count /tmp/testfile | head -1`
    echo firstvar within the loop: $firstvar
    secondvar=$firstvar
    echo secondvar within the loop: $secondvar
    count=`echo $count+1 | bc`
done < /tmp/testfile
echo firstvar outside the loop: $firstvar
echo secondvar outside the loop: $secondvar
```

The following tables summarize all of the previously discussed scenarios. Table 10-1 displays the availability of the variable that is initially set in the loop (firstvar). Note that in all shells except for the manual loop, this variable is not available for use following the loop's completion.

	Ksh	Bash	Pdksh	Bourne
Opt. 1. Pipe to While Read	*No*	*No*	*No*	*No*
Opt. 2. Redirected File to Back of Loop	*No*	*No*	*No*	*No*
Opt 3. Redirected Here-Document to Back of Loop	*No*	*No*	*No*	*No*
Opt. 4. Manual Iteration through Loop	Yes	Yes	Yes	Yes

Table 10-1: Availability of Variables that Are Initially Set in a Loop, After Loop Completion

Table 10-2 displays variable availability within the loop (secondvar) once the loop has completed. These can be values assigned to the initial variable (firstvar), since that variable is accessible within the loop or from any other assignment inside the loop.

	Ksh	Bash	Pdksh	Bourne
Opt. 1. Pipe to While Read	Yes	*No*	*No*	*No*

Opt. 2. Redirected File to Back of Loop	Yes	Yes	Yes	No
Opt. 3. Redirected Here-Document to Back of Loop	Yes	Yes	Yes	No
Opt. 4. Manual Iteration through Loop	Yes	Yes	Yes	Yes

Table 10-2: Availability of Variables that Are Set Within a Loop, After Loop Completion

Pipe to Read Directly

The next example represents a scenario where the script does not pipe to a loop, but instead pipes input to a `read` statement. This method works well in `ksh`. Within both `pdksh` and `bash`, the situation is such that once the following command is executed, both `foo` and `bar` variables are undefined.

```
echo a b | read foo bar
```

The workaround removes the use of the `read` command altogether. This modified version has the same functionality, but it uses two separate commands instead of a pipeline of two commands.

```
set `echo a b` ; foo=$1 bar=$2
```

Using `set` without any options or arguments takes the `echo` output and assigns each output '*word*' using a positional parameter. The parameter can then be reused. This works fine in most instances. However, if $1 is a negative value, the `set` command interprets the - sign as a switch. It then complains about the switch not being valid.

```
set -- `echo a b` ; foo=$1 bar=$2
```

The workaround for this is to use the double dash switch for set. This will tell `set` not to process any further arguments that begin with a + or -.

```
set "@"`echo a b` ; foo=$1 bar=$2
foo=`echo $foo | cut -c1-`
```

One other workaround for this is somewhat of a brute force tactic but may be necessary depending on the age of system or shell you're working with. You prepend some arbitrary character (not a - sign) to the beginning of the echo output to protect against switch evaluation. Once the variables are set, you should strip off the first character of first variable using cut so you will be left with the original value.

Process Input Word by Word

The last example enables you to parse through each word of some input string, consuming two words at a time. Words are assumed to be separated by spaces. This once again uses the set command to assign positional variables the value of each word. The same code as above is implemented, but the core function is now surrounded by a loop that continues until the first word is null.

```
#!/bin/ksh
set `echo a b c d e`
while [ "$1" != "" ]
do
   foo=$1 bar=$2
   echo $*
   shift
   echo foo $foo
   echo bar $bar
done
```

The loop assigns the first two positional parameters to foo and bar. It then outputs the value of all positional variables. The shift command drops the $1 value and promotes $2 and all other variables by one position. It then outputs the values of foo and bar for each iteration. The $* variable that is echoed holds all of the current positional parameters. Thus, after each iteration through the loop, the output of the line is shortened by one element. Note that this script is written in ksh, but it should work in all previously mentioned shells.

Chapter 11: Math from the Shell

$\mathbf{M}$athematical calculations are an important element of writing shell scripts. In the various flavors of UNIX, there are multiple ways to perform just about any task, and mathematical tasks are no exception.

While there are many types of mathematical computations, I am going to limit the discussion in this chapter to the basic operations of addition, subtraction, multiplication, division and remainder, exponentiation, and trigonometric functions. The examples make use of the variables a, b, c, and d.

One note on division: Some programming languages don't perform integer division like you might expect from using your traditional calculator. There are two parts to the quotient of an integer division problem, the *whole* (or *integer*) *part* and the *remainder*. Take the example of 5 divided by 3: The whole part of their quotient is 1 and the remainder upon division is 2. In some of the methods for doing math in the shell that we demonstrate below, there are two distinct operators for integer division. The '/' operator returns the whole part and the '%' operator returns the remainder. Keep this in mind when performing your calculations.

expr

The first of these methods is the use of expr. This is a utility that evaluates various types of expressions, including ones containing string, logical, and mathematical functions. The following are examples of how to use expr to carry out mathematical operations.

Addition:

```
answer=`expr $c + $d`
```

Subtraction:

```
answer=`expr $c - $d`
```

Multiplication:

```
answer=`expr $c \* $d`
```

Division:

```
answer=`expr $c / $d`
```

Remainder:

```
answer=`expr $c % $d`
```

There are no explicit trigonometric or exponentiation functions in expr.

There are a couple of items to keep in mind when using expr. As shown in the examples, single spaces are required between the expr call and its arguments, and between the operators and their arguments. Also, when using the '*' character for multiplication, the shell will interpret it as a wild card and expand it to the elements in your current directory before attempting to evaluate the expression unless you either escape the asterisk '*' or turn off globbing[1] (path and file expansion) using set -f.

Shell Internal Math

The shell itself can also perform mathematical operations. The advantage of using the internal math functions is that your code doesn't have to call an external program, which will reduce the footprint of the code and also allow it to run faster. This method is available in bash and ksh. The Bourne shell does not have this functionality. One note on the use of large numbers in the shell: The largest integer available for internal shell math is $2^{63}-1$, or 9223372036854775807 (in bash and expr; ksh uses scientific notation for large numbers). This is the maximum 64-bit integer. If you need numbers that are larger than this, you will want to use the bc or dc calculators.

---

1   *Globbing* is the term used for the shell's completion of paths and filenames that contain metacharacters.

Addition:

```
answer=$(($c+$d))
```

Subtraction:

```
answer=$(($c-$d))
```

Multiplication:

```
answer=$(($c*$d))
```

Division:

```
answer=$(($c/$d))
```

Remainder:

```
answer=$(($c%$d))
```

Exponentiation:

The first argument raised to the power of the second:

```
answer=$(($c**$d))
```

Order of operations:

The default order can be modified by using parentheses as with all of the methods of performing shell math. Without the use of parentheses to order the calculations as you desire, the common order is as follows: First perform any calculations surrounded by parentheses. These are ones that you may not have specified. Second, perform all calculations that are exponents or roots such as a square or cube root. Third, working from left to right perform any multiplication or division. Last working from left to right, perform any addition and subtraction.

```
answer=$((($c+$d)*$c))
```

A math library is available in `ksh` that can be used to perform more sophisticated mathematical calculations. These are the functions it provides: `abs()`, `acos()`, `asin()`, `atan()`, `atan2()`, `cos()`, `cosh()`, `exp()`, `floor()`, `fmod()`, `hypot()`, `int()`, `log()`, `pow()`, `sin()`, `sinh()`, `sqrt()`, `tan()`, and `tanh()`. The following table gives a basic description of these functions but their use is beyond the scope of this book.

```
answer=$((cos($a)))
```

Trigonometric Function	Description
abs()	Absolute value
acos()	Inverse cosine
asin()	Inverse sine
atan()	Inverse tangent
atan2()	Four-quadrant inverse tangent
cos()	Cosine
cosh()	Hyperbolic cosine
exp()	Exponential
floor()	Round toward minus infinity
fmod()	Floating point remainder of division
hypot()	Square root of sum of squares
int()	Integer portion of a real number
log()	Natural logarithm
pow()	Raise base number to an exponential power
sin()	Sine
sinh()	Hyperbolic sine
sqrt()	Square root
tan()	Tangent
tanh()	Hyperbolic tangent

Table 11.1 Descriptions of Trigonometric Functions Available in `ksh`

bc

The bc utility is an arbitrary-precision calculator. This means that the precision of the answer can be set at runtime through the use of the *scale* operator. Most of the mathematical shell utilities described up to this point focus on operations on whole numbers. The exception is the special library of functions that is available in ksh. With bc, you can set the *scale* (number of decimal places following the decimal point), so that results will be expressed as floating-point numbers of the specified precision. The functional use of bc is very similar to the use of expr.

Addition:

```
answer=`echo "$c+$d" | bc`
```

Subtraction:

```
answer=`echo "$c-$d" | bc`
```

Multiplication:

```
answer=`echo "$c*$d" | bc`
```

Division:

```
answer=`echo "$c/$d" | bc`
```

Remainder:

```
answer=`echo "$c%$d" | bc`
```

Exponentiation:

```
answer=`echo "$c^$d" | bc`
```

Scale:

The scale of a floating-point number is the number of digits that follow the decimal point. Setting the scale when performing a calculation:

```
answer=`echo "scale=5;$c/$d" | bc`
```

Trigonometric functions:

In order to use the trigonometric functions, you must enable the math library by invoking bc using the -1 switch. When the library is enabled, the default scale is set to 20 decimal places. The following examples set the scale to 5 places.

Sine in radians:

```
answer=`echo "scale=5;s($a)" | bc -1`
```

Cosine in radians:

```
answer=`echo "scale=5;c($a)" | bc -1`
```

Arctangent in radians:

```
answer=`echo "scale=5;s($a)" | bc -1`
```

dc

The dc utility is another arbitrary-precision calculator that works much like bc. Its main distinction lies in its use of reverse Polish notation.[2] It uses a stack to store numbers; evaluating a number pushes it onto the stack, and the operations pop their arguments off the stack and push the result back onto the stack. For shell scripting purposes, I have not used the dc calculator. Not that it isn't a valuable program, but the majority of the calculations I've needed are fairly simple and don't require the advantages that it provides. I mention it only for the sake of completeness.

---

2   More information on reverse Polish notation (RPN) can be found at
    http://en.wikipedia.org/wiki/Reverse_polish_notation

Chapter 12: Cron

The system scheduler on UNIX and Linux systems is called cron. Its purpose is to run commands, series of commands, or scripts on a predetermined schedule. This ability would normally be used on systems that run twenty-four hours a day, seven days a week. Writing cron scripts to perform system maintenance, backups, monitors, or any other job that you would want to run on a schedule is a very common task. There are a few subtleties with this application, however, that many users and administrators may be unaware of.

Crontab Entries

On a UNIX or Linux system, the cron daemon process runs all the time. The daemon is started by a run control (rc) script when the system boots. The cron daemon searches for entries in the systemwide or individual user's crontab (short for "cron table") files and loads them into memory. Once each minute, the daemon determines if any of the entries should be run based on its predetermined schedule. A scheduled job can run as often as every minute or as little as once a year.

A crontab entry is a specially formatted line in a crontab file that specifies on which minute, hour, day, day of the week, and day of the month a particular task should be run. To add a task to the cron table, you would run the crontab -e command, which allows an individual user to maintain the entries in the personal crontab file; this launches a session with the editor that is defined by the EDITOR shell environment variable. Each user on a machine may have a crontab file for their own purposes. However, a system administrator can curtail individual users' capabilities according to security policy. The following line is a simple cron entry scheduled to run at 4:15 pm on Tuesdays:

```
15 16 * * 2 /some/path/myscript.sh
```

There are six fields in each entry. The first five fields define the schedule and the remainder of the line is the job that you want to run on that schedule. The last field is what I want to focus on here. Many users are aware that they can run a job within `cron`, although they may not be aware that the task can be quite complex and may therefore contain multiple elements. You can source environment files, set variables, debug the code, put logic into your entry, and call scripts and other commands from the `crontab` file.

This `cron` entry is a more complex example:

```
* * * * set -x ; cron_count=`ps -ef | grep [c]ron | wc -l`\
  ;[ $cron_count -ne 5 ] && echo "Cron Count $cron_count" | mail -s\
  "Cron Count $cron_count" rbpeters
```

The entry first sets the `set -x` expansion flag, assigns a variable, performs a test, and then, based on the results, sends an email message. `cron` entries can be a powerful tool in your scripting arsenal.

Environment Problems

I've worked with many users who have had problems with a script they have coded and debugged for a significant amount of time, only to arrive at the conclusion that "It works from the command line, but not from `cron` ?!" To tell the truth, I have run into this problem from time to time myself, but knowing what the issues are tends to help you find the solution much quicker.

The differences between a script or a program running from `cron` and the same script or program being run manually from the command line is that a script running from `cron` is not run in the same shell environment as a command typed at the prompt. When you log in to a machine and you are at the shell prompt, there are many variables that need to be set to enable your interactive shell session. `cron` is not run from an interactive session, however. A `cron` job only runs with some of the shell environment variables that are set in an interactive shell session. It is a very rudimentary environment. Most problems with users' `cron` scripts that I have seen stem from the assumption that the code runs in an environment with the characteristics of an interactive session, rather than the `cron` environment.

Here's an example to illustrate the difference. This is one of my user environments, which is displayed when I use the `env` command:

```
SSH_CLIENT=172.16.5.199 3433 22
USER=rbpeters
MAIL=/var/mail/rbpeters
```

```
HOME=/home/rbpeters
SSH_TTY=/dev/ttyp1
PAGER=more
ENV=/home/rbpeters/.shrc
LOGNAME=rbpeters
BLOCKSIZE=K
TERM=xterm
PATH=/sbin:/bin:/usr/sbin:/usr/bin:/usr/games:\
  /usr/local/sbin:/usr/local/bin:/usr/X11R6/bin:\
  /home/rbpeters/bin
SHELL=/bin/sh
SSH_CONNECTION=172.16.5.199 3433 172.16.5.2 22
FTP_PASSIVE_MODE=YES
EDITOR=vi
```

I then set up the following `cron` job to run temporarily for illustrative purposes:

```
* * * * * env > /usr/home/rbpeters/env.out
```

After the job ran and created the `env.out` file, I found the following lines in it:

```
USER=rbpeters
HOME=/home/rbpeters
LOGNAME=rbpeters
PATH=/usr/bin:/bin
SHELL=/bin/sh
```

Notice that there is a fairly significant difference between the two environments. For instance, the $PATH variable doesn't have nearly as many directories to search, a state of affairs that can easily break a script. The system `cron` daemon automatically sets the environment variables that make up the minimal environment. It sets the SHELL to /bin/sh, and the PATH to /usr/bin:/bin. The USER, LOGNAME and HOME variables are set based on your entry in the `passwd` file. That's all you get in the default `cron` environment.

If you look at the following slightly modified version of the above `cron` job, you will note the addition of the command to source the .profile file, which sets up some environment parameters prior to running the command. The additional command adds a more useful environment to the `cron` job:

```
* * * * * . /home/rbpeters/.profile >/dev/null ; \
```

```
env > /usr/home/rbpeters/env.out
```

Here is the new output in the `env.out` file:

```
USER=rbpeters
HOME=/home/rbpeters
PAGER=more
ENV=/home/rbpeters/.shrc
LOGNAME=rbpeters
BLOCKSIZE=K
PATH=/sbin:/bin:/usr/sbin:/usr/bin:/usr/games:/usr/local/sbin:\
  /usr/local/bin:/usr/X11R6/bin:/home/rbpeters/bin
SHELL=/bin/sh
EDITOR=vi
```

Now you can see several additional items, as well as a more complete $PATH variable. Another way of getting similar results would be to fully qualify all paths, commands, and other files mentioned in the `cron` script. Supplying the full path to any element that may otherwise rely on the variables set in the interactive shell environment is a good idea in general when writing scripts, since it keeps you aware of the external files that you are depending on.

Finally, you can replace the `env` command with the `set` command and see similar results as shown above. The output is much more extensive, but the same principle still applies.

Output Redirection

When a scheduled `cron` task is run, it may or may not create output. Since there is no interactive session attached to the task, the output, if any, is sent to the owner of the `crontab` file via an email with the subject set to the `cron` entry and the body of the message being the output of the job. This is the email message that I received from the example of a complex `cron` entry shown earlier:

```
++ ps -ef
++ grep '[c]ron'
++ wc -l
+ cron_count=4
+ '[' 4 -ne 5 ']'
+ echo 'Cron Count 4'
```

```
+ mail -s 'Cron Count 4' rbpeters
```

Since the `cron` entry started with a `set -x`, the subsequent commands executed while the job runs are expanded and printed as they are executed. This is a valuable feature when you have to debug the job. Any output from the job will be mailed in the same way. Even though this is useful output, I have found that many users of `cron` will redirect all output to `/dev/null` because once the job is in place, they don't want to become desensitized by too many routine email messages that don't indicate a problem. A typical job might look like this:

```
30 * * * * /usr/local/bin/some_script > dev/null 2>&1
```

This entry, which happens to use a very common pattern, not only redirects normal output (`stdout`) to `/dev/null`, it also redirects all errors (`stderr`) to the same target. This can become a problem. I have seen jobs scheduled like this that have run for years without ever doing anything. They may have environment issues, as described in the previous section. They may have worked at the time of implementation, but at some point a change somewhere else in the system caused the `cron` script to break. In either case, the output that would have warned the user about emerging problems was dropped in the bit bucket. For this and other reasons, I would not recommend using this type of output redirection in a `cron` entry.

Whenever I write a script to be run from `cron`, my goal is to have the script only emit output if a debug flag has been set. Normal usage would not display any output. This way, the `crontab` entry would only send mail when error messages are generated. One level of redirection that I would implement is to redirect only the output (`stdout`) of the script to `/dev/null`. If any error messages were to be created, they would still be sent to the user for diagnostic purposes.

The following modified form of the unsafe `cron` job above would yield the desired result:

```
30 * * * * /usr/local/bin/some_script > dev/null
```

Chapter 13: Self-Linked

Scripts

The technique I am about to discuss allows you to have a single script that can be called in several ways by different names. The script itself contains all the code necessary to perform a number of tasks, but you may want to determine the specific task to be performed at run time by calling the script by a specific name. A possible reason you might want to do this is so that users can invoke an individual task by name, without having to learn specialized command-line switches for the options they want.

There are a couple of ways of specifying the precise behavior of a script. One way is to have the script accept command-line options telling it how to act. This method is covered in Chapter 5, which dealt with the use of getopts. This section will illustrate how to call a script by giving it multiple names.

There are times when you may want to have multiple scripts that perform tasks that are related in some way but with only slight differences. An example, albeit a silly one, would be a script that monitors disk consumption of the / file system.

Filesystem	1K-blocks	Used	Available	Use%	Mounted on
/dev/hda2	18334940	13019804	4383768	75%	/
/dev/hda1	256666	25241	218173	11%	/boot
none	257300	0	257300	0%	/dev/shm
/dev/hdb1	16577308	11732468	4002760	75%	/snapshot

The script will determine the disk utilization percentage from the output of the df command. Above is a sample of df output.

```
#!/bin/sh
fs="/"
fs_total=`df -k $fs | tail -n 1 | awk '{print $2}'`
fs_used=`df -k $fs | tail -n 1 | awk '{print $3}'`
percent_used=$((100*$fs_used/$fs_total))
echo "$fs is at ${percent_used}% capacity"
```

For illustrative purposes, our script doesn't do the obvious and use Use% value from the df output; it will instead calculate disk consumption directly from the 1K-blocks and Used values. So now you have a script that can be used to display the percent utilization of the / file system. We will call this root_check.

Now, suppose that you want to have a similar script, called boot_check, which will perform the same file system capacity check on the /boot partition. First we create a soft link (ln -s) called boot_check pointing to the original root_check script. The following shows the modification to the root_check code that will allow the script to determine how it was called.

```
#!/bin/sh
whatami=`basename $0`
```

The basename command strips off the leading path elements of a file. In this case, the positional parameter $0 containing the name used to invoke the script is supplied. The script could be called with its fully qualified name or with a relative path, and the basename command gives you only the name of the script without those variable items. One thing to note here is that if the script is being run in setuid[1] mode, the shell will drop the environment variables for security reasons, and the value of $0 will become the name of the shell that is running the script.

```
case $whatami in
  root_check)
    fs="/"
  ;;
  boot_check)
    fs="/boot"
  ;;
  snap_check)
    fs="/snapshot"
```

---

1 Setuid is a permission setting which allows a utility to be run *as* the owner of the utility instead of the user that is running the utility.

```
  ;;
  *)
    echo "Don't know what to do. Exiting"
  ;;
esac
```

This `case` structure is what allows multiple command names to work. If the name of the command is `root_check`, we set the `fs` variable to the `/` file system. If it is `boot_check`, we set the `fs` variable to `/boot`, and so on. This example sets only one value in each case, but it could just as easily change many more elements depending on your needs.

```
fs_total=`df -k $fs | tail -n 1 | awk '{print $2}'`
fs_used=`df -k $fs | tail -n 1 | awk '{print $3}'`
percent_used=$((100*$fs_used/$fs_total))
echo "$fs is at ${percent_used}% capacity"
```

Once the `fs` variable is set, all the rest of the code is the same as before. One interesting item to note with this example is that the `Use%` column displayed by the `df -k` command output is significantly different from the output of this script, even though they are both based on the same numbers. The `df` command is likely performing its calculations with some rounding involved for a quick view of the percentage used instead of the exact value.

Chapter 14: Throttling

Parallel Processes

I have been in many situations where I've needed to perform a task across multiple systems. A common example is the installation of a software package on each machine in a large environment. With relatively small environments, you could simply write a script that loops through a list of systems and serially performs the desired task on each machine. Another method would be to loop through the list of machines and submit your job to the background so the tasks are performed in parallel. Neither of these methods scale well when you run a large environment. Sequentially processing the list is not efficient use of resources and can take a long time to complete.

With too many backgrounded parallel processes, the initiating machine will run out of network sockets and the loop that starts all the background tasks will stop functioning. Another problem with this method is that even if you permit an unlimited number of socket connections, the installation package may be quite large and you might end up saturating your network. You might also have to deal with so many machines that the installations might take an extremely long time to complete because of network contention. In all of these cases you need to control the number of concurrent sessions you have running at any given time.

The scripts presented here demonstrate a way of controlling the number of parallel background processes. You can then tune your script based on your particular hardware and bandwidth by timing sample runs. You can then play with the number of parallel processes to control the time it takes to run the background jobs. The general idea of this algorithm is that there is a background job that is spawned whose only task is to take a large list of items and feed them back to the parent process at a rate that is controlled by the parent process as slowly or as quickly as you want.

Since the number of those who have to manage remote jobs on large numbers of machines (hundreds to tens of thousands) is limited, I came up with an example of broader applicability: a script that validates web page links. The script takes the URL of a web site as input. It starts by gathering the URLs found on the input page, and then proceeds to get all the URLs from those pages, up to a specified level of depth. It is usually sufficient to take a level of 2 in order to gather from several hundred to a few thousand unique URLs.

Once the script has finished gathering the URLs, it validates each link and writes the validation results to a log file. The script starts URL validation in groups of parallel processes based on the number specified when the script was called. Once a group is started, the code waits for all the background tasks to complete and then starts the next group. The script repeats the validation process until all web pages passed to it have been checked.

You could easily modify the script to manage any parallel task, such as handling jobs on large numbers of remote machines. If you want to focus on URL validation, you could limit the list of URLs to be validated to those residing within your own domain; you would thereby create a miniature web crawler that validates URLs on your own site.

Parallel Processing with ksh

One feature available within ksh is something called a co-process. This is a process that is run and sent to the background with specific syntax that allows the background child process to run asynchronously from the parent that called it. Both processes are also able to communicate with each other. This version of the web crawler uses this method.

```
#!/bin/ksh
LOGFILE=/tmp/valid_url.log
if [ -f $LOGFILE ]
then
   rm $LOGFILE
fi
```

You start by defining the log file for the script to use and then you have to determine whether it already exists. If there is a previous version, you need to remove it.

```
function url_feeder
{
  while read
  do
    [[ $REPLY = "GO" ]] && break
```

```
      done
```

This function is called by the main loop as the background co-process task. The function starts an infinite loop that waits for the message "GO" to be received. Once the function receives the message, it breaks out of the loop and continues executing function code.

```
for url in $*
do
    print $url
done
}
```

The script passes a variable to this function containing the list of unique URLs that have been collected. The script collects all links based on the starting web page URL and the link depth it is permitted to search. This loop iterates through each of the pages and prints the links, although not to a terminal. Later I will discuss in greater detail when explaining how this function is called.

```
function find_urls
{
  url=$1
  urls=`lynx -dump $url | sed -n '/^References/,$p' | \
      egrep -v "ftp://|javascript:|mailto:|news:|https://" | \
      tail -n +3 | awk '{print $2}' | cut -d\? -f1 | sort -u`
```

The find_urls function finds the list of web pages and validates the URLs. It takes a single web site URL as a parameter (e.g.: www.google.com). This is the function that is called as a background task from the main code of the script, and it can be performed in parallel with many other instances of itself.

The urls variable contains the list of links found by the lynx command on the page defined by the url variable. This command lists all URLs found on a given site in output that is easy to obtain and manipulate in text form. I removed links that do not represent web pages by piping the output of lynx to egrep, and ordered and formatted the links with tail, awk, cut, and sort.

```
urlcount=`echo $urls | wc -w`
if [ "$urls" = "" ]
then
    if [ "$2" != "" ]
```

```
then
    echo $url Link Not Found on Server or Forbidden >> $LOGFILE
else
    echo ""
fi
```

Now you need to determine the number of URLs found on the page that was passed to the function. If no URLs were found, then the script checks whether the second positional parameter $2 was passed. If that is so, then the function is acting in URL validation mode and it should first log a message stating the page was not found. If $2 was not passed, then the function is acting in URL gathering mode and it should echo nothing. This means that it didn't find any links to add to the URL list.

```
elif [ $urlcount -eq 1 -a "$urls" = "http://www.com.org/home.php" ]
then
    if [ "$2" != "" ]
    then
        echo $url Site Not Found >> $LOGFILE
    else
        echo ""
    fi
```

If a single URL was found and it matches http://www.com.org/home.php, then we log that the web page has not been found. This is a special-case page that Lynx reports. As in the previous section of code, if $2 is not passed, the function is acting in URL gathering mode.

```
else
    if [ "$2" != "" ]
    then
        echo "$url is valid" >> $LOGFILE
    else
        echo " $urls"
    fi
fi
}
```

The last case applies when the URL was found to be valid. If this is the case and $2 was passed to the function, you would log that the web page is valid. If $2 was not passed, the unchanged list of URLs would be passed back to the main loop.

```
OPTIND=1
while getopts l:u:p: ARGS
do
   case $ARGS in
     l) levels=$OPTARG
     ;;
     u) totalurls=$OPTARG
     ;;
     p) max_parallel=$OPTARG
     ;;
     *) echo "Usage: $0 -l [levels to look] -u [url] -p [parallel
checks]"
     ;;
   esac
done
```

This is the beginning of the code where the script processes the switches passed by the user. The three possible switches define the levels of depth that the script will check, the URL of the beginning site, and the maximum number of parallel processes permitted to run at the same time. If the user passes any other parameters, the script prints a usage statement explaining the acceptable script parameters. You can find more detail on the processing of switches in Chapter 5.

```
while [ $levels -ne 0 ]
do
   (( levels -= 1 ))
   for url in $totalurls
   do
     totalurls="${totalurls}`find_urls $url`"
     url_count=`echo $totalurls | wc -w`
     echo Current total number of urls is: $url_count
   done
done
```

This nested loop gathers a complete URL list, starting with the opening page and progressing through the number of levels to be checked by the script. The outer loop iterates through the levels. The inner loop steps through all previously found URLs to gather the links from each page. All URLs found by the inner loop are appended to the `totalurls` variable. Each pass through this inner loop will generate a line of output noting the number of sites found.

```
totalurls=`for url in $totalurls
do
   echo $url
done | sort -u`
url_count=`echo $totalurls | wc -w`
echo Final unique total number of urls is: $url_count
```

Now that the whole list has been gathered, we `sort` it with the `-u` option to reduce the list to unique values. In this way we avoid redundant checks. Then we determine and output the final number of sites found by the script.

```
url_feeder $totalurls |&
coprocess_pid=$!
```

This is where the script becomes interesting. You now call the `url_feeder` function as a co-process by using the `|&` syntax; then you pass the total list of URLs to process. As pointed out before, this is a capability unique to `ksh`. A co-process is somewhat like a background task, but a pipe acting as a channel of communication is also opened between it and the parent process. This allows two-way communication which is sometimes referred to as IPC, or 'interprocess communication'.

As I mentioned before, the `url_feeder` function prints out a list of all URLs it receives, but instead of printing them to standard output, the function prints them to the pipe established between the co-process and the parent process. One characteristic of printing to this newly established pipe is that the print being performed by the child co-process won't complete until the value is read from the initiating parent process at the other end of the pipe. In this case, the value is read from the main loop. This allows us to control the rate at which we read new URLs to be processed, because the co-process can only output URLs as fast as the parent process can read them.

```
processed_urls=0
parallel_jobs=0
print -p "GO"
```

Here we initialize a few variables that are used to keep track of the current number of parallel jobs and processed URLs by setting them to zero and then send the GO message to the co-process. This tells the `url_feeder` function that it can now start sending URLs to be read by the parent process. The use of the `print -p` syntax is needed since that is how the parent process communicates to the previously spawned co-process. The `-p` switch specifies printing to an established pipe.

```
while [ $processed_urls -lt $url_count ]
do
  unset parallel_pids
  while [ $parallel_jobs -lt $max_parallel ]
  do
```

The main loop is only permitted to continue executing while there are still URLs left in the list. While this is the case, the variable for the list of process IDs currently running in parallel needs to be reinitialized and then the internal loop started. The internal loop is where the maximum number of parallel jobs are initiated based on the value that was passed to the script.

```
    if [ $(($processed_urls+$parallel_jobs)) -ge $url_count ]
    then
       break
    fi
```

Now we have to determine whether we have exhausted the whole list while in the middle of starting a group of parallel jobs. If we have completed running the whole list, we then have to break out of the loop. As an example, if the total number of URLs to check were 43 and each grouping of parallel jobs were set to a maximum of 20, the third grouping would need to be stopped after 3 jobs.

```
    read -p url
    find_urls $url v &
    parallel_pids="$parallel_pids $!"
    parallel_jobs=$(($parallel_jobs+1))
  done
```

The script reads a single URL from the established pipe of the coprocess. Note that the `read` command, like the `print` command, uses the `-p` switch. Once we have a URL to validate, we call the `find_urls` function with the 'v' switch to validate the URL. We also send the function call to the background as one of the parallel jobs. Finally, we add the process ID of the background task to the list and increment the number of currently running parallel tasks.

```
wait $parallel_pids
processed_urls=$(($processed_urls+$parallel_jobs))
echo Processed $processed_urls URLs
parallel_jobs=0
done
```

To complete the main loop, we wait for all background jobs to complete and then add the total of those completed jobs to the total number of processed URLs. Once that is complete, we output the running tally of validated URLs. Then we reset the number of parallel jobs to 0 and start the loop again until the entire list of web sites is processed.

Parallel Processing with bash

The bash shell doesn't use co-processes. Named pipes, however, fulfill a similar purpose. The term '*named pipe*' refers to the fact that these pipes have an actual name since they are a special file type that reside in the file system. A named pipe, also referred to as a FIFO, or 'first in, first out,' is a special type of file that ensures that whatever data stream is written to the file in a particular sequence, comes out of the file in the same order.

You can create a pipe file with either the mknod or mkfifo command. The mknod command will require the appropriate system-dependent switches, as it can create other special file types as well. You should refer to your systems man page for more detail. A pipe file can be determined by the first character position of a long listing (ls -l) as seen below:

```
$ ls -l dapipe
prw-r--r--  1 rbpeters users 0 Jul  2 21:52 dapipe
```

The permissions and ownership of a pipe file are identical to the permissions and ownership of a traditional file. When writing to or reading from a pipe, the action will appear to hang until the opposite end of the pipe is connected and the data is allowed to pass through.

```
$ cat /etc/hosts > dapipe
```

If you display the output of a file using cat and redirect it to the pipe file, the command would appear to hang until another complementary command is issued from a separate session, for example:

```
$ cat dapipe
```

When this command is run, the output is delivered from the pipe and the initiating command `cat /etc/hosts` would complete. These characteristics of pipe files are used in the following script to emulate the co-process technique from `ksh`. In this way we can asynchronously communicate with separate processes from our script.

This `bash` script doesn't perform any real task. It demonstrates the same technique used in the `ksh` script, but using named pipes. It drives a `bash` version of the URL validation script without duplicating unnecessary code.

```
#!/bin/bash
thevar="one two three four five six"
pipe=/tmp/dapipe
```

First we start the script and assign a text string to the `thevar` variable with some values that will be sent by the background process. We also define the named pipe file that we will be using.

```
some_function () {
  all=$*
  for i in $all
  do
    set -m
    echo $i > $pipe &
    wait
    set +m
  done
}
```

This function is analogous to the `url_feeder` function in the `ksh` script. It is called as a background task and loops through all the values passed to it; it then writes them to the pipe file one at at time, so that the main loop can read and process them.

There are a few interesting items in this function: The first is the `echo` statement that sends the data to the pipe file. This command is sent to the background, and then the `wait` command is issued to wait for the most recent background task to finish executing. The second group of items are the `set -m` and `set +m` lines. These lines taken together allow the pipe file to act like a co-process by sending only one data element at a time. When working with pipe files from the command line as previously demonstrated, this isn't necessary, but it is required when running a script.

The `echo` command requires these steps to send the data to the pipe file and force it to *'hang'* until the data have been read from the other end of the pipe by the parent process. This is somewhat counterintuitive, but this technique is required in order for the script to work.

The `set -m` directive turns on the *monitor* mode, which enables job control. Monitor mode is not set by default for background tasks. Job control allows suspension and resumption of specified tasks. This is the key ingredient to make this script work.

```
some_function $thevar &
for i in 1 2 3 4 5 6
do
  read read_var < $pipe
  echo The read_var is $read_var
  sleep .005s
done
```

The script calls the function as a background task. It starts the loop that will `read` the background function output through the pipe file. The loop simply assigns the variable to the value it receives from the pipe file. After every `read` statement, the background write function completes and loops to its next `echo` output, which is written to the pipe.

The `sleep` command issued here adds a slight delay to the main loop. When we have two asynchronous loops running at the same time, it is often, but not always, the case that the main loop iterates faster than the background task can send the next value. The delay is then needed to align the two loops, although your mileage may vary and you may need to tune the loops since their speeds are ultimately system-dependent.

Chapter 15: Command Line

Editing and History

When working from the command line, you will at some point enter a command multiple times, possibly with minor modifications. In those cases the ability to recall and modify previous commands quickly and efficiently is beneficial. In the old DOS days, there was a utility called *doskey* which would keep your history in a buffer. You could go back or forth through the command history one command at a time by using the up and down arrow keys. Individual commands could be edited by using the cursor and delete or backspace keys to make replacements. This basic form of recall and modification of recently typed commands is also available in bash.

Modern shell versions (ksh and bash) also provide more advanced command-line capabilities. You can set your shell session to act as though you were in a vi editing session. The vi editor has two modes of operation, *insert* and *command*. When typing commands at the prompt, you are working in the shell's equivalent of vi's *insert* mode. You type a command, use the backspace key to fix any typing mistakes, and then hit enter to input the command.

When using the shell's vi editing mode, you can press escape and change to *command* mode. This allows you the additional options to move around on the command line as in vi: 'h' to move left, 'l' to move right, 'b' to move one word left, 'w' to move one word right, and so on. Once you have positioned the cursor where the modification is to be made, you can press 'i' to go back into insert mode and start typing. Many vi commands besides cursor motion are available, too, such as 'x' to delete a character, 'dw' to delete a word, 'A' to append to the end of the line, and many others which, once you are familiar with the vi editor, will be second nature. If you're not familiar with vi, there are many on-line references and tutorials.

In addition to the editing commands, command mode has the ability to move through your command history. If you press the escape key at the command prompt to change to command mode, the 'j' and 'k' keys will move you down and up through the command history list.

Think of your command history as a list in a simple flat file where the earliest commands in your history are at the top of the list and the most recent ones are at the bottom. When you enter command mode you start at the bottom of your history and press the 'k' key to move back up through the list. Pressing the ' j' key moves you forward (down) through the history list. Once you have found the desired command, you can then make any appropriate modifications and press enter to run the command.

One last command history function that has been extremely valuable to me is the ability to search for previous commands that match a pattern. The search is also done in the same way as search in a `vi` session. First press escape to change to command mode and then press the forward slash '/'. This gives you an opportunity to type in a substring to search for within the commands in the history stack. If the first match displayed isn't the correct one, you can press 'n' to see further matches, as you would in `vi`, until you find the command you're looking for.

I have been using this method to work at the prompt for a long time and my fingers are accustomed to moving to the correct keys. This has improved my speed and agility immensely when working at the command line. If you're not overly comfortable with the `vi` editor, I would recommend practicing for a couple of reasons: `vi` is pretty much the default standard text editor on all UNIX/Linux systems and you'll certainly have to use it at some point. The other reason is that while I agree that learning the `vi` editor is not the easiest thing to do, once you are comfortable with it you will be amazed at how powerful it is.

One last thing about editing modes: There is also an `emacs` mode. I recommend the `vi` mode if you have no previous experience mainly because it is a more standard tool, available on all systems. If you're a fan of `emacs` and comfortable with that editor, then by all means use the `emacs` mode. The goal here is to become quicker and more efficient.

Setting It Up

There are a couple of ways to set up `vi` editing for either `ksh` or `bash`. You can configure it system-wide or for individual users. You can also configure it right at the command prompt if you like.

bash

With bash, there are a few ways to enable this mode. The first is to modify the inputrc file. There is a system-wide /etc/inputrc file that all users use who have bash set as their shell. There is also an individual .bashrc file that is usually kept in the user's home directory. Adding the following line to one of those two files will enable vi mode.

```
set editing-mode vi
```

The second way to enable vi mode in bash is to modify either the system-wide /etc/profile or the .bash_profile in an individual user's home directory to include the following line.

```
set -o vi
```

ksh

In ksh this modification can once again either be set system-wide or for an individual user. Modifying the system-wide /etc/profile file would enable this for all users and modifying the .profile in a user's home directory would enable it at an individual level. The line to add to either of these two files is the same as for bash.

```
set -o vi
```

Command and File Completion

One additional option, available in both shells, that increases your efficiency at the command line is command or file completion. With this feature, you can start to type a path or command and once a sufficient number of characters have been typed for it to become uniquely determined, pressing a special key sequence will complete the command.

The key sequence for bash is simply the TAB key. In ksh, the sequence is either the TAB or an ESC-\ (escape and then backslash).

This feature can be explained with a simple example. My shell on the system I'm working on is bash and my home directory is /home/rbpeters. If I wanted to cd to that directory using command completion, I could type the following key sequence:

```
cd /h<TAB>rb<TAB><ENTER>
```

The first TAB would complete the /h to /home/ because there are no other subdirectories of the root directory beginning with "h". The second TAB would similarly complete the /home/rb to /home/rbpeters. Pressing enter then executes the command.

Chapter 16: Scripting from

the Command Line

One of the advantages of working at the shell command line is that you're working in a shell. Now that sounds sort of obvious and dumb, but please bear with me: Pretty much anything that you can do in a shell script can also be done from the command line. I've coded many ad-hoc scripts right at the command line. I wouldn't recommend writing anything significant that way, but for quickies, it's just the ticket.

If you start a loop or conditional, such as a `while`, `for`, or `if/then` statement, while working at the shell prompt, the command line is just extended until you have finished the steps in the code block. In a traditional script, such code would customarily span several lines in a file. Here is a typical interaction with the shell when entering code directly from the command line:

```
$ while : ; do
> clear
> ls -lrt
> sleep 3
> done
```

Note that after the first <enter> is pressed, the command line returns a '>' prompt to continue the code block. You can then keep adding lines until the loop has been completed. Once the last line has been entered, in this case the `done` line, the code will begin to run. In our case, it is an infinite loop, which can be stopped by a <ctrl>-c.

The following examples are formatted using more traditional indentation for the sake of readability. If you were to enter these from the command line, you would see results similar to those shown above. None of the examples are particularly complex; they are just representative of what can be done from the command line.

A Few Examples

This while loop does nothing more than create a long listing of specific files over and over while sleeping for 3 seconds between iterations. It is part of a set of scripts that I use for concurrent package installation on a large number of remote systems. Each concurrent installation produces its own log file which documents its progress and any issues it encounters. All log files are stored in a single directory.

I found that while watching the output of the installation loop, I can tell when an installation at a specific node is complete by the size of the log file. This saves me from having to review each log individually. Successful installations all have log files that end up being of a particular size. Files of a different size stand out and show me that I need to review that log.

Also, watching the growth rate of the files can convey information about how the install is progressing. A typical installation goes something like this: The install package is pushed out to the remote nodes; then the package is uncompressed on each of the remote systems, where the install script is run until it completes. By watching the file size of all log files increase, I can review the status of all installations at once and generally know at which point they have arrived, as well as note any problems, without actually viewing the contents of the log files themselves.

```
while : ; do
   clear
   ls -lrt install_log.*
   sleep 3
done
```

This is a representative example of the mini-script I use for this task. Note that I use the -lrt switch with ls. This sorts the output by modification time with the newest files being listed last.

```
for i in 1 2 3 3 4 5 6 7 8 9
do
   for j in 1 2 3 3 4 5 6 7 8 9
   do
      for k in 1 2 3 3 4 5 6 7 8 9
```

```
    do
       touch $i$j$k
    done
  done
done
```

This next mini-script is nothing more than a series of nested for loops. I've used this type of script to create large numbers of empty files in a directory. It is the result of an effort to test a monitor script which is supposed to send notifications in case the number of files in a directory exceeds a certain threshold. Another use for it would be to perform a task a specific number of times (729 in this case). In the example, I could have replaced the touch command with something that didn't reference any of the counter variables ($i, $j or $k) at all. It could have easily been an echo statement repeating 729 times, but that's just boring.

The last example is something I do fairly regularly. I often want to gather information from each system named in a list of machines. This shows how to get the list of node names by using a command call within back-ticks, ` `. A command string enclosed within back-ticks denotes not the given string, but the string obtained by evaluating the command string and replacing it with what is returned.

```
for node in `cat some_nodelist_file`
do
  if [ "$node" = "cheese" ]
  then
    continue
  else
    rsh $node uname -a
    rsh $node uptime
  fi
done
```

In this case, the `cat some_nodelist_file` would be replaced with an actual list of nodes originally contained in that file. The for loop then iterates through each of the nodes. I've also included an if/then statement which will skip any node named "cheese" to provide an example that includes a conditional.

A final trick for using these kinds of scripts efficiently is command line recall, which is discussed in Chapter 15, Command Line Editing, just prior to this one. If you make a mistake while typing (not too unlikely with this many lines at once), you can return to the previous (mistyped) command in your history and then edit the command sequence using vi-style command-line editing. You can also recall a previously entered mini-script for easy modification and reuse.

Chapter 17: Automating User Input with expect

xpect is a utility whose name suggests precisely what it does: "Expect" some output from an interactive program, and send it some input in response. Expect has much more functionality than I'm going to cover in this chapter, but the example here is a good sample of how it can be used.

You may find that when you try to automate a task, the utilities or tools you are using don't lend themselves well to scripting. In the past, use of the format or fdisk commands have been good examples of procedures that are difficult to automate. Today, we have versions of these utilities, such as sfdisk, which are much easier to use within a script. More modern examples include logging into specialized hardware to gather information or to customize settings, as is required when administering network routers, switches, and firewalls.

I am going to present a pair of scripts used to automate the control of a serial terminal server. This is a type of network accessible hardware that physically looks very much like a network hub or a switch with multiple RJ45 ports. Each physical port can be connected to serial devices, such as serial consoles. Once consoles are attached to the terminal server, you can telnet to a specific network port on the terminal server and establish a connection with the attached console.

The first script is a shell script that processes command-line switches provided by the user specifying what commands to send to the terminal server. The second script, which is called by the first, is an expect script that performs all the manual labor. Expect is an extension to the Tcl scripting language that is designed to communicate with an interactive program. It works well with programs such as ssh, telnet, ftp, and other interactive utilities.

A Shell Script to Customize Parameters for an `expect`

Script

The first script obtains the user input necessary to connect to the desired terminal server(s) and perform the intended tasks. It displays usage instructions and allows the user to specify a specific terminal server or to provide a file containing node names if there are multiple terminal servers with which one wants to communicate in the same way and at the same time. First, we need to define a few variables:

```
#!/bin/sh
NODE=""
CMDS=""
NODEFILE=""
AUTO=""
USAGE="There is a problem with the command, type $0 -h for syntax"
```

The variables are initialized to null strings, except for the USAGE variable, which contains a message that is displayed whenever the script finds a problem with the command line call provided by the user.

```
if [ $# -eq 0 ]
then
  echo $USAGE
  exit 1
fi
```

The script gets the information it needs from the user on the command line, so first we check that switches have been given. If there are no switches passed to the script, the script displays the usage statement and quits with a non-zero return code (here, 1).

```
while getopts idhlc:f:n: opt
do
  case $opt in
```

```
    i) CMDS="$CMDS \"sho ip\""
    ;;
```

The next section is where the command-line switches are handled. The code uses the `getopts` construct, which is explained in greater detail in Chapter 5. The `-i` switch is used to indicate that the terminal server's IP settings should be displayed. It causes the command "sho ip" to be appended to the CMDS variable, which holds the commands that will be sent to the terminal server.

```
c)  CUSTOM_CMD=$OPTARG
    CMDS="$CMDS \"$CUSTOM_CMD\""

;;
```

The `-c` switch is for user-provided terminal server commands that aren't hard coded in the script. The user can provide as many such commands as desired when invoking the shell script, as long as a `-c` option precedes each command and the command itself is double-quoted; most commands interpreted by the terminal server contain multiple words that are space-delimited and so need to be tied together with quotes when the shell script is called.

The OPTARG variable used in handling the `-c` switch is part of the `getopts` construct. Note that this switch is followed by a colon in the `getopts` specification. When a colon ':' follows a switch in the `getopts` command, `getopts` will expect some type of argument to follow that switch whenever it is used. OPTARG is the variable that receives the additional argument to the switch. As an example, if you had a script that takes a command-line parameter to specify an optional input file, the invocation might look something like this: `sample_script -f input_file`. The corresponding `getopts` line would look like this: `while getopts f:<other switches> opt`, and OPTARG would be set to the string `"input_file"`.

```
    h)  cat << EOT
Usage:
 $0 [-idhl]  [-c "custom command"]  [-f node_file]  [-n node]
    where:
            -i          Sends the "sho ip" command to the Xyplex terminal
               server
            -d          Logs in and drops you to the command prompt
            -h          Displays this information
            -l          Logs out ports 1-15
            -c          Takes a custom command and sends it to the xyplex.
                        Double quotes are required. You can have as many of
                        these as you like.
```

```
          -f          Define a file with a list of terminal servers to
                      apply the commands to.
          -n          Define a specific node to apply the command to.
EOT
        exit 0
    ;;
```

The -h switch causes the script to display its usage information. Note that the cat command is used here to format the output, instead of multiple echo commands. There is more discussion in Chapter 28 on the technique of free-format output using cat.

```
    d)  AUTO="no"
    ;;
```

The -d switch is used to indicate that the terminal server session is not automated, and that the user simply wants to be left at a prompt after logging in. The presence of this switch causes the AUTO variable to be set to no. The expect script examines this variable, and if it is set to no, the expect script leaves the user at the command prompt of the terminal server's shell after logging in. If this variable is not set to no, the expect script performs any commands specified via the other options and then automatically logs out. (See the next section.)

```
    l)  CMDS="$CMDS \"logout por 1-15\""
    ;;
```

The -l switch adds a command to tell the terminal server to log out all of its serial ports. On occasion, a terminal server will have a hung and unresponsive serial port. A command to log it out resets the port and it becomes usable again. This is an example of a command that changes settings on managed hardware. This command is specific to the hardware involved.

```
    f)  NODEFILE=$OPTARG
    ;;
```

The -f switch is used to specify a file containing a node list (i.e., a list of terminal servers). The script will loop through the list of terminal servers and perform the specified command(s) against each one.

```
    n)  NODE=$OPTARG
    ;;
```

The -n switch indicates that a specific terminal server node is the target, rather than those in a list of nodes, as specified using the previous switch.

```
   ?) echo $USAGE
      exit 1
   ;;
   *) echo $USAGE
      exit 1
   ;;
 esac
done
```

These last two alternatives have been included for robustness. If anything else was provided in the invocation of the script besides the anticipated options, the script should echo the contents of the USAGE variable to the screen and exit.

```
if [ "$NODEFILE" != "" ]
then
  if [ -s $NODEFILE ]
  then
    for node in `cat $NODEFILE | grep -v '^#'`
    do
      eval ./xyp_connect $NODE $AUTO $LOGNAME $CMDS
    done
  else
    echo There is a problem with $NODEFILE
  fi
else
  if [ "$NODE" != "" ]
  then
    eval ./xyp_connect $NODE $AUTO $LOGNAME $CMDS
  else
    echo $USAGE
  fi
fi
```

Finally, after processing the switches and building the command list, the script calls the expect script to contact the terminal server. If a NODEFILE was specified using the -f switch, it validates the file and then iterates through it, calling the expect script once for each terminal server with the parameters that were supplied by the user. If a NODEFILE was not specified by the user using the -f switch, the script validates that an individual terminal server was specified with the -n switch and that the NODE variable is not null. If so, it calls the expect script with the appropriate parameters; otherwise it displays the usage string.

The eval command is used here to evaluate the variables on that line of code once before the code is actually executed. This is because the CMDS variable may contain terminal server commands that are, as a result of the processing of the switches, surrounded by a backslash ('\')-escaped double quotes; these escaped characters must be replaced with unmodified quotes or else the multiple commands will be read incorrectly as one long command. This is also where the call to the xyp_connect expect script is called that performs the interactive functions.

An *expect* **Script to Automate** *telnet*

The xyp_connect script, an expect script, performs the actual communication with the interactive program used to connect to the terminal server, in this case telnet. The script starts out by initializing some variables to hold the parameters that were passed to it from the shell script. These parameters are accessed by their positions in the argument vector, argv[], of the expect script's process. The -f switch here in the first line is used so the script will accept additional command line options.

```
#!/usr/bin/expect -f
set TERMSERV [lindex $argv 0]
set AUTO [lindex $argv 1]
set USER [lindex $argv 2]
```

The first parameter is the terminal server to which to attach. The second parameter defines if this will be an automated session where the expect script performs the work or an interactive one where the script simply logs you in and leaves you at the terminal server shell prompt. The third parameter is the user who is to be logged in.

```
catch {spawn -noecho telnet $TERMSERV 2000}
```

The next line of the expect script initiates an interactive telnet session with the terminal server. The spawn command starts by trying to establish a telnet connection at the specified port (2000). Port 2000 is being used because of the way this vendor has designed their equipment. Other manufacturers will likely be configured differently. The noecho switch tells expect to avoid echoing on the user's console the command that is being spawned. Finally, a `catch` command surrounds the whole `spawn` command. It *catches* the output that is generated by the spawned `telnet` so that the script can use it later when determining how the `telnet` command responded.

```
set timeout 10
expect {
  timeout { send_user "Telnet timed out waiting for $TERMSERV\n" \
  ; exit }
  "onnection refused" { send_user "Connection was refused to \
  $TERMSERV\n" ; exit }
  "nknown host" { send_user "System $TERMSERV is unknown\n" \
  ; exit}
  "Escape character is '^]'."
}
send "\r"
```

Once the `telnet` connection has been started, a timeout should be set, in order to check that the command completes within a reasonable amount of time. Here we set the timeout period to 10 seconds, and, following the setting of the timeout, is the first true `expect` command. A single `expect` command can handle multiple events, performing the appropriate task based on which one is detected. In this case, there are a number of responses that may be received from an attempted `telnet` connection. A timeout, connection refused or actual connection are a few possibilities. For each type, the code needs to determine the appropriate response to make.

This first `expect` command handles the three error events that may arise from the `telnet` attempt. The first event is the timeout. Once 10 seconds have passed with no response, the script displays an error message and exits. The next two events are represented by patterns matching the error messages that may be caught from the `telnet` invocation in case of failure: "Connection refused" and "Unknown host," respectively. Because the error message may or may not be initial-capped, depending on the `telnet` server, and we want to handle both possibilities, the first character is not included in the pattern used to match against the caught output. In each event, a `send_user` command is used to echo the appropriate error output to the user and exit the `expect` script.

If none of these error conditions occur, then we have successfully begun a `telnet` session with the terminal server. The previous `expect` command then has no effect, and the script falls through to the next statement, `send "\r"`. But the terminal server does not yet know this. Once we are attached to the terminal server, there is no further reply from it until it receives a single carriage return from us. This `send` command delivers that carriage return, at which point both parties know that we have arrived via `telnet` at the point just prior to login. Now comes the interaction for the actual login to the terminal server.

If `expect` succeeds in so establishing a `telnet` connection, the caught output consists of the success string, which for our terminal server is the pound or hash sign #. When the script detects this response, it proceeds with `expect` commands implementing the login dialogue.

```
expect "#"           { send "access\r" }
expect "username>"   { send "$USER\r" }
expect ">"           { send "set priv\r" }
expect "Password>"   { send "system\r" }
expect ">>"
```

Our particular terminal server hardware will by default take anything for the initial username and not require a password. My `expect` script assumes these factory defaults. You may need to change this dialogue to match your environment. (For example, it would be fairly simple to add another switch to the shell script allowing the password to be given from the command line, so that the login/password would not be hard-coded in an unencrypted text file.) In our case, the basic login is complete when the '>' character is received in reply for the username; however, in order to perform administrative tasks on the terminal server, one must upgrade privileges via a 'set priv' command. As shown above, the default password for this level of access is 'system', and once logged in at the privileged level, a '>>' prompt is received.

```
if { "$AUTO" == "no" } {
  send_user "Script ended: You have been dropped to the command line\n"
  send "\r"
  interact
  exit
}
```

Next we check whether the AUTO variable is set to no. Recall that the value of this variable was passed to the `expect` script as a parameter, and allows the script to determine whether the user wants to perform a command or a set of commands on the terminal server, or simply wants to be left logged in to perform their own administration. In the case where AUTO is set to no, a message is sent to the user that the script has completed its run and control of the terminal server session will now be handed over to the user. The next-to-last `interact` command in this part of the script carries out this handover before exiting.

```
set argc [llength $argv]
for {set i 3} {$i<$argc} {incr i} {
  send "[lindex $argv $i]\r"
  expect ">>"
}
```

If the script reaches this point, then AUTO has not been set to no, and there may be terminal server commands that were intended for the expect script that were included in the shell script's command line as described earlier. We next determine the number of these parameters and assign that value to argc. This lets us know when to stop looking in the expect script's argument vector argv for terminal server commands. Each time through the for loop, a terminal server command is sent, and after the command has finished running, a '>>' prompt should be received before the next command is issued. (The loop starts at 3 because the first few parameters, at index positions 0, 1, and 2, are those that were used earlier by the expect script: AUTO, TERMSERV, and USER.)

```
send "^]"
expect "telnet>"
send "quit\r"
send_user "\n"
```

When the list of commands has been processed and all commands have been sent, we perform the telnet logout dialog. The first send command in this code segment contains a single special character, not a caret followed by a right square bracket. It is actually a CTRL-] character. To enter the special character in vi's insert mode, you would press CTRL-v and then CTRL-]. The CTRL-v command tells vi to insert the following key sequence as a CTRL character sequence, without attempting to interpret it. (Another example would be obtained by replacing the CTRL-] with an ENTER, which would specify a CTRL-ENTER sequence and be displayed as ^M.)

Sending the '^]' special character causes the script to break out of the active telnet connection and drops you to the telnet's interactive prompt. At this point the script sends a quit command to the terminal server and the telnet session closes. After the telnet port connection closes with the quit command, a final carriage return '\n' is issued. This is just to ensure that when the script finishes cleanly, the user will then be back at their usual shell prompt.

Chapter 18: User Input

Timeout

There are instances when you want a program that accepts user input to run automatically. If the user does not type anything within a specified amount of time, the program should continue running and use a default value for input.

A boot loader is a good example of this type of application. It would give the user a prompt where they will be able to choose the OS or kernel to be booted, but if the user lets the timeout expire, the boot loader uses a previously defined default operating system to boot the system.

An automated system build script is another example. I wrote one to perform an automated system build while running from a bootable CD. This script would allow the user to choose how to build the system. If there was no response within a predetermined amount of time, the script would continue, using the default build option.

There are several ways to write a script that will time out while waiting for user input, yet continue to run. The first method which I am going to outline is one I devised that is a brute force method. It is simple and demonstrates what you can do with multiple processes. The second and third methods are a bit more elegant.

Manual Timeout Method

The code in the following set of three scripts doesn't perform any real action, but it does demonstrate a general framework that can be used to perform timeout-enabled input. The first script was originally a main shell program that prompted the user to decide whether to perform or to skip a specific type of disk partitioning. The main script called two other scripts. The first subsidiary script prompted the user to enter a choice and the second subsidiary script kills the process running the first subsidiary script after a timeout has elapsed, thereby allowing the main script to continue even if no user response was received.

This set of scripts operates as follows: First, the main script invokes the subsidiary `killit` script to run in the background where it waits for a set amount of time. After the time period has passed, this helper script wakes up and checks to see if a second process spawned by the main script to read the user's input (`readit`) is still running. If the `readit` process is still running, the `killit` process terminates it. If the `readit` process does not exist, the `killit` process exits quietly. In either case, the main script continues with other tasks after the `readit` process has terminated.

```
#!/bin/sh
HOMEDIR=$HOME/scripts
$HOMEDIR/killit &
$HOMEDIR/readit
ans=$?
echo The return code is: $ans
```

This code is a template for the initiating script, called `buildit`. It calls the two helper scripts (`killit` and `readit`), and its purpose is to determine and display the return code from the `readit` script. In a "genuine" application, the main script would then be able to establish its next course of action based on that return code.

```
#!/bin/sh
echo Timeout in 3 seconds...
echo -e "Do you want to skip or not? (y or n are valid):"
read ans
ans=`echo $ans | tr "[A-Z]" "[a-z]"`
if [ "$ans" = "y" ]
then
  exit 1
else
  exit 2
fi
```

Next, is a template for a `readit` script. This template displays the chosen timeout value and asks for input from the user. It only requires a simple yes or no answer, but it could just as easily accept a more complex question with more than two possible answers. Once the user has given a response, the script exits with the appropriate return code.

```
#!/bin/sh
sleep 3
readit_pid=`ps -ef | grep readit | grep -v grep | awk '{print $2}'`
if [ "$readit_pid" != "" ]
then
   kill $readit_pid
fi
```

Finally, here is an example of a `killit` script. It puts itself to sleep for the predetermined timeout period (3 seconds) and then checks the process table for a running the `readit` script. If such a process is found, the `killit` script assumes after awakening that the user hasn't answered the question from the `readit` script yet and that the `readit` script has waited long enough. The `killit` script then kills the `readit` process, thereby allowing the calling script, `buildit`, to continue.

There are a couple items to note when using this method for timing out while waiting for user input. First, the return code returned by the `buildit` script may be a value other than what is defined in the `readit` code and probably won't be intuitively obvious. When the `readit` script terminates normally, after the user enters an appropriate value, the return code displayed by the `buildit` script will be either a 1 or 2. However, if the `readit` script is killed by the `killit` script there is no return code generated by the `readit` script. The shell recognizes that a process has been terminated and it assigns a return value to that process that is the sum of a specified value and the `kill` signal that was used to kill it. The specified value returned by the `buildit` script depends on the shell. The specified value in `bash` is 128, whereas in `ksh` it is 256. Assuming `bash` for our example, the signal of a plain kill would be 15 and the return code would be 143. If the *'kill it no matter what'* signal of 9 were used, the return code would be 137.

Second, when the `readit` process is killed, it will generate a message, which will be sent to the `stderr` (standard error) I/O stream of the main `buildit` script, stating that the process was killed. If you don't want to see that message, you will have to deal with that output, for example by redirecting `stderr` of the `buildit` script to a file or to `/dev/null`.

Timeout Using *stty*

The second method of handling a user timeout is based on some cool features of `stty`. It is also more elegant, as you don't need to write several scripts or spawn jobs that run in the background. The two features of the `stty` command we are going to use are the *min* and *time* settings. Both are used with the `-icanon` switch.

```
#!/bin/sh
```

```
/usr/bin/echo -n "Input a letter or wait 3 seconds: "
stty -icanon min 0 time 30
```

The *min* value is the minimum number of characters for a complete read of requested input from the user. We set the value to 0 so it will always be complete even if there is no input from the user. The *time* value is the timeout measured in tenths of a second. This is much more fine-grained than the example code above which uses full seconds to measure time using the `sleep` command.

```
ANSWER=`dd bs=1 count=1 2>/dev/null`
stty icanon
echo ; echo Answer: $ANSWER
```

Once the `stty` values have been set, the script then uses the `dd` command as shown below to receive input from the user and to save that input (if given within the timeout period) in the ANSWER variable. In this case, only a single character will be received. If user input is to exceed one character, you would need to increase the *min* value of `stty` and also to modify the *count* value of the `dd` command to match the required input.

Here the `stty` settings are afterward reset to normal and the answer displayed. However, in a "real" application script, the presence or absence of an answer from the user would have to be tested and handled by subsequent code.

In current versions of both the `ksh` and `bash` shells, the built in read command has a timeout option (-t seconds). This takes all the difficulty out of user input.

General Timeout Utility

This final utility[1] is much like the design of the manual method previously discussed but is much more simple and self contained. Instead of requiring three separate scripts, this single function handles all the work. It is also not specific to user input applications. It can be used for any type of command that you may want to have a timeout value applied to. Since this is a self contained function, it is also another good candidate for addition to a shell library discussed in Chapter 2.

I recently used this method for setting a timeout value within a system monitor that attempts an `ssh` to a remote machine. In some cases a system will be seemingly alive based on a `ping` result, but an attempted connection to the machine will hang forever. This is where the timeout ability is required.

```
timeout()
{
```

---

1   Found at Heiner's SHELLdorado (http://www.shelldorado.com/) from September 2000.

```
waitfor=5
command=$*
$command &
commandpid=$!
```

The first half of the function sets that timeout value and the command that is received from the function call. It then runs the command in the background and determines that process ID.

```
(sleep $waitfor ; kill -9 $commandpid >/dev/null 2>&1) &
watchdogpid=$!
wait $commandpid
kill $watchdogpid
}
```

The last half is where the cleverness lies. First it sends a combination of commands to the background. The first of these two commands is a sleep which will delay for the specified amount of time. The second will kill the original process after the sleep completes. Once this combination of commands is backgrounded, the background process ID is determined. The function then waits for the original backgrounded process to complete, whether it was killed or not. It finally kills the backgrounded watchdog process. This is in the event that the original backgrounded process completes normally and doesn't need to be killed.

Chapter 19: Instant Keyboard Response

There are times you may want to enter some input or perform an action without having to use the enter key. A while back, I encountered this problem when I needed to view the numerical output of ballistic equations. I wanted to be able to increment or decrement an input value and recalculate the results by only pressing just one key. I came up with a script that would do this, and display both the changed input value and the new results calculated from it. The example script here, while interesting, is just a simple demonstration of how to process instant response.

The script accomplished its task quite well. The following script is a simplified version that calculates and displays the values for a projectile's trajectory. The user can set the launch angle and the firing velocity in the manner described. The script will then display the distance, maximum height, and duration of flight of the projectile.

```sh
#!/bin/sh
old_stty_settings=$(stty -g)    # Save original settings.
stty -icanon
theta=0
velocity=0
distance=
height=
time=
```

First we initialize some variables and, because we will alter the terminal settings, we save the current settings so that we can restore them later. To do the keystroke processing, we have to first set up the terminal using `stty`. Keystrokes are then obtained using the `head` (or `dd`) command, as described below. Here, setting `stty` with the `-icanon` switch enables `erase`, `kill`, `werase` and `rprnt` characters for terminal manipulation. The first two attributes (`erase` and `kill`) enable the special characters that will erase the last character typed and erase the current line, respectively. The last two attributes (`werase` and `rprnt`) aren't very common. The `werase` attribute enables the special character that will erase the last word typed, whereas `rprnt` enables the special character that redraws the current line on the screen. For more information, review the `stty` man page.

The script consists of a loop that repeatedly computes trajectory values based on the current inputs and then updates the input values based on the user's keystrokes.

```
while :
do
# convert the angle from degrees to radians
angle=`echo "scale=5;$theta/57.29578" | bc -l`
# gravity is 9.8m/s^2
distance=`echo "scale=5;(($velocity^2)*2*(s($angle))*\
    (c($angle)))/9.8" | bc -l`
height=`echo "scale=5;(($velocity*s($angle))^2\
    /(2*9.8))" | bc -l`
time=`echo "scale=5;(2*($velocity*s($angle))\
    /(9.8))" | bc -l`
```

This is where the calculations are performed for the values we seek. Every iteration of the loop recalculates the projectile's distance, height, and duration[1]. The value of the `angle` variable is the radian equivalent of the `theta` value, which is expressed in degrees. The `bc` utility performs trigonometric functions in radians, so this conversion must be performed before angles can be used. The `-l` switch used with `bc` is required to load the standard math library allowing `bc` to evaluate trigonometric functions, such as the cosine of the angle. The scale value that is passed to `bc` sets the number of decimal places that follow the decimal point. More information on shell math functions can be found in Chapter 11.

```
clear
echo "j to decrease launch angle     --- k to increase launch angle"
echo "h to decrease launch velocity --- l to increase launch velocity"
echo
echo "x or q to exit."
```

---

[1] Trajectory calculations can be found at: http://hyperphysics.phy-astr.gsu.edu/hbase/traj.html

```
echo
echo "Launch angle deg.=$theta   Velocity M/s=$velocity"
echo
echo "Distance: $distance meters"
echo "Maximum height: $height meters"
echo "Flight Time: $time seconds"
```

Next the script outputs usage instructions informing the user how to vary the launch angle and velocity, how to quit the program and displays the values just calculated from the current values of launch angle and velocity. The next command is the central for handling the input of the script.[2] Here each character entered by the user is assigned to the Keypress variable.

```
Keypress=$(head -c1)
# Or Keypress=$(dd bs=1 count=1 2> /dev/null)
```

Note that there are two possible commands that could be used. The head command on many UNIX systems normally only displays the first few lines of a file. The GNU version of the head command, however, has a -c option, as shown here. The -c switch is used to specify how many bytes or characters of data to display. The line of code that has been commented out uses the dd command to do the same thing: This command, with the bs (block size) set to 1 byte and a count of 1, is functionally the same as the head -c1 command. You will only need one of these lines. The reason both are shown is that not all UNIX systems have the GNU version of head that has the -c switch, and I wanted to include an alternative command that can be used on both GNU and non-GNU systems. The head command seems a bit cleaner and more intuitive.

```
case $Keypress in
  j|J)
    if [ $theta -ne 0 ]
    then
      theta=$(($theta-1))
    else
      theta=90
    fi
    ;;
  k|K)
```

---

2   Thanks to Stephane Chazelas who supplied the keypress detection code found on
    http://www.dimi.uniud.it/~antonio/LabOS/abs-guide/system.html

```
    if [ $theta -ne 90 ]
    then
        theta=$(($theta+1))
    else
        theta=0
    fi
    ;;
```

Once the `Keypress` variable has been assigned, we have to decide what to do with it. For each of the valid value-updating keystrokes, the new values are validated. In the case of the launch angle, the valid values lie between 0 and 90 degrees. If the angle is going to become greater than 90 or less than 0, we roll the variable to the opposite end of the valid range. If the current angle `theta` was 90 degrees and you wanted to add another degree, the value of `theta` would be reset to zero. The converse happens when decrementing an angle of 0 degrees.

```
h|H)
    if [ $velocity -ne 0 ]
    then
        velocity=$(($velocity-1))
    else
        velocity=0
    fi
    ;;
l|L)
    velocity=$(($velocity+1))
    ;;
```

The launch velocity should of course only have a positive value. If the value, for some reason, goes below 0, we reset it to 0. There is no upper bound on this value, so you can increase the initial velocity as much as you like.

Note that the keys used to increment and decrement the input values were chosen to match the keys used for cursor movement within `vi`, where '*j*' is down, '*k*' is up, '*h*' is left, and '*l*' is right.

```
q|Q|x|X)
    break
    ;;
```

```
    esac
done
```

If one of the keys to quit was pressed, we break out of the loop. Otherwise the next iteration of the loop displays the recalculated trajectory values and waits for more input.

```
stty "$old_stty_settings"
exit 0
```

Finally, the script resets the terminal settings to the original values and exits cleanly.

Chapter 20: Directory Copying

Copying files from one place to another seems a trivial task hardly worth mentioning in an advanced shell scripting book. However, upon closer inspection, it turns out that copying groups of files with the typical cp command doesn't result in a true copy. You might expect an exact duplicate of the source files, but there may be soft links, hard links, subdirectories, pipes, dot files, and regular files, among others, and the cp command doesn't work as you might expect with all of them. You need to add a few tweaks to get a copy command that performs well for all file and link types. For testing purposes, I created a directory that contains some of each of these file types that can be used to check whether the copy has been performed correctly.

```
cp -Rp * /dest/dir
```

This is the cp command that comes the closest to duplicating the test directory. The -R option tells cp to recurse through the directory structure it is copying; the -p option preserves permissions, ownership, and access and modification times of the original files. The copy is based on the access rights of the user performing the copy.

However, the actual functionality of the cp command falls short of expectations. Symbolic links in the destination directory are created with the modification time noting when the copy was performed, not when the original files were created, although this shouldn't be a significant issue since the actual files that are linked keep their original modification time. The main issue with the cp command is that hard links are not maintained. Hard links are copied as individual files; they are not treated as links to the same file. This may result in a significant storage issue if you have many hard links whose copies no longer conserve disk space as duplicate files.

```
cp -a * /dest/dir
```

Newer versions of the `cp` command have a `-a` switch. This option will preserve as many source file attributes as possible, including hard links. The way this works is that the `cp` command keeps track of files that contain a link count greater than one in its application memory. This works fine for relatively small copies, but has the potential downside that during execution the process could run out of memory and fail because of an excessive number of hard links that need caching.

```
tar cvf - * | (cd /dest/dir && tar xvfp -)
```

One possible alternative to the `cp` command is `tar`. `tar` was originally intended for backup tape archives, but it also has the ability to send its output to `stdout` and to receive `stdin` as input. Thus, you can create a `tar` archive with the `c` option (create; often used with `v` for verbose, `f` for file) and use the `-` switch to send output to `stdout` through a pipe. On the other end of the pipe you have to attach a succession of commands: First, a `cd` to take you to the intended destination directory. Second, an extracting `tar` command that receives the data stream via `stdin` and then saves the files to the intended target. This `tar` command is combined with the first using the short-circuit `&&` operator to make its execution dependent on the success of the `cd`.

With this method, the files are copied correctly, and hard links and their modification times are preserved. Soft links still have the date of archive extraction as the creation date, instead of the creation date of the original link that was being copied. The main problem with this command is that the wild card `*` does not capture all files hiding in the source directory. It will miss dot (or hidden) files. I have seen examples where regular expressions are used to gather all files, but there is another way.

```
find . -depth | xargs tar cvf - | (cd ../tar_cp/ && tar xvfp -)
```

Replacing the wild card that gathers all the files in the source directory with a `find` command is a simple way of retrieving all files and directories. The `-depth` option minimizes permission problems with directories that are not writable or not searchable; the latter can be dealt with by processing a directory's contents before the directory itself. The list of files found by recursively searching the source directory is then passed to the `tar` command via `xargs`. The rest of the command is the same as in the previous example.

```
find . -depth | xargs tar cvf - | ssh machine_name \
    'cd /dest ; mkdir dir ; cd dir ; tar xvfp -'
```

These commands will not only copy directories from one location on an individual machine to another, but also copy files across the network using `ssh`. Simply add the `ssh` command to the pipeline and the files will arrive at the correct place. Please note that in the example, I create the destination directory prior to extracting the archive. This can also be performed using `rsh` instead of `ssh`, but I wouldn't recommend it because `rsh` is not an encrypted protocol and is therefore vulnerable to interception.

```
find . -depth | cpio -dampv {/dest/dir}
```

If you are more familiar with `cpio` than with `tar`, this command is the equivalent of the combination of `find` and `tar`. The modification times of destination soft links and directories are still set to the time when the command was run. The options to `cpio` used here are as follows: The `-d` will create directories as needed, `-a` resets the access time of the original files, `-m` preserves the modification time of the new files and `-v` lists the files being processed to keep you apprised of the command's progress. The most important option here is `-p`. This switch puts `cpio` into a "copy pass-through" mode which acts like a copying operation as opposed to an archive creation. This is somewhat like the *tar create piped to tar extract* command example above, but it achieves its goal with only one command.

```
find . -depth | ssh machine_name 'cpio -dampv /dest/dir'
```

As with `tar`, you can combine `cpio` with `ssh` and copy files across a network connection to another machine. The main concern is to ensure that the destination directory exists. You could add directory creation commands to the `ssh` command line as shown in the earlier example, so that you won't have the archive files incorrectly dumped in the destination's parent directory.

```
rsync -av /src/dir /dest/dir
```

One final option for copying a directory is `rsync`. This program was originally intended to be an expanded version of `rcp`. The `rsync` utility has an archive switch `-a` that allows it to perform a copy of a directory including dot files while maintaining all permissions, ownership and modification times. The `-v` switch is used for verbose mode. Once again, the destination soft links still have the modification time of when the copy was performed but that shouldn't matter much. This is a very slick way of copying files.

```
rsync -av -e ssh user@remotehost:/src/dir /local/dest/dir/
```

Rsync has the added benefit for which it was originally intended of performing copies to remote machines across the network as well as many other options that are outside of this discussion. Remote copies can also be performed with `ssh` (using the `-e` switch to specify the remote shell to use) for increased security. In this example, the source directory is located on a remote machine but the remote machine could either be the source or destination.

```
rsync -avz -e ssh user@remotehost:/src/dir /local/dest/dir/
```

One last `rsync` command has the addition of the `-z` switch. This performs the remote copy in the same way as before but also includes compression in the remote transfer to reduce network traffic.

Most of these options and syntax variations are rather cumbersome to remember, and I decided to write a small script that copies directories so that I wouldn't have to remember the code.

```
#!/bin/sh
if [ $# -ne 2 ]
then
    echo Usage: $0 {Source Directory} {Destination Directory}
    exit 1
fi
```

This script is used much like a standard `cp` command, except that the source and destinations aren't files but directories. It first validates the number of parameters passed to it and outputs a usage statement if the count is incorrect.

```
SRC=$1
DST=$2
if [ ! -d $DST ]
then
    mkdir -p $DST
fi
```

Now you need to set the source and destination variables. This isn't a required step but variables like SRC and DST are more readable to humans than 1 and 2. You also need to determine whether the destination directory exists or not. If the directory does not exist, it will be created. Some additional code to validate the existence of the source directory might be useful here.

```
find $SRC -depth | xargs tar cvf - | (cd $DST && tar xvfp -)
```

Finally, you can now perform the directory copy using the command line that uses `find` and `tar`. You could easily replace the `find`/`xargs`/`tar` combination with whatever copy method you want to use such as `cpio` or `rsync`.

Chapter 21: A Brief Tour of the X Display Environment

This section is not going to be an exhaustive discussion of the X Window System architecture since there are many books devoted to this topic. I will, however, explain how to send windows to remote displays. Saying that it is possible to send the *display* of a program to another system may seem to involve the use of familiar concepts in unfamiliar ways. In short, an X-enabled application (`xterm`, `xclock`, `xeyes` etc.) can be run from one system and the display (i.e., the window) can be viewed on a totally separate system.

The variants of the Microsoft Windows operating system do not have this capability. If an application runs on one of those systems, the user can only see the display on that system if he is logged in directly to the console. A separate application, called a *remote desktop manager*, makes it possible to view the whole desktop remotely across the network; these include products such as VNC, Windows Remote Desktop Connection (RDC), and LANDesk. X-enabled programs are different in that they have the ability to set display details at the individual application level. The X Window System (or 'X') allows a user to run individual programs on multiple remote systems while viewing them all locally on a single display. We will demonstrate this functionality in Chapter 22 when discussing the X Navigation Window.

Now, how is this related to shell scripting? Part of scripting consists in understanding system capabilities that you can exploit in your scripts. This section will explain some of the basic settings and utilities for displaying X client applications that can be exploited by a shell script.

The Display

X applications consist of a client and a server. In X however, the relationship between clients and servers is a very confusing topic because it is quite different from what you might intuitively assume. The X client is an application program, such as `xclock` or `xterm`, and the location of the viewable display is called the server (or display server), since it is *serving* the graphical display functions needed by the application.

Some common X servers are XFree86 and Xorg on Linux and other UNIX-related operating systems. There are also X servers for Microsoft Windows, such as Exceed by Hummingbird and Cygwin/X. There are many more.

Once you have one of these X servers running on your system, you can send to it the display data of the user interface of an X-enabled application. Let's assume that you're running an X server on a laptop and the X application (i.e., client) that you want to run is located on a remote system. You can arrange to have the application output display on the laptop. The following paragraphs will throw more light on this scenario.

First, we need to understand the `DISPLAY` variable. The `-display` option is critical to all X applications because this option denotes the network location to which the display output will be sent. A display consists of nothing more than a system name or IP address followed by a colon and a number. An example is `ron.mydomain.com:0`, which is display 0 on the system with the domain name `ron.mydomain.com`. If you are working on the console of a system that has an X server running and you start an X application on that system, it is not necessary to specify the local system name as it is the default value. Thus the display for a local system where the X server and client are both running on it is commonly just called `:0`. An X server can be configured to have multiple displays, each of which is identified by a number; zero is the most commonly used as the primary display.

Here is what an invocation of `xclock`, specifying the display on the command line, would look like:

```
/usr/bin/xclock -display ron.mydomain.com:0 &
```

Another way to set your display is with an environment variable. The environment variable checked by all X applications when they run to determine the display server is `DISPLAY`. If `DISPLAY` is set correctly prior to running the application, the `-display` switch is not required. Setting the value is simple but is dependent on the shell you're running:

```
export DISPLAY=ron.mydomain.com:0
```

Once the `DISPLAY` variable is set, any X applications then started will use that value and the application window will show up on that X server. Of course I could set my display variable to `rons_friend.mydomain.com:0` and send the application display to that system instead of to my own. Technically, this is perfectly reasonable. However, while there can be valid reasons for this action, you can see how it could present you with a security problem when anyone can send the display of an arbitrary application program to your system.

This brings us to the `xhost` utility. It gives you the ability to allow or to restrict X applications from displaying on your X server. This power is traditionally called *access control*. The `xhost` command to limit access has the form `xhost [+|-]nodename|username` where the + sign allows access and the - sign dis-allows access. This gives you fine-grained control of what systems and users have access to your X server. Using the `xhost +` command will disable all access control and any users or systems will be able to send displays to your X server, although this is not what you would normally want. By default, the security denies access to those not specifically allowed.

X Traffic through `ssh`

One of the downsides of X network traffic is that it isn't secure. A malicious third party able to view X network traffic can listen in on your sessions and log keystrokes, view the windows you are viewing, or even hijack and completely take over the session. This isn't a good thing. One good way to tighten up the security of X traffic across the network is to use `ssh`, the secure shell.

The `ssh` utility can be used to tunnel pretty much any network protocol across an encrypted connection, including X traffic. In this case, the insecure X protocol is being packaged and carried within the secure encrypted ssh protocol. As long as the `ssh` server and client are configured correctly, X traffic is tunneled securely, but otherwise acts exactly the same as if there was no encrypted connection. There is a little overhead, since all traffic has to be encrypted before being sent.

There are a few settings that you need to configure on the `sshd` server and the `ssh` client in order to implement X protocol tunneling. The option for `X11Forwarding` in the `sshd_config` file should be set to `yes`. Then the `sshd` process should be restarted to enable the new configuration. There is also an option on the `ssh` client side to enable X forwarding or tunneling. To enable it from the command line, you add -X (when using OpenSSH) to the `ssh` command. However, I have observed on Linux and Solaris systems that X forwarding is enabled without the need for using the switch; I have also observed that the Cygwin `ssh` client requires the `-X` switch.

There are many `ssh` clients, each of which has a number of settings to enable X forwarding. One popular client is PuTTY, which is a free implementation of `telnet` and ssh for Windows and UNIX platforms. Once you have created a session, you enable X forwarding by clicking on the category 'Connection', and then 'SSH', and finally 'X11'. There is a check box on this screen to 'Enable X11 Forwarding'.

Once the `ssh` session is configured, you would start your X server. You would then open your `ssh` session to the remote system and log in. At that point, you can start an X application using the `ssh` session, and the application window will come up on your local X server.

I should add that when enabling tunneling under X, there is a file in the user's home directory on the remote system called `.Xauthority`. It contains the authorization information for connecting to the X server. This file should only be readable by its owner. If there is another user on the remote system who has the ability to read that file, that user will be able to access to your display through the forwarded connection. They may then be able to monitor keystrokes processed by your X server.

X Applications through a Third Party System

As just mentioned, the `.Xauthority` configuration file contains the authorization for a specific user to attach to and use a specific display. Here is an example: You have an environment comprising various systems that you want to access via the Internet, and you want to use X applications from those systems. However, for security reasons you only have `ssh` access through a single portal system, and thus you don't have direct access to all of the machines in your environment.

What do you do? Well, if your Internet-facing system has its `ssh` daemon set as described, then once you open your initial `ssh` session you will have a secure connection through which to send X traffic. Enabling all other systems in the environment to use this secure link is just a matter of giving them the appropriate authority to link up to the original session.

To make this simple, let's create an example consisting of a three-system environment. System A is the machine you're working on, and it has an X display server running. The Internet-facing remote `ssh` server B is the machine with which you open an `ssh` session; this is where you will create a secure tunnel through which to pass X traffic destined for the X server on A. Machine C is the box behind the `ssh` server; the `ssh` server portal machine can access it, but that machine is not directly accessible from the Internet. We'll assume that system C does not have `ssh` enabled, although there is an X application there that you need to access.

First, we open an X-enabled `ssh` session between systems A and B. Then we obtain the X authority information for that session. You can view this information by running the command 'xauth list'; you run this command on system B and it shows you all sessions and displays contained in your `.Xauthority` file. Here are a few sample lines from the output on my system:

```
casper:17   MIT-MAGIC-COOKIE-1   47c872e9b9e62080749e3f6cb601e173
casper:16   MIT-MAGIC-COOKIE-1   d778834a45880121769f333b41a119d1
```

```
casper:15   MIT-MAGIC-COOKIE-1   427868f7541d8f1a84538841fd362a3f

casper:14   MIT-MAGIC-COOKIE-1   95bacf26a4e6ab10c6a5bf95ac228ad8
```

Each record of this `xauth` output represents a specific display, shown in the first field. The second field shows the protocol used for creating the token to allow access to that display. The last field is the 128-bit hex token itself that is presented to the X server by the client that authorizes the application to be displayed.

To extract the authority information for the current display in a usable form and send it to a file, `xauth-cookie_file`, `run the following command:`

```
xauth nextract - $DISPLAY > xauth_cookie_file
```

The `DISPLAY` variable is automatically set when the `ssh` session is opened, so this should work. You will need to take note of the `DISPLAY` value, though. The output from this `xauth` command consists of a long list of characters that represents the token as noted above for the current session. The `xauth_cookie_file` can then be moved to the remote system (machine C) and merged into the `.Xauthority` file on that system. This is done by running the following command on machine C after copying the file there.

```
xauth nmerge - < xauth_cookie_file
```

To validate the entry that has been added, run the '`xauth list`' command again, but this time on machine C. Now that authorization for machine C to connect to the display on machine A is in place, the last task is to set the `DISPLAY` variable for the X client on system C to use. For our example, we'll take the last line from the '`xauth list`' sample output above to be our current `DISPLAY`.

```
export DISPLAY=casper:14
```

Note that the display number is 14, instead of 0, as we saw earlier. Since the `ssh` server can have many tunneled X sessions attached at the same time, the display number increases with the number of sessions attached to the `ssh` server. Also, when you set the `DISPLAY` variable, you may need to fully qualify the name of the display system (Machine B) in order for machine C to know which system should be attached. You may recognize a small oddity in that the `DISPLAY` variable is set to Machine B instead of Machine A where the X server is running. This is because you are attaching to one end of the ssh tunnel. The other end of the tunnel is on Machine A which is where the application is actually displayed.

The authority and display are now set on machine C. You should now be able to run an X application on Machine C, and its display will be sent to the X session that is being tunneled through machine B via `ssh`. The display information will travel through the tunnel and show up on machine A.

One item to note in this model is that the X traffic traveling between machine C and machine B is *not* encrypted, and the usual security concerns for unencrypted X traffic should be noted for this connection. Our model assumes that systems B and C are part of a single trusted environment, and that the security boundary is between them and system A.

User Profile Entry

One way to make this procedure a lot simpler is to include commands in the system or personal profile (i.e., in the /etc/profile or ~/.profile file that runs on login) that create a file containing the current authorization cookie and the current value of the DISPLAY variable. Additional code then checks for that file, merges the authorization cookie into the remote system's .Xauthority file (using xauth -nmerge), and sets the DISPLAY variable. This makes the X experience seamless. Keep in mind that security issues relating to remote file access still apply.

If your home directory is NFS-mounted to a central location, the process is even easier. All that is required is to add these entries to your personal .profile or .bash_profile. All the systems in the environment will then have access to the same ssh tunnel session.

The following is the code that would be used in your personal .profile or .bash_profile file in an environment where home directories are NFS-mounted. The main idea of the code is that you would create the configuration files that contain the .Xauthority information and the DISPLAY value when you initially log into the machine used to set up the encrypted tunnel via ssh. After that, when you log into any other system in the environment, you then simply gather these settings from the configuration files that were created, using them to import the saved authority value into the .Xauthority file and set the DISPLAY variable.

```
if [ "`uname -n`" = "casper" ] && \
   [ "$REMOTEHOST" != "casper" ] && \
   [ "$DISPLAY" != "" ]
```

This first if statement applies when you log in to the node in your environment where the ssh server used to tunnel X is located (It is assumed that you are using an ssh client with X forwarding enabled). An X session is only created on a single system. If the three conditions in this test are fulfilled, then we are on that machine and the files containing the display and authority information should be created. The first condition checks if the node logged into is named 'casper' This is the name of my ssh server, and you'll want to modify this accordingly.

The second condition checks whether the value of the REMOTEHOST variable is 'casper' or not. The check is needed for the window.sh script that is called in the body of the if statement (This is an X utility called the X Navigation Window and is explained in Chapter 22). It is also needed because you don't want to recreate the configuration files if you ssh to the local system (casper in this case).

The final condition determines if the DISPLAY variable is set or not. The DISPLAY variable will be set when ssh'ing into a system with a session that has X forwarding enabled. If you don't have X forwarding enabled in your ssh client, there won't be any DISPLAY variable defined, and thus no need to create your X environment files.

```
then
    xauth nextract - $DISPLAY > $HOME/.xauth.$LOGNAME
    chmod 600 $HOME/.xauth.$LOGNAME
    echo $DISPLAY > $HOME/.xdisp.$LOGNAME
    chmod 600 $HOME/.xdisp.$LOGNAME
    ~/scripts/window.sh
```

If all these checks turn out to be true, you can create the files that hold the X environment settings for this session. If you then log into some other system that has your home directory mounted, you'll have access to the .Xauthority and DISPLAY information that you need in order to set both correctly on that system and allow X-based clients running there to attach to your X server.

The action creates two files based on your current X server settings: .xauth.$LOGNAME and .xdisp.$LOGNAME. It also changes the permissions on the files so that they are only accessible by the owner of the files. The security issue mentioned earlier about protecting the .Xauthority file still holds true, because your files exist on an NFS server and its administrators have access to your files. The last command calls up a script that opens the X Navigation Window application that I mentioned before. You can read about it in Chapter 22.

```
else
    if [ -f $HOME/.xauth.$LOGNAME ]
    then
        cat $HOME/.xauth.$LOGNAME | xauth nmerge -
        DISPLAY=`cat $HOME/.xdisp.$LOGNAME`
        export DISPLAY
    fi
fi
```

If the three conditions of the if statement are not satisfied, you are on a machine other than the one where the X tunneling takes place and need to determine whether .xauth.$LOGNAME exists. The hope is that it does, but we shouldn't count on this. If the file does exist, you have to import the authority information into the local .Xauthority file. You also have to set the DISPLAY variable appropriately. The assumption here is that if one of the files exist, they both do. To be prudent, you would want to implement another check for the existence of the display file. Once this is done, all X clients that you run from this remote node will be able to access the ssh session where X is being tunneled.

Similar code could also be added to the system /etc/profile on each of the nodes in your environment, so that it will be effective for all users instead of just one. This may be a somewhat tedious task if you have many systems and operating system types, each with its own configuration details; you will have to address these issues if you pursue this option.

Root Profile Entry

If you intend to add similar code to the system /etc/profile, you may be interested in also entering the following code to the root user's personal profile. The purpose of this code is to handle the scenario where an administrator has logged into a system as himself and became the root user via the su - command. The code determines which user became root. Then it imports the original user's X environment settings. Thus, the administrator can run X client applications and have them display with his personal settings.

```
XAUTH=`which xauth`
MYPPID=`ps -fp $$ | tail -n 1 | awk '{print $3}'`
MYPPPID=`ps -fp $MYPPID | tail -n 1 | awk '{print $3}'`
MYID=`ps -fp $MYPPID | tail -n 1 | awk '{print $1}'`
MYOID=`ps -fp $MYPPPID | tail -n 1 | awk '{print $1}'`
```

First the code determines which xauth utility to use; it also needs the parent and grandparent process ids of the running shell (MYPPID and MYPPPID). Once the values have been found, the script determines the owners of those processes (MYID and MYOID). The reason for this is that the parent id (which represents the su utility) is sometimes owned by root, and sometimes owned by the user that is becoming root depending on the system you're on. We have to check for both.

```
if [ "$MYID" != "root" ] || [ "$MYOID" != "root" ]
then
   for user in $MYID $MYOID
   do
     if [ "$user" != "root" ]
     then
```

```
        MYID=$user
    fi
done
```

If either of those two variables (MYID and MYOID) is not root, you have to assume that someone has become root using su. The for loop then determines which variable is not root and sets MYID to that user.

```
MYHOME=`grep "^$MYID:" /etc/passwd | cut -d: -f6`
if [ -f $MYHOME/.xauth.$MYID ]
then
   cat $MYHOME/.xauth.$MYID | $XAUTH nmerge -
   DISPLAY=`cat $MYHOME/.xdisp.$MYID`
   export DISPLAY
  fi
fi
```

Now that MYID is set to the appropriate user, the script needs to find that user's home directory. In an NIS environment, you'll want to change the MYHOME command to get the value from the appropriate NIS map. Once the home directory is known, we determine whether the .xauth.$MYID file exists. If it exists, we import .Xauthority and DISPLAY information into the current shell environment. Once again you may want to check for the existence of the display file instead of assuming it does. Root should now be able to start X client applications and have them display on the users X server.

Throw a Temporary Root Window

In some environments, there are times when application owners need root access on a system. This can happen when applications that are owned and managed by someone other than the administrator need to run as root because of their design (or need to be modified by the root user). There are obvious security implications when root access permissions are given to ordinary users.

Of course you have to be very selective about extending root access. The following script sets this up in a reasonable fashion by restricting access with a timeout value that will kill the root window after a preset time. The code assumes a user who has the profile code described earlier set up, so that .xauth and .xdisp files are created.

```
#!/bin/sh
if [ $# -ne 1 ]
```

```
then
   echo "This script will send a root window to a \
     user's display who is using"
   echo "ssh to access  the environment"
   echo
   echo "Usage: $0 {username}"
   exit 1
fi
```

First the code checks the number of parameters passed to the script. If the count is not one, some information about the script and its usage is echo'ed out.

```
user=$1
userhome=`grep "^$user:" /etc/passwd | cut -d: -f6`
```

Next the user variable is set to the username and the corresponding home directory is found by searching the /etc/passwd file. Once again, if you are in an NIS environment, you will need to modify this command appropriately.

```
if [ -f $userhome/.xdisp.$user ]
then
   cat $userhome/.xauth.$user | \
     /usr/openwin/bin/xauth nmerge -
   DISPLAY=`cat $userhome/.xdisp.$user`
   export DISPLAY
else
   echo "SSH Display information not available \
     for $user. Is $user using it?"
   exit 1
fi
```

If the .xdisp file for this user exists, the script imports his X display and authority information into the current shell environment. If not, it echoes an error message and exits.

```
RIP="This root@`uname -n` xterm window expires in \
   1 hr from `date '+%H:%M'`"
```

Now that the X environment has been set up, we set a variable holding a message that will be sent in the title bar of the xterm window, notifying the user of the window's expiration date. An xterm window can be launched with a switch that allows you to specify what is displayed in the title bar of the resulting window, as shown below.

```
nohup /usr/bin/xterm -ls -sb -T "$RIP" &
PID=$!
echo "kill $PID" | at -m now + 1 hour
```

The xterm is started using the -ls and -T switches. The -ls switch qualifies the shell within the window as a login shell and thus gives the full root user environment. The -T switch changes the title bar to the value following the switch. Then the PID variable is set to the process id of the xterm. Finally, the script sets up an at job which is a scheduled task (somewhat different from a cron job) that will kill the PID after one hour.

Chapter 22: X Navigation Window

The scripts we are about to analyze are an X-based application that gives you a way of easily accessing systems based on their system names or IP addresses. When managing environments with a machine count in the hundreds or more, saving every bit of time is vital. The utility has grown and matured over many years and now we have a cleaned-up version that's running on both Linux or Solaris-based X displays as well as on X servers that run on Windows-based systems.

Another purpose for this utility is that users also need to access these systems and this provides a simple method for them. Having users set up their own environment is sometimes problematic because of varying skill levels. Providing a utility that is easy to use and is owned and used by the administrators can help remove some their issues.

With this utility, you have a small `xterm` window somewhere on your desktop with a "`Node:`" prompt. The usage is simple enough: just type in the node name or IP address of a remote machine, and an `xterm` window will pop up connecting you to that system. Depending on your method of connecting to the remote machine, you may still need to provide a password. Other logic in the script makes the user interface and connection type (`ssh`, `telnet`, etc.) configurable.

Note that there is no explanation of X or display values. That is really outside of the scope of this chapter. An overview of X display usage information is explained in more detail in the Chapter 21.

Navigation Window Usage

When the `window` script is run, you will see a window much like figure 22-1. To use the utility, simply type in a node name or IP address and the script will do the rest to bring up an `xterm` with a remote connection to the desired machine.

22-1: X Navigation Window

To specify the connection type to the remote machine and override the pre-configured value, enter the node name or IP address followed by a space and one of the following switches:

- s specifies an `ssh` connection
- r specifies an `rlogin` connection
- t specifies a `telnet` connection

If you don't add a switch indicating a connection type, the script will default to the `any` connection option. This attempts to establish a connection to the remote machine by first trying `ssh`, then `rlogin`, and finally `telnet`, in that order.

Navigation Setup

The code consists of a set of two scripts. The first script (`window`) sets up the configuration environment and then opens a small window in which it starts the `where` script itself. The second script is what is run within the window. It performs all the logic for the new connection. It determines the connection type, opens the connection, and configures the colors and appearance of the new window now connected to the remote system.

```
#!/bin/sh
CONFIG_FILE=$HOME/.whererc.$LOGNAME
RLOGIN_TITLE="Where..."
RLOGIN_FG=red
RLOGIN_BG=ivory
```

First we set up some default variables for the `where` window initialization. We also set up variables for the location of the configuration file the initial window's title, and the foreground and background colors.

```
if [ -f $HOME/.whererc ]
```

```
then
  . $CONFIG_FILE
else
  cat > $CONFIG_FILE <<EOF
# These are the environment settings for the where... window
#
# These are the foreground and background
# color settings for systems on production subnets
FONT=fixed
PROD_FG=yellow3
PROD_BG=black
# systems on non-production subnets
NON_PROD_FG=lightblue
NON_PROD_BG=black
# These are the foreground and background color settings for
# systems on all other subnets
OTHER_FG=DarkSeaGreen2
OTHER_BG=black
```

Now the script has to check for a preexisting configuration file. This file mainly contains color and font information, as well as a few other items. If the configuration file is found, it is `sourced` to put its contents into effect in the current shell environment. If the configuration file does not exist, the script creates it using a here-document and populates it using default values. Then it has to source the newly created file. The configuration file is located in the user's home directory so that each user can make his or her own customizations.

```
# This is the default connection type to use.
# Options are rlogin, telnet, ssh and any. Any will
# try ssh first, then rlogin, then telnet as a last
# resort.
CONNECTION_TYPE=any
# These are the foreground, background and other
# settings for the where window itself
RLOGIN_TITLE="Where..."
RLOGIN_FG=red
RLOGIN_BG=white
```

```
WHERE_WIN_GEOM="20x1+1200+0"
XTERM=`which xterm`
EOF

    . $CONFIG_FILE
```

The CONNECTION_TYPE variable specifies the type of connection that the user would like to have as their preferred method of attaching to a remote system. The connection types include ssh, rlogin, and telnet, among others. The ability was added to automatically switch over to an alternate connection type if the initial attempt is unsuccessful. This came about because some users wanted to connect with a specified default protocol instead of the original default of rlogin. For instance, some devices only have a telnet daemon to which a remote machine is able to attach; the users of those devices would want telnet as their default connection method.

When nmap became available, it was then possible to determine what ports were available on the remote machine. nmap is an open source utility for network exploration and auditing. In our script, nmap is used to determine if a specified port on a remote machine is open; the code will then choose the appropriate connection method. If the value of the CONNECTION_TYPE variable is '*any*', the code will first try ssh, then rlogin, and then telnet. It will attach to the remote machine using the first available protocol. Note that for security reasons, you may not want to make nmap available to the general user population.

Some other connection types that could be added here are rdesktop to attach to Microsoft Windows systems, ftp or sftp to send and receive files, or some other connection type based on local needs. Customizations can be quite varied, but I'm going to limit this demonstration to simpler uses.

```
xmessage -fn 12x24 "Note:  If you don't like the \
    colors of the windows, modify this file: $CONFIG_FILE." &
fi
```

If the configuration file didn't exist and one was just created, we let the user know how to modify their interaction with the remote machine and adjust the interface colors and settings. This window only comes up when the user logs in with this script for the first time.

This utility evolved over quite a long period of time. There were many instances where the script was being run by multiple users at the same time that changes were being made to the code. A solution had to be found for keeping existing users up to date with the current configuration values. The expanding list of configuration options needed to be checked against each user's personal configuration file. Options not present in the user's file had to be added using the default entries.

```
changes=0
for conf_val in NON_PROD_FG.lightblue NON_PROD_BG.black \
    CONNECTION_TYPE.any WHERE_WIN_GEOM."20x1+1200+0" \
    XTERM.`which xterm`
do
  var=`echo $conf_val | awk -F. '{print $1}'`
  val=`echo $conf_val | awk -F. '{print $2}'`
  is_there=`grep $var $CONFIG_FILE | grep -v "^#"`
  if [ "$is_there" = "" ]
  then
    echo "${var}=${val}" >> $CONFIG_FILE
    changes=1
  fi
done
```

This code starts a `for` loop that iterates through the possible configuration entries, some of which may need to be added to the user's configuration file. In this example, there are five of them. Notice that each entry is a two-part value, where each part is separated by a '.' (dot). The first part is the configuration variable name and the second part is the default value for that variable. For each of these entries, the code then splits the VARIABLE.default_value pair apart into the variable and value pieces. Next, it determines if this particular variable is already in the user's configuration file. If it isn't, it appends the new variable and its default value to the user's configuration file and sets the value of the `changes` variable to 1 to note that a modification was performed.

```
if [ -f $CONFIG_FILE -a $changes -eq 1 ]
then
  . $CONFIG_FILE
fi
```

Then we check the `changes` variable, and re-source the configuration file to make sure the environment has been updated.

```
nohup $XTERM -cr $RLOGIN_FG -fg $RLOGIN_FG -bg \
    $RLOGIN_BG -fn 12x24 -rw -geom $WHERE_WIN_GEOM -T \
    "$RLOGIN_TITLE" -ls -e \
    /usr/local/bin/where.sh >/dev/null &
```

Now that the environment has been set up completely, the code will start up the small window on the local X display and call the `where.sh` script in that window. This script will make the actual connections to the remote machines. The purpose of the `nohup` command that calls the '*where*' `xterm` window is to avoid interrupting any of the child windows when the parent window is closed. This completes the first script in the pair.

Navigation Window

The `where.sh` script is run within the original small window appearing on the user's X display. The only output this small window gives is a Node: prompt for user input. The script determines the type of connection and the color of the output of the new window containing the remote system connection. First, the script defines a few variables.

```
#!/bin/sh
CONFIG_FILE=$HOME/.whererc.$LOGNAME
LOG_FILE=$HOME/.whererc.${LOGNAME}.log
stty intr '^C'
stty erase '^?'
```

The `stty` commands set up the backspace and CTRL-C (interrupt) key sequences for use in the small `where` window. The actual text of two characters (^C and ^?) are actually single control characters. To insert these correctly in the script on your system while using `vi`, you start by typing CTRL-v and then the desired key sequence. The CTRL-v sequence tells `vi` to ignore the actual usage of the next key sequence typed (e.g. CTRL-c, backspace, enter etc) and insert it as a control character instead. The CTRL-v sequence thus works somewhat like an escape character. So as an example, to input the ^? character for a backspace, in `vi` you would be in insert mode, press CTRL-v and then press the backspace key.

```
while true
do
   if [ -f /usr/ucb/echo ]
   then
     /usr/ucb/echo -n "Node: "
   elif [ -f /bin/echo ]
   then
     /bin/echo -n "Node: "
   else
     /usr/bin/echo "Node: "
```

```
fi
```

Now the script starts an endless loop which accepts the user's input specifying remote system names or IP addresses. In order to make the code more portable in heterogeneous environments, we first check for the echo command in various places. The script then reads in the nodename and the connection type if one is specified. Earlier I discussed how the script chooses from different connection types, and that if a switch is given following the nodename entered, the script will open a connection using that connection type.

```
read nodename conn
if [ "$nodename" = "" ]
then
   continue
fi
```

If the nodename variable is null, the script should just continue to the next iteration of the infinite loop. This step may seem superfluous, but it keeps the script from hanging. For a long time the code had this problem, until the 'continue' statement was added.

```
nodename=`echo $nodename | tr "[A-Z]" "[a-z]"`
if [ -f $CONFIG_FILE ]
then
   . $CONFIG_FILE
fi
```

Once again, we have to source the configuration file. This allows any configuration updates to appear when the next window is started. This is done so that changes to the available configuration options can be made without having to restart the script to reflect any changes. The script also makes sure that the nodename variable is always translated to lowercase to qualify the user input.

```
if [ "$CONNECTION_TYPE" = "any" ]
then
   S=`nmap -p 22 --max_rtt_timeout 100 $nodename \
     | grep open`
   R=`nmap -p 513 --max_rtt_timeout 100 $nodename \
     | grep open`
   if [ "$S" != "" ]
   then
```

```
      CONNECTION_TYPE=ssh
   elif [ "$R" != "" ]
   then
      CONNECTION_TYPE=rlogin
   else
      CONNECTION_TYPE=telnet
   fi
fi
```

If the preferred connection type is *any*, the script uses `nmap` to check for open ports to determine the type of connection to be opened. `Nmap` will listen for a port for 100ms before timing out; the script then moves on to the next connection type. It currently checks for `ssh` and then `rlogin` (login), and if those attempts fail, `telnet` is used. This is the place in the code where other connection types could be added.

```
if [ "$conn" != "" ]
then
   case $conn in
      r) # Use rlogin
         CONNECTION_TYPE=rlogin
         ;;
      s) # Use ssh
         CONNECTION_TYPE=ssh
         ;;
      t) # Use telnet
         CONNECTION_TYPE=telnet
         ;;
      *) # make no change and use the default.
         echo
         ;;
   esac
fi
```

If the user adds a space and one of the characters `r`, `s`, or `t` after inputting the node name, the character specifies the type of connection to use for this specific remote session. This allows the user to override the defaults and attach to a specific system with a specific type of connection. This can be useful for remote systems to which one can connect in multiple ways.

158

```
echo `date` $nodename $CONNECTION_TYPE \
  $conn >> $LOG_FILE
third_ip=`grep -w $nodename /etc/hosts | \
  grep -v '^#' | tail -1 | awk '{print $1}' | \
  cut -d\. -f3`
if [ "$third_ip" = "" ]
then
  third_ip=`echo $nodename | awk -F. '{print $3}'`
  if [ "$third_ip" = "" ]
  then
    nohup $XTERM -fn $FONT -bg $OTHER_BG -fg \
      $OTHER_FG -sb -sl 500 -T "$nodename" -e \
        "$CONNECTION_TYPE" -l $USER $nodename \
        >/dev/null &
    continue
  fi
fi
```

We're now about ready to open the connection to the remote system. First we create an entry in the user's log file for tracking and debugging purposes. Next, the script tries to determine the subnet that the node is a part of. This is because systems that are critical to the environment may be segregated by subnet, and you may want the window foreground and background colors to distinguish the critical systems from less important ones. The subnet can be determined in various ways. You could look in the /etc/hosts file or see if the node name is actually an IP address. You could also add an nslookup or dig query, or possibly an NIS lookup of the hosts map. If the subnet can't be determined, we open the connection with the 'other' foreground and background colors as defined in the users configuration file.

If the script can determine the subnet, the connection should be opened with the appropriate foreground and background colors. Many color groupings could be set up but I only show you a few combinations here. Using windows with meaningful color settings can help reduce the risk of making a mistake of typing the wrong command in the wrong window.

```
if [ $third_ip -ge 1 -a $third_ip -le 10 ]
then
  nohup $XTERM -fn $FONT -bg $PROD_BG -fg \
    $PROD_FG -sb -sl 500 -T "$nodename" \
```

```
         -e "$CONNECTION_TYPE" -l $USER $nodename >/dev/null &
   elif [ $third_ip -ge 11 -a $third_ip -le 20 ]
   then
      nohup $XTERM -fn $FONT -bg $NON_PROD_BG \
         -fg $NON_PROD_FG -sb -sl 500 -T "$nodename" \
         -e "$CONNECTION_TYPE" -l $USER $nodename \
         >/dev/null &
   else
      nohup $XTERM -fn $FONT -bg $OTHER_BG -fg \
         $OTHER_FG -sb -sl 500 -T "$nodename" \
         -e "$CONNECTION_TYPE" -l $USER $nodename \
         >/dev/null &
   fi
done
```

This part of the code is where the new xterm windows are launched. The main difference between the three xterm launch lines are the colors used for the foreground and background. The if statements determine whether the remote machine is in a specific IP address range. If it is, we start the xterm with the appropriate color combination. The switches passed to xterm are for the font, color combination, scroll back configuration, and title bar definition. All of these can be specified in the users configuration file. The -e switch to xterm defines what you want to have executed within the xterm window. In our case, it will be either an ssh, rlogin, or a telnet connection to the remote machine.

Chapter 23: Command Line

Email Attachments

I often send email to myself containing information gathered from a running system. Most of the information comes as flat text obtained from various files or output from system commands. From time to time, the file that I would like to send is a binary of some type. Sometimes I want a file to show up as an attachment regardless of whether it is a binary or not. This is a more complex task.

I wrote a few scripts that can perform such a task. They encode the binary file as flat text for transmission and then email the file. The file can then be decoded at the receiving end manually or, more conveniently, by the email client receiving the file. Each script takes as input the binary file and the destination email address.

uuencode

The first method uses uuencode to convert the binary file to flat text. This method works, but some email clients, for instance my web based Squirrelmail client, will not recognize the encoded file. If that is the case, you can simply save the text and decode it yourself with uudecode to obtain the original binary file.

```
#!/bin/sh
tmpfile=/tmp/uu_output.$$
usage="Usage: $0 {filename} {email_address}"
```

First we define a variable specifying the temporary file that will contain the encoded message and a the variable that holds the script usage string.

```
if [ ! -z $1 ]
then
  file=$1
  if [ ! -f $file ]
  then
    echo $usage
    exit 1
```

Now we validate the input by determining whether the positional parameter holding the binary file is defined. If it is, we assign the `file` variable to its value. This is the file that will be encoded later in the script. If the parameter is not defined, we output the script usage and exit. Please note that the `exit` command is used with a value that will be the return code of the script. In this case it is non-zero (1), indicating that there was an issue encountered during execution.

```
  else
    if [ ! -z $2 ]
    then
      address=$2
    else
      echo $usage
      exit 1
    fi
  fi
```

Next you have to validate the positional parameter for the email address that is passed to the script. This is done in the same way as for the file argument.

```
else
  echo $usage
  exit 1
fi
```

Finally, if no parameters were passed to the script, we display the script usage and exit with the non-zero return code as before.

```
basefile=`basename $file`
echo "A uuencoded file is attached called: $basefile" > $tmpfile
echo >> $tmpfile
```

```
uuencode $file $file >> $tmpfile
mail -s "$basefile attached from $from" $address < $tmpfile
rm $tmpfile
```

Next is the heart of the script: it is the part that encodes the file and then sends the file to its destination. First a `tmpfile` is created containing a summary of what is attached for the reader of the message. A blank line is added using the `echo` command between the text of the email and the text of the encoded binary file. The file is encoded with the `uuencode` utility and appended to the `tmpfile` following the text of the message. The `uuencode` and `uudecode` commands were originally designed for this very purpose, to transmit a binary file via a transmission method that only supports text. After the file has been encoded, we send the `tmpfile` to the destination email address with the `mail` command; the `tmpfile` is then removed.

If the `uuencode` and `uudecode` commands are not installed on your system, you can find the appropriate installation package of the UNIX `sharutils` utilities, and both commands will be included. A version of `sharutils` should be available for most current platforms.

MIME Encoding

The next script performs roughly the same task as the first, but it uses MIME encoding. This type of encoding is more current; it is also standard for email clients that have to be able to process a message with an attachment.

The code here is very similar to the code used in the previous example except that it doesn't create an encoded file that is emailed; instead, the script creates a specially formatted file constituting an email message that contains the appropriate headers for email clients to process and recognize as an attachment.

```
#!/bin/sh
tmpfile=/tmp/mime_output.$$
from="$USER@`cat /etc/dnsdomainname`"
usage="Usage: $0 {filename} {email address}"
```

Once again we first define the temporary file that contains our message and the usage statement. The difference here is that we need to identify the sender of the message. The sender's identity will be manually added to the mail message.

```
if [ ! -z $1 ]
then
    file=$1
```

```
  if [ ! -f $file ]
  then
    echo $usage
    exit 1
  else
    if [ ! -z $2 ]
    then
      address=$2
    else
      echo $usage
      exit 1
    fi
  fi
else
  echo $usage
  exit 1
fi
```

Validation of the parameters passed to the script is the same as in the uuencode script.

```
basefile=`basename $file`
cat > $tmpfile << EOT
From: $from
To: $address
Subject: $file attached from $from
MIME-Version: 1.0
Content-Type: multipart/mixed;boundary="mime-attachment-boundary"

--mime-attachment-boundary
Content-Type: text/plain; charset="iso-8859-1"
Content-Transfer-Encoding: 8bit

A MIME encoded file is attached called: $basefile
--mime-attachment-boundary
Content-Type: application/octet-stream; name="$basefile"
Content-Transfer-Encoding: base64
```

```
Content-Disposition: attachment; filename="$basefile"
```

```
EOT
```

Next, the email message is created, which includes a simple text message specifying which file is attached. The way I determined how to create the headers was to use my email client to attach a binary file to a basic text message, and then send it to myself. When I received it, I copied the headers in the the test message. I have intentionally preserved the line spacing of the copied message.

You'll notice that there is a line above that defines a *boundary* string. This is what bounds the beginning and end of the text as well as the MIME-encoded portions of the message.

```
mimencode $file >> $tmpfile
echo --mime-attachment-boundary--   >> $tmpfile
```

Once the headers have been created, we encode the binary file using the `mimencode` utility and then append the encoded file, which includes another boundary statement, to the temporary file to complete the message.

```
/usr/lib/sendmail -t < $tmpfile
rm $tmpfile
```

Now that the temporary file containing the message is ready, we send it with the `sendmail` program using the `-t` option. This option tells `sendmail` to look in the input for the `To:` header instead of specifying the destination address manually. And finally remove the temporary file for cleanup.

Again, the `mimencode` utility might not be installed on your system. In case `mimencode` is not available, you will be able to find it by installing the `metamail` package, which includes this utility.

One modification that could be performed to upgrade either of these two scripts would be to reverse the order of the input parameters so that the destination email address comes first. That way, you could accept multiple files and attach them all to a single message. With the `uuencode` version, it would simply be a matter of adding white space between the text segment for each encoded file. The `mimencode` version would be a bit more complex. You would need to separate the encoded sections with the appropriate boundary strings to signify the beginning and end of each attachment. To see exactly how this is done, send a test message to yourself containing a couple of small attachments, and mimic the results.

Chapter 24: Text Processing

One-Liners

Even though this book is about using the shell's command language, I use a fair number of calls to other utilities for text processing. Sed, awk, and grep are the primary UNIX text processing utilities, although I have used others. This chapter gives you a collection of short and useful one-liners, and they illustrate quite a few methods for gathering specific information from various textual sources.

Very often when writing a script, you need to first know source data locations, before you start pruning the data for further processing. For instance, you can find the load average of a running Linux system from the first line of the output of the top utility, the output of the uptime command, the output of the w command, as well as in the /proc/loadavg file. There are almost always multiple ways to to gather and process information, and the tools introduced in this chapter should give you an excellent start on what you will need to do in many situations.

For more information about any of these utilities, you may find reference information in Appendix C or the man pages of individual utilities. This chapter is not intended to cover these utilities exhaustively; indeed several of these utilities have had complete books written about them.

An extremely common use of the utilities discussed in this chapter is to modify or filter a string that is obtained from any one of a number of sources such as stored in an environment variable or output from a system command. For consistency in these examples, a common variable is echoed and piped to the utility to illustrate the mode of use, and its value will be the following:

```
VAR="The quick brown fox jumped over the lazy dog."
```

Display Specific Fields

The following example is a simple `awk` statement to extract data fields from a string containing a record with multiple fields, assuming that white space characters separate the fields. The `awk` field variables start at `$1` and increment up through the end of the string. In our example string, there are nine fields separated by white space. The `awk` positional variable `$0` is somewhat special in that it holds the value of the whole string. This is a technique I use heavily. Quite often, the `print` statement will only target a single field, but this example shows how to extract and reorder several of the input fields.

```
echo $VAR | awk '{print $1, $8, $4, $5, $6, $7, $3, $9}'
```

Output:

```
The lazy fox jumped over the brown dog.
```

Specifying the Field Separator

Here is another simple use of awk where the field separator is specified using the `-F` command line switch. Using this option causes the source string to be split up based on something other than white space. In this case it is the letter 'o'.

```
echo $VAR | awk -Fo '{print $4}'
```

Output:

```
ver the lazy d
```

Simple Pattern Matching

Matching specific fields of the input is very useful in finding data quickly. A `grep` command can easily return lines that match a given string, but `awk` can return lines that match a specific value in a specific field. The following example finds and displays all lines whose second field is equal to the string 'casper' in `/etc/hosts`. The test used for the second field could be changed from equal (`==`) to not equal (`!=`) to find the lines in the file that do *not* contain the string 'casper' in the second field, and more complicated conditions can be constructed in the usual way.

```
awk '$2 == "casper" {print $0}' /etc/hosts
```

Output:

```
172.16.5.4    casper    casper.mydomain.com
```

Matching Fields against Several Values

Another pattern-matching technique that is similar to the previous one is to look for one of several alternatives in a specific field. The example here extends the previous one a bit by looking for lines in my /etc/hosts file whose IP addresses (in field 1) start with either 127 or 172. Note that each alternative between the '/' marks is separated by the pipe '|' character; this is awk notation for the regular expression specifying the pattern "starting with 127 or starting with 172." The pattern-matching operator '~' could also be replaced with the negated operator '!~' to return the lines in the file that don't match the expression.

```
awk '$1 ~ /^127|^172/ {print $0}' /etc/hosts
```

Output:

```
127.0.0.1    localhost
172.16.5.2    phred    phred.mydomain.com
172.16.5.4    casper    casper.mydomain.com
```

Number of Fields

This one-liner illustrates the use of a special awk internal variable NF whose value is the number of fields in the current line of input. You may want to try changing the field separator as shown in the earlier example and note the difference in the result.

```
echo $VAR | awk '{print NF}'
```

Output:

```
9
```

The Last Field

This is a slightly modified version of the previous example which adds a '$' in front of the NF variable. This will print out the value of the last field instead of the number of fields.

```
echo $VAR | awk '{print $NF}'
```

Output:

169

dog.

Second to Last Field

Continuing the previous examples, we can use NF to get the second-to-last field of the string as shown below. This could be easily modified to reference other positions in the input relative to the last field. These last three examples all relate directly to the standard numeric awk field variables. From our example string, $NF would be equal to $9. The true value is that this variable is one layer more abstract than directly referencing a positional variable. It allows you to reference any particular field of an arbitrary string length through logic.

```
echo $VAR | awk '{print $(NF-1)}'
```

Output:

```
lazy
```

Passing Variables to awk

In some cases you may not know until the command is run which field is wanted. You can deal with this by passing a value to awk when it is invoked. This example shows how you can pass the value of the shell variable 'TheCount' to an awk command. The -v switch to awk is what specifies that you are going to set a variable. Following the -v switch is the variable being assigned within awk.

```
TheCount=3
echo $VAR | awk -v counter=$TheCount '{print $counter}'
```

Output:

```
brown
```

Using a Variable Passed to awk in a Condition

Here is another use of shell variables with the awk command. The NODE=$node assignment sets the internal awk variable NODE to the value of the shell variable $node. The awk command then checks each line of the input file for $2 to equal to the value of NODE. If it is equal, then $3 is output. In this example, the /etc/hosts file was used. The code works like that in the simple pattern matching example shown earlier, except that the value to compare against can be specified independently of the field that is output.

```
cat /etc/hosts | awk -v NODE=$node '$2 == NODE {print $3}'
```

Output: The output will depend on the contents of your /etc/hosts file, but the intended effect will be to display the domain name corresponding to the specified node name, if it is found. Try setting the node variable to the name of your system before running this command. My system is named "casper" and this is its hosts file entry:

```
172.16.5.4        casper  casper.mydomain.com
```

Thus, if, on some line in the /etc/hosts file, the system name stored in the node variable is in field 2, then the third field of that line will be displayed. When I run this command after setting the shell variable $node to casper, the output is the third field of the /etc/hosts entry for casper: casper.mydomain.com.

Display a Range of Fields

Printing out a range of fields from an input line cannot in general be expressed using simple syntax. Unless the range is fixed, you generally need to have awk loop through a previously specified list of fields, printing each one in turn. In this example, the for loop starts with a fixed field number (here, 3) and ends with the value of the NF variable. This can be easily be modified to permit any range. The printf (formatted print) command in the body of the loop prints the current field, followed by a space. The last print statement outside the loop adds a final carriage return at the end of the output.

```
echo $VAR | awk '{for(i=3; i<=NF; i++) {printf "%s ",$i}; print ""}'
```

Output:

```
brown fox jumped over the lazy dog.
```

Display a Range of Fields (alternate method)

One last use of external variables being passed to awk is related to potential problems with awk versions. In some cases, the versions of awk, nawk or gawk handle the -v switch differently. There are also issues when passing variables that have spaces included in literal strings. Most awk commands from the command line are contained within single quotes "'". When passing external shell variables to awk, the space within the awk command where the variable containing spaces would normally be applied, you should embed the shell variable directly into the command by surrounding it with more single quotes. In the example below, the awk command starts with a single quote and then begins a for loop. The counter variable 'i' is set to the initial value of 3 and will continue while 'i' is less than or equal to $end. $end is a shell variable that is embedded between two single quotes. The first of these quotes ends the initial `awk` statement and the shell is then used to expand the value of the $end variable. The second single quote that follows the $end variable reopens the `awk` command which includes the loop increment value as well as the `print` statements. The final single quote ends the whole `awk` statement.

This example is very simple and nearly the same as the range printing solution. It illustrates the use of a shell variable within an `awk` command. The difference is that the ending variable ($end) is passed from the shell environment and it is not contained within the single quotes of the `awk` command. The shell variable $end is set to the value '6'.

```
echo $VAR | awk '{for(i=3; i<='$end'; i++) {printf "%s ",$i}; print ""}'
```

Output:

```
brown fox jumped over
```

Length of a String Using `awk`

The 'length' value in `awk` is another internal variable that contains the number of characters in the current line.

```
echo $VAR | awk '{print length}'
```

Output:

```
45
```

Length of a String Using `expr`

Another solution for this task uses the internal length function of `expr`.

```
(expr length "$VAR")
```

Output:

```
45
```

Displaying a Substring with `awk`

Substring extraction can be performed using a built-in function of `awk`. The function has the following form:

substr (*string, position of first character of substring, number of characters in*

substring)

The following example extracts a substring of three characters from the third field of the VAR variable, starting from the second character in the field.

```
echo $VAR | awk '{print substr($3,2,3)}'
```

Output:

```
row
```

Displaying a Substring with expr

Here is a method of extracting a substring using expr. It uses the substr() function of expr. As before, the first argument is the string, the second is the position of the starting character of the desired substring, and the last is the number of characters in the substring. The example gets 4 characters from the string stored in VAR, starting at character number 12.

```
(expr substr "$VAR" 12 4)
```

Output:

```
rown
```

Simple Search and Replace with sed

This is an example of a simple search and replace using sed. It searches for space characters within each line of input and replaces them with the string %20. The form of the search and replace syntax follows the pattern of s/search string/replacement string/. The 'g' at the end of the expression is optional. The trailing 'g' (global) indicates that you want to replace all instances of the search term found in the line. Without the 'g', the command replaces only the first instance of the search term.

```
echo $VAR | sed -e "s/ /%20/g"
```

Output:

```
The%20quick%20brown%20fox%20jumped%20over%20the%20lazy%20dog.
```

Disregard Blank and Commented Lines from a File

This example is a little more involved. First it uses a sed command to filter all lines in a specified file (here, /etc/ntp.conf) that have been commented out. The output is then piped to awk, which is used to print only those lines that are non-null (i.e., for which the line length is not 0). The sed command checks whether each line starts with a '#' and is followed by a string matching the further pattern '.*', which denotes "any any number of any characters." If a line matches this overall pattern, sed produces no output; otherwise, it echoes the line. The effect of this is to echo the original contents of the file, minus any commented lines (those beginning with '#'). The sed output is piped into an awk one-liner that filters out lines of length 0. The resulting sequence is a quick way to remove all blank and commented entries of a file.

```
sed -e "s/#.*//g" /etc/ntp.conf | awk '{if(length !=0) print $0}'
```

The output will of course be specific to the file used as input.

Dual Search and Replace with sed

A more advanced search and replace first checks the input for a string other than the one that is going to be replaced, and performs the search-and-replace only if this string is found. For instance, you might have a file in which each line contains a name and address, and want to change "Portland" to "Gresham," on the lines containing the name "Ron Peters."

This can be accomplished using sed by including a pattern before the search expression. This example first searches for the word 'quick' in the input and then replaces all instances ('g') of the string 'he' with the replacement string 'she' on the line if the word was found.

```
echo $VAR | sed -e "/quick/s/he/she/g"
```

Output:

```
Tshe quick brown fox jumped over tshe lazy dog.
```

Filtering Lines with sed

Sometimes filtering out certain lines is desirable. For instance, when parsing ps output, you might not want the header line displayed. The following sed example will remove the first line from the stdout of a call to ps. This is similar to the head command, but it has the opposite effect: While a head command grabs the specified number of leading lines and drops the rest, our example removes the specified number of initial lines from the output of `ps` (here, 1) and displays the rest. (The `tail` command could be used, but you would need know the total number of lines.) Removing more than the first line is as simple as changing the specified line to a range of lines: To remove the first three lines, you would change the '`1d`' to '`1,3d`' .

```
ps -ef | sed -e '1d'
```

Output (The italic line is the header that was removed):

```
UID         PID   PPID  C STIME TTY          TIME CMD
root          1      0  0 22:32 ?        00:00:05 init [5]
root          2      1  0 22:32 ?        00:00:01 [keventd]
root          3      1  0 22:32 ?        00:00:00 [kapmd]
...
```

Search for Multiple Strings with *egrep*

`Egrep` is a utility that works in much the same way as the traditional `grep` command. The special feature that I have found to be most useful is that it will search for more than one string at a time. In this example, I search for any one of three alternative search strings within the `/etc/passwd` file.

```
egrep "desktop|mysql|ntp" /etc/passwd
```

Output:

```
ntp:x:38:38::/etc/ntp:/sbin/nologin
desktop:x:80:80:desktop:/var/lib/menu/kde:/sbin/nologin
mysql:x:27:27:MySQL Server:/var/lib/mysql:/bin/bash
```

A Clean Method of Searching the Process Table

Traditionally, a command to find a specific process in the process table would look something like this:

```
ps -ef | grep some_string
```

When this command is run, the output will include not only the process data you were looking for, but also the data for the `grep` process itself since the search string is also contained in the invocation of `grep`. To clean up the output you can add an additional pipe to `grep` out the `grep` process, like this:

```
ps -ef | grep some_string | grep -v grep
```

There is a little trick for performing this task without the additional pipe. It looks like this:

```
ps -ef | grep "[s]ome_string"
```

This turns the original search string into a regular expression. The new `grep` command has the same effect as the previous one because the regular expression evaluates to the same string as in the original `grep` command (`some_string`). The entry for the `grep` process, however, shows the command as it was issued, prior to the evaluation of the regular expression (`[s]ome_string`). The entry for the `grep` process thus fails to match the `grep` and is not included in the output.

Random Numbers using `awk`

I don't use random number generators very often. The only times when I've needed one was when writing simple games and when starting multiple tasks at random intervals so that they wouldn't conflict with each other.

The following command generates a random number between 0 and 100. The `rand()` function of `awk` generates a number between 0 and 1. The `srand()` function initializes the random number generator using the seed value passed to it as an argument. If the seed expression is left out (as in the example), the time of day is the default value used for the seed. For testing purposes, you may want to remove the `srand()` function from the code so the "random" number returned won't be random but predictable.

```
echo | awk '{srand(); print int(100 * rand())}'
```

Output: A random number between 0 and 100.

Random Numbers from the Shell

Both `bash` and `ksh` have the ability to generate random numbers. There is a built in shell variable called RANDOM that you can use for this purpose. This variable will generate a random integer between 0 and 32767 every time it is accessed.

```
echo $RANDOM
```

Output: A random number between 0 and 32767.

Character-Based Field Display with sed

Awk is very good at displaying fields separated by white space or by specific delimiters. It is more challenging to extract a specific character or range of characters from a string whose length is not known in advance. Now, you could find the length of the string with awk and then use the cut command to grab specific characters, but that requires more than one command. The same effect can be achieved more simply by using sed.

Sed can be used to split strings based on character patterns rather than fields. A pattern describes the elements into which the string will be split. These elements are represented by parentheses containing one or more dots (.), which stand for single characters. Each element in the pattern corresponds to a field in the input string when it is split.

The possible elements are shown here:

(.) - One character

(.*) - An arbitrary number of characters

(...) Here, 3 consecutive characters; in general, as many consecutive characters as there are dots

The split instruction consists of two parts separated by forward slashes before and after. The first part is the pattern and the second specifies the field or fields from the string that should be displayed. When sed is invoked, the entire split instruction, including the pattern, is quoted, and the parentheses in the pattern are escaped with backslashes.

Here are a few examples to clarify this technique. In the first example, the first element in the pattern specifies an arbitrary number of characters leading up to the second, final element. The second element consists of a single character. The $ sign used here signifies the end of line or in this case, the end of the input string. The output is the second field of the input string. Thus, this command prints the last two characters in the input string. In our case, this is the last character of the phrase and the period at the end of the sentence.

```
echo $VAR | sed 's/\(.*\)\(..\)$/\2/'
```

Output:

---

g.

The second example has three elements in the pattern. The first consists of the first four characters in the string. The second consists of all characters apart from the first four,

Shell Script Pearls

leading up to the final element. The third element consists of the last three characters in the string. The first and third elements are then printed. Note that the fourth character in the output is a space.

```
echo $VAR | sed 's/\(....\)\(.*\)\(...\)$/\1\3/'`
```

Output:

```
The og.
```

Escaping Special Characters

We have seen several occasions in which special characters had to be escaped, since they were not to be evaluated using their normal meanings. This occurs frequently in sed operations, particularly replacements. These replacements can be somewhat tricky because of all the backslashes and forward slashes.

The next few examples show the code for several replacement operations. The code works within a script as written, but because of the way escape characters are evaluated by the shell, the code will not work from the command line in case you want to test the code manually. There are two possibilities for most of these example. The first uses escapes to search for and replace the special characters. The second uses square brackets to specify the character in the search. This option doesn't always work, such as in searching for a square bracket or an escape character itself. See Chapter 25 for another method of escaping special characters.

You have to escape all characters with a special meaning, such as !, @, #, %, ^, ., and *. This example shows how to escape a period:

```
some_var=`echo $some_var | sed -e s/\\\./\\\\\\\./g`
some_var=`echo $some_var | sed -e s/[.]/\\\\\\\./g`
```

To escape the dollar sign:

```
some_var=`echo $some_var | sed -e s/\\\\\$/\\\\\\\\\$/g`
some_var=`echo $some_var | sed -e s/[$]/\\\\\\\\\$/g`
```

To escape the ampersand or parenthesis:

```
some_var=`echo $some_var | sed -e s/\&/\\\\\\\\\&/g`
```

To escape forward slashes:

```
some_var=`echo $some_var | sed -e s/\\\\\//\\\\\\\\\\\//g`
```

178

```
some_var=`echo $some_var | sed -e s/[/]/\\\\\\\\\\\//g`
```

The longest and ugliest of all is escaping backslashes themselves. This one is the most tricky since you're trying to escape the escape character '\'. The code speaks for itself.

```
some_var=`echo $some_var | sed -e s/\\\\\\\/\\\\\\\\\\\\\\\/g`
```

`grep` *for a Pattern and Return Lines that Follow the*

Matches

We have seen many times when I've needed to grab certain lines from a file or output identified by running `grep` with a regular expression. What isn't quite so simple is getting lines that follow the lines matching the `grep` search expression. An example of this is a log file in which a particular entry precedes the record of a certain type of sequence of events, and you want to grab both the initial entry and the sequence that follows from the log.

The following `awk` command performs the task by searching for a line containing the STRING which identifies the initial entry. The `getline` command can then be used to get the next line of the input. Several 'getline' statements with a `print` statement between each could be used to retrieve more than one line. You can print each retrieved line, or any field or range of fields within it. The example shows a `print` statement applying only to the first field of the two lines following the initial line containing the STRING.

```
some_command_output | awk ' $1 ~ /^STRING/ \
  { getline;print $1;getline;print $1}'
```

You can also omit printing selected lines. In that case, you would perform several `getline` commands in a row without a `print` in between.

Note that STRING is preceded by a caret '^'. This forms a regular expression specifying STRING occurring at the beginning of the string being matched, $1 in this case. This match works if you want to find text that starts with STRING, possibly followed by additional text. If you want to match STRING exactly, you can add the '$' to the end of the regular expression to specify the end of line character like so: '/^STRING$/'. To match STRING anywhere in the line, remove both the '^' and the '$'.

The current GNU `grep` utility has the ability to return an arbitrary number of lines following a match already built in. This feature is accessed using the -A switch.

grep *for a Pattern and Return Lines Prior to the Matches*

This technique is a bit more involved as you need to cache previous lines and print them out when necessary. I outline three examples here, each more complex than the previous one.

The first command searches through the file for the 'pattern' string. As it processes each line of the file, it saves the line prior to the match, and its record number, in the variables p0 and pNR, respectively. (The awk internal variable NR represents the number of records in the current line of input.) When a line containing the 'pattern' is found, the record number of the previous line (pNR) and previous line itself (p0) are displayed. Here the record number is simply used to display the line number of the line that is being output.

```
awk '/pattern/{print pNR, p0}{pNR=NR;p0=$0}' /some/file
```

The next example works in almost the same way except that it saves and prints out the two lines preceding each line matching the pattern.

```
awk '/pattern/{print ppNR, pp0,"\n", pNR, p0}\
   {ppNR=pNR;pNR=NR;pp0=p0;p0=$0}' /some/file
```

The last example pushes the limits of what I would consider a reasonable one-liner. It grabs and retains previous lines as in the first two examples but in a more general fashion. Instead of using distinct variables as in the second example, it saves the data in an array which it populates with a loop.

The first part of the command is a for loop that iterates through an array containing the previous lines of input. The loop moves the second through the last elements to the bottom of the array and then saves the current line ($0) in the highest element of the array. This loop is executed once for each line in the file.

Once it finds the 'pattern' string, it prints an entry delimiter '*Entry*'. This isn't required, but when you see the final output, it can easily get confusing without some type of demarcation between groupings of lines. Then another loop iterates through and prints out the lines stored in the array.

To configure this command for your own purposes, change the upper value of the 'j' loop to the number of previous lines you want to return, plus 1. If you want the 3 previous lines for each of the 'pattern' entries, set this value to 4. Also change the array assignment which sets the highest element $0 to 4 as well.

Next, modify the upper value in the 'k' loop to the number of previous lines you want printed. If you want 3 as before, use 3. If you would like to include the 'pattern' line as well as the previous lines, make the upper limit of the 'k' loop the same as that of the 'j' loop. In this case it would be 4.

Since this is a somewhat complex command sequence, a generic example and a more specific one are presented below. It is worth some experimentation time to get a feel of how this works.

Generic:

```
awk '{for(j=0;j<='prevlines+1';j++){a[j]=a[j+1];a['prevlines+1']=$0}}\
   /some pattern/{{print "Entry"}\
   {for(k=0;k<'prevlines or prevlines+1';k++)\
   {print a[k]}}}' /some/file
```

More specific:

```
awk '{for(j=0;j<=4;j++){a[j]=a[j+1];a[4]=$0}}\
   /some pattern/{{print "Entry"}{for(k=0;k<3;k++)\
   {print a[k]}}}' /some/file
```

One last note: The current GNU version of the grep utility has the ability to return an arbitrary number of entries found prior to the matches found. This feature is accessed with the -B switch.

Chapter 25: Editing Files in Place

There are times when you want to modify a file as part of the tasks run from a shell script. Although the use of `sed` to modify files on the fly is common, the use of `ed` is less familiar to many. `Ed` is a line-oriented editor that works much like any other text editor. It opens a file, makes modifications, saves the changes, and exits. We can script these interactive sessions with `ed`. The advantage of `ed` is that the modification is performed directly on the file itself and the results are neither redirected to another file, nor used to overwrite the file itself.

For example, you might want to process a large list of files, applying a single modification to all of the files. In most of these cases, the modification may not be more than a simple search-and-replace operation. You could pipe the file through `sed` and then redirect the `sed` output to another file; once the output has been validated, you can move the modified file back into place and either overwrite the original or, more conservatively, back up the original file to another location before replacing it with the modified version.

The alternate method discussed here carries a little more risk because the original file itself is modified. There is a chance that the system might crash for reasons not related to editing during the editing process. Disk failures do occur on occasion, and it is also possible that another user might be modifying the file at the same time that you make changes of your own or simply that your modification is incorrect and isn't validated. The upside is that it works well and there isn't any need to create temporary files while modifications are in progress, although you may want to back up the original files for safety.

Our procedure uses the `ed` utility to modify files in place. `Ed` is not a full-screen interactive editor, and any modification you want to perform on a file needs to be specified by an `ed` command. These commands include moving to specific locations in a file, searching and replacing, inserting and deleting data, and so on. When you script the use of `ed`, you first create a file containing all the modification commands you want to apply to the target file. Once that command file is created, you then apply all the commands at once to the target file.

This discussion will focus mainly on performing search and replace commands, plus a couple of other types of edits. The `ed` editor can do much more than what I'm going to suggest here, but this will give you a good start on this style of editing.

```
g/search/s/search/replace/g
w
q
```

This listing is the simplest example. It shows the contents of a file named `ed.script` containing an `ed` script consisting of a single search-and-replace-command. The script then saves the newly modified file and quits. A more advanced script would contain many more commands, but the final two write 'w' and quit 'q' lines would remain the same. The script can then be applied to a target file.

```
ed -s /target/file < ed.script
```

The `ed` command file is first redirected into `ed` which is then run against the target file. The `-s` switch is used to suppress diagnostic information.

```
ed -s /target/file <<EOF
g/search/s/search/replace/g
w
q
EOF
```

This is a slightly different method of creating `ed` input without the need for a separate script file. Note that the text of the script is redirected into the `ed` command using a here-document. This is done by opening a here-document for input, in this case the delimiter is EOF. You then give the commands you desire and then complete the here-document with an ending delimiter. This is very similar to the discussion of free formatted output using `cat` found in Chapter 28.

Now that the mechanics of how to create the command file and use it are set, let me explain some of the commands in more detail.

Search and Replace Using *ed* Dissected

Now I want to explain, using the search-and-replace command from the above ed.script, what parts make up the search-and-replace instruction and what they do.

g/*search*/s/*search*/*replace*/g

The command is made up of six elements delimited by forward slashes '/'. The first element, 'g' for "global," instructs ed to perform the search-and-replace task throughout the entire target file. This element is optional. Without it, ed would default to editing only the *first* line that is found to match the search.

The second element just describes what you are searching for in the target file.

The third element, the 's', is fairly simple as well: It tells ed to search for the fourth element. At first this doesn't seem to make sense, as the search string was already given by the second element. On to the next element.

The fourth element is a secondary search term. It qualifies the search specified by the first search term (the second element of the command). For example, say, you had a file containing names and addresses where the first field of each line was either "Name" or "Address," indicating what information follows. If you wanted to modify a particular street name and did a simple search and replace, you might end up modifying some personal names as well as the desired street names. With the technique shown here, you could search for all lines starting with "Address," and then (using the secondary search term) search for and modify a specific street name within these lines. This gives you more control over how the term that is to be modified is matched.

The fifth element is what you will replace the fourth element with. Once again, this is pretty straightforward.

The final element is another 'g', once more representing a global replacement. Again, this element is optional. This 'g' tells ed to make the replacement for *all* instances of the secondary search term on lines that match the primary search string. If the second 'g' is not present, the replacement will only be performed on the first match of the secondary search string. Any subsequent matches of the secondary string on that line will be ignored.

Examples of *ed* Commands

The following listing represents the target file for each of the examples of ed search-and-replace commands given below. As you can see, it is part of a hosts file. I am also going to leave out the final 'w' and 'q' entries from the displayed ed scripts. In practice, you wouldn't want to forget these, as the changes then wouldn't be saved when ed completes. After the entry or entries that would be in the ed.script file, I explain what the code will do, and finally show you the modifications.

```
172.16.5.1          node1 node1.somedomain.com alias1.somedomain.com
172.16.5.2          node2 node2.somedomain.com alias2.somedomain.com
172.16.5.4          node3 node3.somedomain.com alias3.somedomain.com
```

The command below will search for occurrences of somedomain in the lines of the file and, on each line where this string is found, replace all entries of somedomain with newdomain.

ed **Command**

```
g/somedomain/s/somedomain/newdomain/g
```

Modified File

```
172.16.5.1          node1 node1.newdomain.com alias1.newdomain.com
172.16.5.2          node2 node2.newdomain.com alias2.newdomain.com
172.16.5.4          node3 node3.newdomain.com alias3.newdomain.com
```

The next example replaces all occurrences of somedomain with newdomain on the first line where the somedomain string is found.

ed **Command**

```
/somedomain/s/somedomain/newdomain/g
```

Modified File

```
172.16.5.1          node1 node1.newdomain.com alias1.newdomain.com
172.16.5.2          node2 node2.somedomain.com alias2.somedomain.com
172.16.5.4          node3 node3.somedomain.com alias3.somedomain.com
```

This replaces the first instance of somedomain with newdomain on the first line where the somedomain string is found:

ed **Command**

```
/somedomain/s/somedomain/newdomain/
```

Modified File

```
172.16.5.1        node1 node1.newdomain.com alias1.somedomain.com
172.16.5.2        node2 node2.somedomain.com alias2.somedomain.com
172.16.5.4        node3 node3.somedomain.com alias3.somedomain.com
```

Here we replace all instances of the `somedomain` string with `newdomain` on all the lines where the IP address `172.16.5.2` is found.

ed **Command**

```
g/172.16.5.2/s/somedomain/newdomain/g
```

Modified File

```
172.16.5.1        node1 node1.somedomain.com alias1.somedomain.com
172.16.5.2        node2 node2.newdomain.com alias2.newdomain.com
172.16.5.4        node3 node3.somedomain.com alias3.somedomain.com
```

To replace all instances of `somedomain` with `newdomain` in the file whenever an entry for the `172.16.5` subnet is found[1].

ed **Command**

```
g/^172.16.5/s/somedomain/newdomain/g
```

Modified File

```
172.16.5.1        node1 node1.newdomain.com alias1.newdomain.com
172.16.5.2        node2 node2.newdomain.com alias2.newdomain.com
172.16.5.4        node3 node3.newdomain.com alias3.newdomain.com
```

In the next example, we search for `node2` and insert a new entry prior to the line that is found. Note that there are three commands: First, the search for the term where you want to insert the new text. Second, the '`i`' for inserting the new text. This command switches the editor into insert mode instead of command mode, similar to the `vi` editor. Now comes the text of the line you want to insert. The final command is the single period '.'. This returns the editor back to command mode.

---

1 Note the leading '^' carat in the subnet that specifies lines beginning with that subnet. Without this character, IP addresses that ended with 172.16.5 would also be replaced.

ed **Commands**

```
/node2
i
172.16.5.14      node14 node14.newdomain.com alias14.newdomain.com
.
```

Modified File

```
172.16.5.1       node1 node1.somedomain.com alias1.somedomain.com
172.16.5.14      node14 node14.newdomain.com alias14.newdomain.com
172.16.5.2       node2 node2.somedomain.com alias2.somedomain.com
172.16.5.4       node3 node3.somedomain.com alias3.somedomain.com
```

In the next example, we search for node2 and insert another entry following the line that was found. This command sequence is nearly identical to the previous example with only a slight modification so the new text follows the line that was found in the search. The 'i' command to insert the new text example has been replaced with the 'a' to append the new text. The text and the closing '.' remain unchanged.

ed **Commands**

```
/node2
a
172.16.5.14      node14 node14.newdomain.com alias14.newdomain.com
.
```

Modified File

```
172.16.5.1       node1 node1.somedomain.com alias1.somedomain.com
172.16.5.2       node2 node2.somedomain.com alias2.somedomain.com
172.16.5.14      node14 node14.newdomain.com alias14.newdomain.com
172.16.5.4       node3 node3.somedomain.com alias3.somedomain.com
```

The last example shows how to delete a line entirely. We search for a line containing the string node2 and delete it. This command only deletes the first line that is found in the file. A leading 'g' on the command would implement the deletion for all lines found in the file.

ed **Commands**

```
/node2/d
```

Modified File

```
172.16.5.1        node1 node1.newdomain.com alias1.newdomain.com
172.16.5.4        node3 node3.newdomain.com alias3.newdomain.com
```

You should now be able to start using ed effectively. Take note again that the ed input can contain multiple entries to perform several tasks on a single file. Often the desired search strings or their replacements only become known just before the target file is manipulated. For example, your ed command input may be dependent on accessing variables that were set prior to creating the ed script. For more examples of this technique in action, take a look at the scripts in Chapters 36 and 37.

Escaping Special Characters in a File

The following is a short script I wrote to escape all the special characters in an file that is specified from the command line. The script is meant to be a baseline that can escape any character though you will likely tailor it to your own needs. The script performs its task using here-document syntax. The here document notation can be found in the shell manual page.

```
#!/bin/sh
usage="$0 {file you want to have special characters escaped}"
if [ $# -eq 0 ]
then
  echo $usage
  exit 1
fi
if [ ! -f $1 ]
then
  echo File $1 does not exist
  echo $usage
  exit 1
else
  file=$1
fi
```

The script starts simply enough. The usage is defined and then the input is validated to make sure a file is specified and that it exists. If these requirements aren't met, the script displays the usage information and exits.

```
ed -s $file <<EOF
g/[\]/s/[\]/\\\\\\\/g
```

This starts the here-document for input to the `ed` command. The first search and replace is for the escape character itself. This replacement must be first or it will replace the backslash of characters that had already been escaped.

```
g/ /s/ /\\\ /g
g/!/s/!/\\\!/g
g/@/s/@/\\\@/g
g/#/s/#/\\\#/g
g/,/s/,/\\\,/g
g/%/s/%/\\\%/g
```

These replacements are the most simple of the bunch.

```
g/\\$/s/\\$/\\\\$/g
g/\\&/s/\\&/\\\\&/g
g/\\*/s/\\*/\\\\*/g
```

This grouping of replacements could have been written with the search character being surrounded by square brackets instead of the double escape. There isn't any difference in the length of the lines and it can be written either way.

```
g/\\;/s/\\;/\\\;/g
g/\\:/s/\\:/\\\:/g
g/\\[/s/\\[/\\\[/g
g/\\]/s/\\]/\\\]/g
g/\\^/s/\\^/\\\\^/g
g/\\\`/s/\\\`/\\\\\`/g
```

This set of replacement characters doesn't work with the search character surrounded by square brackets. They must be escaped so they aren't interpreted by the shell.

```
g/[/]/s/[/]/\\\\//g
g/[(]/s/[(]/\\\(/g
g/[)]/s/[)]/\\\)/g
```

```
g/[+]/s/[+]/\\\+/g
g/[=]/s/[=]/\\\=/g
g/[{]/s/[{]/\\\{/g
g/[}]/s/[}]/\\\}/g
g/[|]/s/[|]/\\\|/g
g/[']/s/[']/\\\'/g
g/["]/s/["]/\\\"/g
g/[<]/s/[<]/\\\</g
g/[>]/s/[>]/\\\>/g
g/[?]/s/[?]/\\\?/g
g/[~]/s/[~]/\\\~/g
g/[-]/s/[-]/\\\-/g
g/[_]/s/[_]/\\\_/g
```

This large section of replacements demonstrates the search character being specified by containing them within the square brackets. The replacement is still an escaped value.

```
w
q
EOF
```

The script completes by closing the here-document. This finishes the input to the ed command and the modifications are then made to the input file.

Chapter 26: Evaluating

Variables in a Flat File

One common scripting technique is to create a flat file that is one of potentially a number of canned messages for users to receive. Messages such as notifications of downtimes, changes in the environment or use of system quota. Based on the logic in the script, the proper message will be sent to the user or users. A more advanced use of this technique provides a template referring to environment variables containing customizable elements so the message can be tailored specifically to the recipient.

In Chapter 36, I present a script that checks every morning for user passwords that are aging and therefore should be changed. In that script, when a password has reached the predetermined cut-off age, the script sends an email to the account owner stating that the account will be locked if they don't update their password. The script annoys the user every day for a couple of weeks, after which the account is locked. The user still wanting to use the account would then have to call and explain why he didn't heed the friendly email warnings.

The canned template file looks like this:

```
The $ENVIRONMENT UNIX account password for \\"$USERID\\" will expire in
$REMAINING day\\(s\\)
================================================================
++ ACTION NEEDS TO BE TAKEN OR YOUR ACCOUNT WILL BE LOCKED   ++
++                  IN $REMAINING day\\(s\\)                      ++
================================================================
```

If the password is not changed within $REMAINING day\\(s\\), the account
will be locked.

Instructions for changing passwords are located at:
\\<a href=\\"http://server.company.com/chg_passwd.html\\"\\>
http://server.company.com/chg_passwd.html\\</a\\>

If you are unable to change your password or need further assistance,
please call the Help Desk.

If you no longer need this account, please reply to this message and let
us know so we can remove it.

System Administration

Note in particular the shell variables (ENVIRONMENT, USERID, and REMAINING) and
their escape sequences. When the script executes, the account expiration date for each
possible USERID is checked, and the script determines how many days REMAINING there
are before the account is frozen. The ENVIRONMENT variable specifies the environment
from which the message is being sent. The occurrences of these variables must be
replaced with their values before the script is run and the message is sent. Likewise, each
escape sequence '\\' evaluates to a single backslash that causes the following special
character to be escaped, so that it is treated as plain text when the script executes.

For each user with a soon-to-expire password, the template file is evaluated at run
time in order to replace the included variables with their contents. The code to perform
the replacements in each case is fairly simple. It consists of one small loop that looks at
each line in the flat file and replaces any variables with their assigned values. You can
easily modify the code for other purposes, for example to display the modified file.

```
cat $flat_file | while read a_line
do
   place_holder=`eval echo $a_line`
   echo $place_holder
done | $MAIL -s "$ENVIRONMENT UNIX Account Notification" $RECIPIENT
```

The loop processes each line of the file using the eval statement, which causes the
variables to be replaced with their string values. The expanded line is assigned to the
variable place_holder so that it can be echoed to standard output. Once all lines have
been processed, the complete output is sent via email to the specified RECIPIENT by the

email command in the final element of the command pipeline. The specific email command would be left up to you, but a couple of common would be `mailx` or `mail` depending on your operating system.

There are many potential uses for this technique. The example script here is much like a traditional mail merge where you customize the message based on specific users. You could also use this technique for creating and maintaining configuration for an application or custom files for individual users patterned after a default file.

Chapter 27: Read Piped Input

The following short script demonstrates several techniques: It shows how to use a function, how to use `eval` to construct commands on the fly, how to read piped input from the command line, and how to send data to a `while` loop.

The script reverses its input and prints this to `stdout`. The script provides two ways to perform this task. The first method works by calling the script with the name of the file to be reversed as an argument. Alternatively, you can pipe output from some other command into the script, and it will then perform the reversal on its standard input.

```
#!/bin/sh
counter=0
```

First we initialize a counter variable that will be used to track the lines of input received by the script.

```
populate () {
  counter=$(($counter+1))
  eval COUNT${counter}='$LINE'
}
```

Next, we define the `populate()` function. This function creates a new variable by calling the `eval` command. The `eval` command performs variable and meta character expansion in what follows before passing the result to the shell to evaluate; it is used here to construct a line of code (an assignment statement) out of the contents of preexisting variables. This is a fairly powerful method for creating command lines at run time and is explained in more detail in Chapter 7.

The `populate()` function first increments the counter variable and then creates a variable called COUNT*nn* where *nn* is the value of the counter which in this case refers to the specific line of input to be reversed. The collection of these variables behaves analogously to an array, except that the limit to the number of elements is based on the amount of memory the shell makes available, rather than the preset limit for the shell's array construct.[1]

```
if [ "$1" != "" ]
then
 if [ -f $1 ]
 then
while read LINE
do
        populate
done < $1
 else
echo "$1 Does not exist, please try again"
 fi
```

Now we check to see whether a filename has been passed to the script. If that is the case, the script tests whether the file exists. If the file is validated, the script redirects it into the back end of the while loop. This loop calls the populate function for each line of the file. If the file named in the command line doesn't exist, we just output a simple error message.

You may think that performing a cat of the file and piping the result into the front of the while loop would work, but this can have unforeseen results. It does work in ksh without a hitch, but not in pdksh or in bash. For more information about piping data into a while loop, see Chapter 10. Redirecting the file into the back end of the while loop always works.

```
else
 while read LINE
 do
        populate
 done
fi
```

---

1 The maximum number of elements in an array in ksh88 is 1024. In ksh93, it is increased to 4096. bash has no range limit.

If there was no filename passed to the script from the command line, we assume that the data is being piped into the script. Each line is read in sequence, and the `populate` function is called to expand the variables to their values.

```
while [ $counter -gt 0 ]
do
  eval echo '$COUNT'$counter
  counter=$(($counter-1))
done
```

Once the script has finished processing all the data, the counter variable contains the number of the last line of data that was processed. This `while` loop then counts down from the counter value, decrementing by one each time, outputting the contents of each of the newly created variables. Thus we reverse the order of the lines from the input.

Chapter 28: Free-Format

Output Using `cat`

There are many ways to send script output to the screen or to a file. The technique for creating pre-formatted output demonstrated below is simple to code. Many times I have coded scripts that write entries to a log, create a configuration file or generate formatted usage output one line at a time by redirecting the output of `echo` statements. While this works perfectly well, the code looks a bit ugly and becomes tedious; it is also more difficult to make changes because each `echo` statement has to be formatted individually.

The original version of the gold Linux build script in Chapter 38 was written in that way. The original script created a temporary file used to partition a hard disk by outputting each partition table entry individually. The script has since been updated to use the technique in this chapter. Here are some sample lines of that code.

```
echo "# partition table of /dev/hda" > $PARTTAB
echo "unit: sectors" >> $PARTTAB
echo >> $PARTTAB
echo "/dev/hda3  : start=0,size=0,Id=0" >> $PARTTAB
echo "/dev/hda4  : start=0,size=0,Id=0" >> $PARTTAB
```

Note that if the partition file already exists, the first command overwrites the file using a single '>', and if the file does not exist, the file is simply created. All subsequent `echo` statements append their output to the file. With this method, there is the danger of using the incorrect redirect (overwrite '>' or append '>>'). As an example, if the last line in the above four lines of code had a single redirect '>' instead of a double redirect '>>', the output of all the lines previous to the error would be eliminated. Troubleshooting this error is somewhat difficult since both versions work, are very similar in appearance and only differ by a single character.

In contrast, the technique described here uses the `cat` utility in a form that is not necessarily intuitive. Instead of echoing lines one at at time, you create the formatted text all at once and then output it to the screen directly using a technique called a here-document. Alternatively, you can redirect it to an output file either in append or overwrite mode.

This method is performed by using double input redirect characters '<<' followed by a unique delimiter, in this case SOMETAG, but it could be anything and does not matter if it is all upper case or not. The delimiter immediately precedes the pre-formatted text, to mark its start. On the line following the last line of the text, a matching end delimiter is issued that closes the here-document. With this technique, you can create free-format output of as many lines as you like in the exact format you want. Once the here-document is closed, the output stream is terminated and the command completes.

```
cat > $PARTTAB <<SOMETAG
# partition table of /dev/hda
unit: sectors
/dev/hda3   : start=0,size=0,Id=0
/dev/hda4   : start=0,size=0,Id=0
SOMETAG
```

This code is functionally the same as the first code segment, except that the code has been modified to use `cat` instead of `echo`. There are a few things to note about this example. It is much cleaner and easier to read, since nearly all the `echo` statements, quotes, and redirection syntax has been removed. Also, commented ('#'), blank, and quoted lines can be entered without further issues arising, as they won't be evaluated by the shell.

Some characters may need to be escaped if you want them to be included in your output. The dollar sign and the back-tick or back-quote '`' will need to be escaped with a backslash '\' because otherwise the shell will evaluate them and attempt to use them with their normal meaning.

```
cat > $PARTTAB <<-SOMETAG
     # partition table of /dev/hda
     unit: sectors
     /dev/hda3   : start=0,size=0,Id=0
     /dev/hda4   : start=0,size=0,Id=0
```

```
SOMETAG
```

This slight modification of the here-document adds the - sign following the initial redirection. This strips any leading tab characters from the pre-formatted text allowing the indentation of the code to look more readable and be viewed in more of a code block.

There are a few examples of this technique that you can see at work in this book. You can find the here-document technique in Chapter 22, where a default user configuration file is created if one doesn't already exist. I also already mentioned Chapter 38, where the partition layout file is created to build a Linux gold system.

The method of opening a file handle for arbitrary input as a replacement for a file can be used for more than just output using cat. Any utility that you might redirect a file into can use this technique. Some examples can be found in Chapters 10 and 25 where the need for a temporary file is removed.

Chapter 29: Automating FTP

Automating commands that are normally used interactively is something I've done many times. The simplest and most common script of this sort that I've used automates an `ftp` session to copy files from system to system. I'll concede that for security reasons, `ftp` is not a good method for moving files around, especially when the session requires login/password authentication as a user other than "anonymous." User names and passwords are then sent across the network unencrypted. Even in a controlled environment, this has its risks, which should be considered carefully. Using this method out in the wild means asking for trouble.

In any case, the point of this section is not to weigh the pros and cons of using `ftp`, but to demonstrate how to script an interactive session using file copying as an example. In this case it is gathering the latest blacklist from the SquidGuard[1] project to automatically update your Squid web proxy from less than desirable Internet locations.

The script presented here is just a simple `ftp` session to get a file. Note the tags for the beginning and the end of the interactive session. In this case EOF is used, but it could just as well have been FLOOBY or CaMeLCaSe (or anything that doesn't appear at the start of a line within the session itself). Also, the closing tag needs to be present at the beginning of the line that follows the final command of the `ftp` session, because the shell recognizes it in that position as the closing delimiter. I would prefer to align the closing tag with the last line of the `ftp` session to make the indentation match up, but if I did this, the end of the session wouldn't be recognized and any following lines of code would be considered part of the session.

```
#!/bin/sh
SGCONFDIR=/opt/apps/squidguard/conf
```

---

1   SquidGuard is a plugin for the Squid proxy server acting as a filter, redirector, and access controller. More information can be found at http://www.squidguard.org.

```
SERVER=ftp.teledanmark.no
FILE=blacklists.tar.gz
DIR=/pub/www/proxy/squidGuard/contrib
```

First, we set up the variables to be used for the `ftp` session, such as the source and destination file locations and the Squid server name.

```
echo "FTPing current squidguard blacklist"
ftp -n $SERVER << EOF
```

Next the script outputs some text about what it is doing and then starts the `ftp` session. The `-n` switch for `ftp` is used to disable the auto-login feature. You need to add the `-n` switch so that you can pass the user name and password from the script.

```
user anonymous you@yourdomain.com
```

The first line of the `ftp` session passes credentials to the `ftp` server. It is generally considered poor security practice to include a user name and password in a script. In this case, it isn't really a problem, since it is an anonymous session. Below I will explain how you can remove the credentials from the script itself and store them in a separate file for `ftp` to use.

```
cd $DIR
hash
lcd $SGCONFDIR
get $FILE
bye
EOF
```

These lines are the `ftp` commands that make up the session. In this case, the commands change to the appropriate remote and local directories, then they fetch the file and close the session.

If you would like to avoid having the user name and password inside the script, there are a few changes to make. First, you should add an entry to the `$HOME/.netrc` file of the user who is running this script. The `.netrc` file contains credentials to use for sessions with specific `ftp` servers by the owner of the file; it looks something like this:

```
machine ftpserver.your.domain.com login johndoe password Vuln3rabl3
machine ftpserver login johndoe password Vuln3rabl3
machine ftp.teledanmark.no login anonymous password you@yourdomain.com
```

The new .netrc entry corresponds to the ftp server that is being used. Then, after modifying the .netrc file, you have to remove the -n switch that was used in the ftp command at the beginning of the script.

You can set up ftp sessions to as many sites as you like in the .netrc file. Remember the security concerns; you'll want to make sure the file is only readable by the owner. One potential gotcha is that ftp will look for the server name used in the script (or command line) invocation of ftp verbatim. In other words, if you ftp to the fully qualified domain name (FQDN), that FQDN must be in the .netrc entry. If you use the short name without the domain in the ftp invocation, then the short name must have an entry in the .netrc file. One can't be substituted for the other. Both types are shown in the example above (in the entries for the server with the FQDN ftpserver.your.domain.com), and I also added an entry for the Squid site used in the script.

It would be more secure to use sftp (secure ftp), which uses an encrypted connection; unlike ftp, it doesn't send your user name and password across the network in plain text.

This is a very quick and simple example of a scripted session with an interactive program. If you prefer a more interesting life, you could use the expect utility, which implements a whole language designed for scripting interactive programs. More information on using expect can be found in Chapter 17.

Chapter 30: Automating Email

with `procmail`

Procmail is an autonomous mail processor. It is a utility that allows you to process your email based on rules. This is much like setting up rules in your email client for the handling of messages based on, for example, the sender's email address or on specified strings in the subject line. One of `procmail`'s advantages, compared to traditional email clients, is that the rules can be defined in such a way that when specific criteria are met, a script is called to perform a task.

Whatever you can do in a shell script, you can do with `procmail`. Once you have mastered the art of writing `procmail` scripts, it is a very powerful skill to have in your arsenal. I have used `procmail` for quite a few tasks. One processed customer feedback surveys and generated reports for use in managing a technical support group. Another received email messages that contained system setup parameters for numerous remote systems, such as patch level or the names of installed applications. `Procmail` would process these messages based on their subject lines and categorize the received information for later review. It was a very convenient way of tracking system configuration information and dutifully ran for many years.

The example I will demonstrate here is a simplified version of one I set up a long time ago that is no longer in use. I had a system at home that I could not access directly from work, and I didn't have convenient access to my system at work when I was at home. My home system, however, periodically dialed my ISP to gather email. From time to time, I would want to get a file from the home system, or to find out a system setting on the work system while I was at home. Because of this need, I set up `procmail` to receive specially formatted mail messages specifying files to retrieve or commands to be run on the remote machine, whose results would be returned back to me through email.

The thing to do in order to make this work is to send all your email to `procmail`. The way this is done depends on your email system. My systems used `sendmail` and my explanations assume this, but the concepts should apply to other mail systems as well. I first created a `.forward` file in my home directory that would pipe all my mail to `procmail`. This is the content of that file:

```
| /usr/bin/procmail
```

Not much to it, except that the path may vary on your machine. `Sendmail` has to be configured to recognize and use the `$HOME/.forward` files, but that is a common configuration. On some systems, `sendmail` is configured to recognize the use of `procmail` by looking for the existence of a `.procmailrc` file; this is the file that contains all of your `procmail` rules. In this case, `sendmail` then sends the mail to `procmail` automatically, without the need for a `.forward` file.

The `.procmailrc` file

Now that we have arranged for mail to be sent to `procmail`, the mail handling rules need to be configured. The `.procmailrc` file lives in the user's home directory and contains their mail rules. The rules are applied in the order that they appear in the file; if none of the rules apply to a mail message, or if the `.procmailrc` file is empty, the message will drop out of `procmail` processing and end up in your inbox as usual.

This is the `.procmailrc` I used:

```
PATH=/bin:/usr/bin:/usr/local/bin
MAILDIR=$HOME/Mail
LOGFILE=$MAILDIR/procmail.log
VERBOSE=yes
LOGABSTRACT=yes
SUBJECT=`formail -xSubject:`
FROM=`formail -rt -xTo:`
#
# Grab mail messages and feed the body of the message to the pipe
#
:0 getthisfile.lock
 * ^Subject:.*getthisfile
{
:0 b
| /usr/local/bin/getthisfile
```

```
}
```

Here is a more detailed explanation of the elements that make up this file.

```
PATH=/bin:/usr/bin:/usr/local/bin
MAILDIR=$HOME/Mail
LOGFILE=$MAILDIR/procmail.log
```

The first few lines set up some path and mail logging variables.

```
VERBOSE=yes
LOGABSTRACT=yes
```

The next two lines configure the amount of logging information that your log files will receive. These values are useful to get logging set up and ensure that the script is working, but normally you'll want to set these to 'no', so that the log file doesn't take over your hard disk.

```
SUBJECT=`formail -xSubject:`
FROM=`formail -xFrom:`
```

The last two lines in the first section are crucial, as they extract the subject and sender lines from the incoming message and save them in environment variables. The variables can then be accessed from within the script. The values are pulled out of the message headers using the `formail` utility. `Formail` is a filter especially designed for email.

```
:0 getthisfile.lock
```

Now we finally come to the body of the rules file. Here is the main rule for processing special-purpose mail messages. This is the beginning of the rule. It creates a lock file that exists while the message is being processed. The lock file is used to prevent the next applicable message in the mail queue from being processed until the processing of the current message is complete. If our system receives lots of mail, and the script to process mail messages takes a while to finish, there could arise several instances running simultaneously on different messages, all trying to access the same temporary files at once. The presence of the lock file indicates that an instance of the script is already running and another should not start.

```
* ^Subject:.*getthisfile
```

The next line of the rule checks the `Subject:` header line for an occurrence of the string 'getthisfile'. If the string is matched, then the body of the rule will be applied. The body of the rule follows the condition, in this case the subject matching 'getthisfile', and is enclosed in braces. I'm not going to talk in detail about the syntax of the procmail rules, since the procmail man page is very good and there is also a man page for procmailex which is dedicated to examples of rules for the .procmailrc file.

```
{
 :0 b
 | /usr/local/bin/getthisfile
}
```

Assuming that the subject line of the message contains 'getthisfile', the message itself is sent to the script. The single 'b' character in this expression stands for the body of the message. The message body is piped to the getthisfile script, which does the actual mail processing. This is the way you would generally send the information contained in the mail message to the script. In our case, most of the header and the body of the mail don't contain anything of value, and the subject line is really all the information we need. If the body of the message were actually required, the script would just need to be ready to receive standard input from the pipe. This would probably be done through a read loop. An example of this type of processing can be found in Chapter 27.

The email account is now set up to receive and process the special messages. Any mail sent to this account with a subject line of the following form will be processed by the getthisfile script.

```
Subject: getthisfile {binary|command|help} {path/file|command}
```

Now let's look at what the script really does. The following section shows the usage of the script.

Usage Examples

Here are a few examples of subject lines and the actions they would cause to be performed:

Subject: getthisfile help

Will send getthisfile usage information back to the sender.

Subject: getthisfile /etc/resolv.conf

Will mail the /etc/resolv.conf file back to the sender.

Subject: getthisfile command ls -l /tmp

Will send the output of ls -l /tmp back to the sender.

Subject: getthisfile binary /usr/bin/diff

This will uuencode the binary file /usr/bin/diff and mail the text back to the sender for later decode. Uuencode is a utility that encodes a binary file (executable, data etc) into simple ASCII. This way the file can be easily sent through email and decoded on the receiving side.

The Code

```sh
#!/bin/sh
warn_mail=my_email@mydomain.com
me=`uname -n`
LOG=/home/username/scripts/filetoget.log
echo `date` >> $LOG
echo Subject: $SUBJECT >> $LOG
```

The gettthisfile script first sets up some variables containing information such as the system name, the log file to write to, and the email address where warnings should be sent if somebody tries to use this tool without authorization. It then adds a couple of entries to the log, like the date and the mail subject.

```sh
filetoget=`echo $SUBJECT | awk '{print $3}'`
echo filetoget: $filetoget >> $LOG
whattodo=`echo $SUBJECT | awk '{print $2}'`
echo whattodo: $whattodo >> $LOG
command=`echo $SUBJECT | cut -d\ -f3-`
echo Command: $command >> $LOG
```

Next, it starts parsing the subject line to find out what is being requested. The variables should be self-explanatory. It is possible that some of them won't be defined at this point, but will be defined later. The values of these variables are also entered into the log.

```sh
if [ "$FROM" != " user1@good_domain.com" -a \
  "$FROM" != " user2@good_domain.com" ]
then
 echo "Invalid user $FROM trying to get procmail info: \
$SUBJECT" >> $LOG
 tail -10 $LOG | mail -s \
```

```
"$FROM attempting to get procmail info" $warn_mail
 exit 0
fi
```

This next part of the script is important if you don't want just anyone having access to your system. The script checks the address of the requester, where the requested information is to be sent. If the requester is not one of the *approved* addresses, a warning is sent to the email address stored in the warn_mail variable, notifying them of the potential intruder. The script then exits.

There is still potential for a breach, however, so don't be lulled into a false sense of security. If someone knew that this utility exists, they could craft a message that works as a spoof, pretending to be sent from one of the allowed addresses. The message would contain a subject line that would cause the getthisfile script to be replaced with a file of the intruder's choosing. The output of the intruder's commands would be sent back to the real allowed email addresses, but by the time they were noticed, it would likely be too late and the intruder would have access (although only to the account that has the procmail setup, which is hopefully not root). Careful setting of permissions and ownership of this script and of the .procmailrc files would makes intrusion a lot more difficult, but still not impossible.

While this isn't the most secure method of transferring files or information, it does demonstrate the use of procmail, which is our goal here. Keep in mind, however, that this is not a setup that I actually have running on a real system, for the reasons just noted. One other detail to note about this section of the code is that in the condition of the if statement there is a leading space in the email addresses. This is the way in which the email address is received from procmail. This could be handled in a few ways, but just adding the space in the if/then conditional works sufficiently well.

```
if [ "$whattodo" = "binary" ]
then
  echo "binary filetoget: $filetoget" >> $LOG
  echo "sending it to: $FROM" >> $LOG
  cd /tmp
  filename=`echo $filetoget | awk -F/ '{print $NF}'`
  uuencode $filetoget $filename > /tmp/$filename.uue
  echo "cat /tmp/$filename.uue | \
mail -s \"uuencoded $filetoget from $me\" $FROM" >> $LOG
  cat /tmp/$filename.uue | \
mail -s "uuencoded $filetoget from $me" $FROM >> $LOG
```

```
rm /tmp/$filename.uue
```

Next we examine the parsed subject line and determine what action to perform. Each action adds an entry to the log file. If a command is received to send a binary file, the process moves to the `/tmp` directory and then `uuencodes` the requested binary file. The script then emails the encoded output back to the requester for later decoding.

There is another way of performing this task that would be an excellent upgrade to this script: Craft an email message that, when received, would attach the binary file to the message. This can be done through manipulation of the email headers and proper encoding of the binary file. See Chapter 23 for a script that can perform this task.

```
elif [ "$whattodo" = "command" ]
then
 echo Running command $command >> $LOG
 echo "$command | mail -s \"Output of $command on $me\" $FROM" >> $LOG
 $command | mail -s "Output of $command on $me" $FROM >> $LOG
```

If the script determines that the requester wants to run a command, it performs the command and then emails the output back to the requester.

```
elif [ "$whattodo" = "help" ]
then
 echo "Sending usage to $FROM" >> $LOG
 echo "Subject: getthisfile {binary|command|help} \
{path/file|command}" | mail -s "Usage" $FROM
```

If the requester needs help in formatting his email subject line correctly, and inserts the proper subject line to get help, the script will send back usage information. OK, it's not the best method, since you do have to know a little about how it works before you can ask for help.

```
else
 filetoget=$whattodo
 echo "filetoget: $filetoget" >> $LOG
 echo "sending it to: $FROM" >> $LOG
 echo "cat $filetoget | mail -s \"$filetoget from $me\" $FROM" >> $LOG
 cat $filetoget | mail -s "$filetoget from $me" $FROM >> $LOG
fi
```

The final part of the script is the most basic. If the file to get and the command to run are the same, the script sees that there is no command to run. In this case the user just wants to receive a simple flat file, which will be mailed back to the requester. Another improvement to this script would be to first check the type of file that is being requested to make sure it is being processed correctly. This can be done by using the 'file' command.

Chapter 31: Process

Management Monitor

System process monitors can be a vital tool in determining the health of a running machine. Ensuring that the required processes are running and that the total number of each type of running process is appropriate is a good way to maintain system stability. The downside of these types of monitors is that they only let you know which processes are running and how many there are. They don't actually give you an indication of the health of each individual process.

This script dives in a little deeper into the condition of processes. By using the `ps` command with a customized format, we'll be able to monitor the age, proportion of cpu usage, virtual memory consumption, and amount of cpu time consumed by a particular process. If there are multiple instances of any given process that you are monitoring, each instance will be held up to the standard being monitored.

One other feature of this process monitor is that it can be configured not only to warn you of impending peril from processes whose operational values are out of bounds, but also to take action in the form of killing the aberrant process when necessary. The monitor could be easily modified to perform other actions besides killing a process.

Using historical data, you can sometimes predict when a specific application will start to consume too many resources. It was one such application that I was working with that prompted me to write this monitor. The monitor helped in characterizing exactly when the application ran out of control and in finding the actual cause of the behavior. Both were very helpful in fixing the problem.

```
kill_plist="dhcpd:pcpu:15:30:1 sshd:pcpu:15:30:1"
```

The syntax for monitor configuration is fairly straightforward, with five colon-separated fields as shown in the above example. The fields are as follows: the process command, the indicator to track, a lower threshold, an upper threshold, and the kill option. You can configure multiple processes by including several records in the configuration string.

The first field is the process command itself. This will be slightly different, and hopefully more simple, than the traditional `ps -ef` output. The `ps -ef` default output (`-e` for all processes, `-f` for formatted output) includes the commands that are running as well as any arguments that they were passed. The `ps -eo comm` output is formatted to only include the commands that are running on a system without any path or argument information. With this switch combination (`-eo`), you can also format your output in many ways to show many other options, such as memory size, process age, process cpu time, and so on. (On some UNIX systems, you may need to define the `UNIX95` variable within the script for the `ps -eo` command to function properly. The `UNIX95` variable can be set to anything you'd like; it just needs to not be undefined.) When specifying the process for our script to monitor, you'll want to use only the command name, as this is what the script will be looking for.

The second field contains the indicator you want to track. The options are `cputime`, which measures the number of minutes the cpu has allocated to the process; `etime`, which is the elapsed time in minutes since the process began running; `pcpu` which represents the current percentage of the cpu capacity the process is consuming; and `vsize`, which shows the virtual memory size in kilobytes for the process.

The third and fourth fields contain the desired lower and upper thresholds for the indicator you're tracking.

The fifth and final field is the kill option. It is a value from 0 to 3:

- 0: Send a notification when either the low (warning) or high (error) threshold have been crossed but *don't* kill the process.

- 1: Send a (warning) notification when the low threshold has been crossed or an (error) notification when the high threshold has been crossed *and* kill the process.

- 2: Send only a low level (warning) notification when either the low or high threshold have been crossed *and* kill the process.

- 3: Kill the process without any notification at all.

Note that for safety, if the kill option is not set, or is set to anything but one of the above values, processes will not be killed. Please take account the fact that there are two levels of notification. I have used alphanumeric paging for the high level (error status) and email for the low level (warning status). You may want to implement the notification method as appropriate for your needs.

```
#!/bin/sh
debug=1
sleeptime=3
kill_plist="dhcpd:pcpu:15:30:1 sshd:pcpu:15:30:1"
```

The first section of the script sets up a few configuration variables, which alternatively could be stored in a separate configuration file and sourced each time the script runs through the loop. This would allow for live configuration changes to the script. The debug value is for testing and the sleep value represents the amount of time to delay between each run. The `kill_plist` variable is the main configuration value that lets the script know what processes and values it should be watching.

```
notify ()
{
  case $2 in
    0)
      # Warn/error level and don't kill..
      echo "$1: $3 process id $4 found with $5 $7. \
        Should be less than $6."
    ;;
    1)
      # Warn/error level and kill..
      echo "$1: $3 process id $4 found with $5 $7. \
        Should be less than $6."
      test $debug -eq 0 && kill $4
    ;;
    2)
      # Warning level only...
      echo "Warning: $3 process id $4 found with $5 $7. \
        Should be less than $6."
      test $debug -eq 0 && kill $4
    ;;
    3)
      # Just kill, don't warn at all..
```

```
        test $debug -eq 0 && kill $4
    ;;
    *)
        echo "Warning: killoption not set correctly, \
          please validate configuration."
    ;;
  esac
}
```

This function performs all notifications and process terminations in the script. It is called with seven sequentially numbered parameters. The positional variables are somewhat difficult to understand and their values could have been assigned to more meaningfully-named variables before they were used, for ease of debugging later. To streamline the script a little, I didn't do this, and you are likely to modify this section at a later stage anyway.

Here, for ease of reference, I define all of the command-line arguments passed to this function:

$1: Text passed used for building the notification string. Used for the difference between Warning and Error.

$2: The kill option which has a possible value of 0-3.

$3: The process name that is being monitored.

$4: The process ID of the process being monitored.

$5: The current value of the indicator you are tracking.

$6: The lower threshold of the monitor.

$7: The text equivalent of the indicator that you are tracking.

This is also a good example of how a function can reduce the length and complexity of a script. The body of this function is code that would have to be repeated eight times throughout the script if it were not placed in a function. An older version of this script was written this way. Putting the code into a function reduced the script's length by roughly 40%.

```
while :
do
  for pline in $kill_plist
  do
```

```
process=`echo $pline | cut -d: -f1`
process="`echo $process | sed -e \"s/%20/ /g\"`"
type=`echo $pline | cut -d: -f2`
value=`echo $pline | awk -F: '{print $3}'`
errval=`echo $pline | awk -F: '{print $4}'`
killoption=`echo $pline | awk -F: '{print $5}'`
```

This is the beginning of the main loop. The script is intended to be run at system start up; it will then be run continuously through an infinite loop. After each iteration completes, the script will sleep for a predetermined time before the next iteration. The first part here is a nested loop that progresses through each record in the configuration string to parse its fields and set up the monitor.

The `process` variable is assigned the first field in the configuration record (`pline`). It is possible that the process command name you're monitoring will consist of more than one word, separated by spaces. Such spaces are replaced (here using the `sed` command) with '`%20`', which is a commonly used substitute for the space character, as for example in URL encoding.

The `type` variable is the second field in the configuration record. As mentioned, it specifies the performance indicator to watch: `cputime` (amount of cpu time consumed), `etime` (elapsed time or age of process), `pcpu` (current percent of the total cpu consumed), or `vsize` (virtual memory size).

The `value` variable holds the lower warning threshold for the monitored value, taken from the third field.

The `errval` variable is assigned the value of the upper error threshold for the monitored value, taken from the fourth field.

The `killoption` variable is assigned the final field of the configuration record and specifies an action to perform when the process deviates from the normal range.

```
if [ "$killoption" = "" ]
then
    killoption=0
fi
test $debug -gt 0 && echo "Kill $process processes if \
    $type is greater than $errval"
```

If the kill option was not specified, we set it to be the default kill option. This makes sure that no processes are killed unless one of the options for doing so is explicitly used.

```
for pid in `ps -eo pid,comm | egrep "${process}$|${process}:$" |\
  grep -v grep | awk '{print $1}'`
do
```

Next we pare down the full list of processes running on the system to the ones running the command being monitored. Then we start a loop that iterates through the remaining processes.

```
test $debug -gt 0 && echo "$process pid $pid"
pid_string=`ps -eo pid,cputime,etime,pcpu,vsize,comm |\
  grep $pid | egrep "${process}$|${process}:$" | grep -v grep`
```

For each process id, the script has to gather the pertinent information. The embedded ps command gathers only the specific information we want.

```
case $type in
  "cputime")
    proc_time=`echo $pid_string | awk '{print $2}'`
    fields=`echo $proc_time | awk -F: '{print NF}'`
    proc_time_min=`echo $proc_time | awk -F: '{print $(NF-1)}'`
```

This case statement is the heart of the monitor. The script tests for the monitor type (cputime, etime, pcpu, or vsize); the cputime is the first listed. The code for each type is slightly different, but all are very similar. Here we obtain the process time from the ps output, as well as the number of fields that the proc_time variable contains.

Both of these are needed because the format of the time value varies depending on the amount of time it represents. The cputime and etime variables have values of the form 'days-hours:minutes:seconds' or 'hours:minute:seconds'. A low value might look something like 00:28 for 28 seconds. A high value could be 1-18:32:29 for 1 day, 18 hours, 32 minutes, and 29 seconds. Both of these types have to be processed and converted to minutes. (Seconds are dropped for simplicity.)

```
if [ $fields -lt 3 ]
then
  proc_time_hr=0
  proc_time_day=0
else
  proc_time_hr=`echo $proc_time | awk -F: '{print $(NF-2)}'`
  fields=`echo $proc_time_hr | awk -F- '{print NF}'`
```

```
        if [ $fields -ne 1 ]
        then
          proc_time_day=`echo $proc_time_hr | awk -F- '{print $1}'`
          proc_time_hr=`echo $proc_time_hr | awk -F- '{print $2}'`
        else
          proc_time_day=0
        fi
    fi
```

Of the four performance indicators, the logic for handling the cputime and etime values is the most complex because the format used to report them changes.

```
    curr_cpu_time=\
    `echo "$proc_time_day*1440+$proc_time_hr*60+$proc_time_min"\
    | bc`
    test $debug -gt 0 && echo "Current cpu time for \
      $process pid $pid is $curr_cpu_time minutes"
```

Once all time values have been determined, we convert them to minutes for comparison with the monitor thresholds.

```
    if test $curr_cpu_time -gt $value -a \
      $curr_cpu_time -lt $errval
    then
        notify "Warning" $killoption $process $pid \
          $curr_cpu_time $value "minutes of CPU time"
```

If the current cputime value is between the warning and error thresholds, we call the notify() function with the appropriate switches. It will handle output and process termination, as described earlier.

```
        elif test $curr_cpu_time -ge $errval
        then
          notify "Error" $killoption $process $pid \
            $curr_cpu_time $value "minutes of CPU time"
```

If the current cputime is greater than the error threshold, we call the notify() function with a different set of options.

```
        else
            test $debug -gt 0 && echo "process cpu time ok"
        fi
    ;;
```

The final condition handles the case where there is no issue with the running process: The script just issues a message saying so.

```
"etime")
    proc_age=`echo $pid_string | awk '{print $3}'`
    fields=`echo $proc_age | awk -F: '{print NF}'`
    proc_age_min=`echo $proc_age | awk -F: '{print $(NF-1)}'`
```

The etime monitor is nearly the same as the cputime monitor. The primary difference is the field that is extracted from the ps output in order to get the current process age.

```
        if [ $fields -lt 3 ]
        then
            proc_age_hr=0
            proc_age_day=0
        else
            proc_age_hr=`echo $proc_age | awk -F: '{print $(NF-2)}'`
            fields=`echo $proc_age_hr | awk -F- '{print NF}'`
            if [ $fields -ne 1 ]
            then
                proc_age_day=`echo $proc_age_hr | awk -F- '{print $1}'`
                proc_age_hr=`echo $proc_age_hr | awk -F- '{print $2}'`
            else
                proc_age_day=0
            fi
        fi
```

Once again, you convert the age of the process to values that will then be used to calculate the age in minutes.

```
        curr_age=\
            `echo "$proc_age_day*1440+$proc_age_hr*60+$proc_age_min" \
            | bc`
```

```
        test $debug -gt 0 && echo "Current age of $process pid \
          $pid is $curr_age minutes"
```

Once again, expressing the process age in minutes makes the threshold check very simple.

```
        if test $curr_age -gt $value -a $curr_age -lt $errval
        then
           notify "Warning" $killoption $process $pid \
             $curr_age $value "minutes of elapsed time"
        elif test $curr_age -ge $errval
        then
           notify "Error" $killoption $process $pid \
             $curr_age $value "minutes of elapsed time"
        else
           test $debug -gt 0 && echo "process age ok"
        fi
    ;;
```

We now perform the comparison checks against the monitor thresholds as before. The first check determines if the current process age is between the low and high thresholds. The second sees if the current age is above the high threshold. In both these cases, call the notify() function for end user output and process termination. The final possibility is that there is no issue, and in this case the script gives a message stating that the process is OK.

```
    "pcpu")
        curr_proc_cpu=`echo $pid_string | awk '{print $4}' | \
          awk -F. '{print $1}'`
        test $debug -gt 0 && echo "Current percent cpu of \
          $process pid $pid is $curr_proc_cpu"
```

The test for percentage cpu usage is quite simple. The value to be compared to the thresholds is obtained directly from the ps output. There is no need for further calculation, as was needed in the code for the cputime and etime monitors.

```
        if test $curr_proc_cpu -gt $value -a \
          $curr_proc_cpu -lt $errval
        then
```

```
        notify "Warning" $killoption $process $pid \
          $curr_proc_cpu $value "percent of the CPU"
      elif test $curr_proc_cpu -ge $errval
      then
        notify "Error" $killoption $process $pid \
          $curr_proc_cpu $value "percent of the CPU"
      else
        test $debug -gt 0 && echo "process cpu percent ok"
      fi
    ;;
```

Once again, we compare the percentage cpu value with the configured low and high thresholds and call the `notify()` function to alert the user and perform any required process termination. If the cpu percentage is below either of these values, output an "OK" message.

```
"vsize")
  curr_proc_size=`echo $pid_string | awk '{print $5}'`
  test $debug -gt 0 && echo "Current size of $process pid \
    $pid is $curr_proc_size"
```

The `vsize` monitor is as simple as the percent cpu monitor. We obtain the current process memory footprint directly from the `ps` output.

```
      if test $curr_proc_size -gt $value -a \
        $curr_proc_size -lt $errval
      then
        notify "Warning" $killoption $process $pid \
          $curr_proc_size $value "blocks of virtual size"
      elif test $curr_proc_size -ge $errval
      then
        notify "Error" $killoption $process $pid \
          $curr_proc_size $value "blocks of virtual size"
      else
        test $debug -gt 0 && echo "process virtual size ok"
      fi
    ;;
```

You have to check the current memory size against the monitor thresholds one last time. If they are within a low or high warning status, we call the `notify()` function for output and termination. If not, output that the process size is OK.

```
        esac
      done
    done
    sleep $sleeptime
done
```

Finally, we close the monitor case statement and the two inner processing loops. The script then goes to `sleep` for the configured amount of time before starting all over again. It will then continue its monitoring until the monitor itself dies or is killed, or the system is shut down.

Chapter 32: Managing File

Counts

System administrators have to manage the computing resources available to their users. One resource consists of the directory queues for email and print servers. These directories contain the files waiting to be processed by the server. The number of files in these directories will vary over time depending on the volume of work on the server. There are times when no one is using the service and the queue empties out. There will also be times when the server is heavily loaded and the queue will be full. Usually, though, the number of files will stay within stipulated limits.

Of course from time to time you will have problems with a queue filling up faster than the server can process the requests. This might be due to a bubble of extremely heavy load or because of some type of problem that prevents the server from processing the requests. You will want to monitor the queue directories so that you can take proactive measures when a problem arises.

The script presented in this chapter is a simple monitor that counts the files in the specified directories. Our script gives you the necessary core functionality; you will, however, want to modify the directory locations and notification methods for your own site and needs.

```
#!/bin/sh
FILENUM="/var/spool/mqueue:50:100:root \
  /var/spool/lp:50:100:root@yourdomain.net /:50:100:rbpeters"
```

First we define the directories to be monitored. It would probably be a bit cleaner to place this definition in a separate file so that you don't have to modify the script in order to make configuration changes. Each entry in the FILENUM variable is a colon-delimited set of fields. The fields specify the directory name to monitor, the warning threshold, the maximum limit, and finally the email address to which to send notifications.

```
for monitor in $FILENUM
do
    set -- `echo $monitor | sed -e 's/:/ /g'`
    file_count=`ls $1 | wc -l`
```

Now we start looping through each of the configured directories to check the file counts. First, sed is used to swap colons with spaces in the configuration entry; then, the set command is used to assign, to each of the positional parameters $1 through $4, the corresponding element of the output, which consists of the items in the original colon-separated fields. Once the fields are assigned to the variables, the script determines the number of files in the directory.

```
    if [ $file_count -lt $2 ]
    then
        continue
    elif [ $file_count -ge $2 -a $file_count -lt $3 ]
    then
        echo "Warning: File count in $1 is $file_count, should be less \
          than $2" | mail -s "Directory file count warning for $1" $4
    else
        echo "Error: File count in $1 is $file_count, should be less \
          than $2" | mail -s "Directory file count error for $1" $4
    fi
done
```

The script completes by comparing the current file count with the three possible situations. There is the state where everything is normal, when the file count is lower than the warning threshold. In a warning state, where the count is between the warning threshold and maximum limit. Finally, in an error state the count is above the maximum limit. In either the warning or error state, the script will send a notification via email specifying the condition of the directory.

To make this script more useful, you would need to call it with cron, or possibly surround the code with an infinite loop that a perpetual process would run in order to continually monitor your machine. The main function of the script is carried out in the assignment of the file_count variable by performing an ls on the target directory and then piping the output to the wc utility. This is one of a number of ways to get queue status information. Two other ways of determining the file count in a directory are to use the echo and find commands. Here are some possible solutions:

```
file_count=`ls $1 | wc -l`
file_count=`find $1 -type f | wc -l`
file_count=`echo $1/* | wc -w`
```

Note that the wc -l switch has been replaced with -w for the last solution. This is because the result of the shell's expansion of the asterisk will appear in the form of a single line of filenames separated by spaces.

Testing File Count Methods

The different methods of counting the files in a directory are not all created equal. Some older operating systems cannot handle large numbers of files when the ls or find command is used. I encountered problems where the find-oriented solution would return incorrect results on directories containing somewhere between 12,000 to 15,000 files. Also, I have worked on systems with file counts of more than one million in a single directory; in these cases ls would return an *argument list too long* error. I have not yet found the echo solution to fail.

On my current Gentoo Linux system, both find and ls seem not to suffer from these earlier limitations, and I have used both to successfully count files in a single directory numbering well above 800,000. While testing, I also noticed that there is a speed difference between the three solutions.

The find solution is by far the fastest .It took about .4 seconds with just over 300k files in a directory. The second fastest is echo *. It took about 1.5 seconds. This measure is most accurate if you work in the directory whose files are to be counted. If a full path is supplied with the asterisk (e.g., /some/full/path/*), the command takes longer because each element in the shell expansion contains the full path and all that extra text needs to be processed. The slowest was ls. It took about 4 seconds to complete. Both find and ls seemed to take similar amounts of time regardless of whether the full path was supplied.

Realistically speaking, with a current operating system, any of these solutions should work fine. It is not very likely that you will be dealing with this kind of extreme number of files in a single directory, and the performance differences will almost surely be insignificant.

Chapter 33: Processes

Running from Inittab

In several chapters[1] of this book, I discuss system monitors and some methods of running them on your machine at all times. There are multiple ways of accomplishing this task without user interaction by automatically starting a process at the system level. There is `cron`, the system scheduler, as well as `at`, another scheduling utility. You can start a process with an `rc` (run control) startup script; these are traditionally located in the `/etc/rc` directories, which are processed automatically at boot time.

The utility that I want to discuss here is the `init` process. The `init` man page states that it is "the parent of all processes." `Init` runs the scripts that, in turn, run the startup scripts living inside the `/etc/rc` directories.[2] It also controls the run-level of the running system. `Init` is started as the last step in the system boot process. If you are looking for the `init` configuration parameters, they are kept in the `/etc/inittab` file.

The main problem with monitors that need to run on the system permanently is that if they die or have to be killed, it is challenging to get them restarted automatically. The methods for automatically starting processes have some unexpected limitations on their ability to keep processes running.

System startup scripts will start a process, but have no notification or recovery method that can be used if a process ends. In addition, these scripts are only run at boot time, and many systems run continuously for long periods between reboots.

---

1   Log file monitoring in Chapter 7, process monitoring in Chapter 31, file count monitoring in Chapter 32 and network monitoring in Chapter 42.

2   The startup scripts may be found in different locations depending on your operating system. /sbin/rc#, /etc/init.d/rc#, and /etc/rc# are some of the locations that that I have seen.

Cron and at jobs that start processes can be scheduled to run frequently, but the process code would need to be written so that it recognizes if another instance of itself is already running. As we shall see, scheduled tasks are not a terribly efficient use of system resources. Although a process may run for long periods of time without issues, the scheduler also uses some resources to continuously check and/or start the process. The problem also exists that if a process does die or get killed, there is a period of time before the next scheduled job when the monitor is not running.

This is where init comes in. There is an action value among the /etc/inittab entries called *respawn*, which is a feature that I don't use often, but is quite useful for certain tasks. When an entry is added to the inittab and the action defined for that entry is *respawn*, init makes sure that a process corresponding to that entry is always running. If the process dies, or is killed for some reason, init will automatically restart or "respawn" it. The process restart is nearly instantaneous, and the amount of time during which no instance of the desired process is running is negligible.

```
1:2345:respawn:/sbin/mingetty tty1
2:2345:respawn:/sbin/mingetty tty2
3:2345:respawn:/sbin/mingetty tty3
4:2345:respawn:/sbin/mingetty tty4
5:2345:respawn:/sbin/mingetty tty5
6:2345:respawn:/sbin/mingetty tty6
```

An /etc/inittab entry takes the form of a line with four colon-separated fields. The first field is a unique identifier for the entry, of one to four characters in length. The second field is a list of the runlevels in which the entry should be run. In the examples above, each of the entries will be run in runlevels 2 through 5. The third field names the action to be taken, which in this case is respawn. There are a number of actions besides respawn that init can perform on a process, such as once, off, boot, wait, and several others. The last field is the script or program that you want to run.

Respawn entries are likely to be part of the default /etc/inittab file for starting the boot-time rc scripts or getty login sessions as seen in the sample entries above.

In the case of monitors which are critical to tracking system health, I have used init in this way to make sure they are always running. The init process is the top dog of all processes on a running system; if it can't keep processes running, your system is probably fairly "sick" and you are likely to have bigger problems than deficient monitors.

```
im:35:respawn:/bin/nice /usr/local/bin/MyMonitors >/dev/null 2>&1
```

Here is an example of an entry that I have used for my system monitors in the /etc/inittab. The `im` identifier is arbitrary and only needs to be unique in the file as a whole. It simply identifies the entry in the file. The process is run on runlevels 3 and 5 and is respawned if it dies. It executes the `MyMonitors` script.

Entries can be added to the /etc/inittab file at any time, but `init` won't automatically reread the `inittab` file when it is modified. This can be done by issuing the `init q` command as root which will reread the file and implement the current configuration.

One potential issue to watch for if you create a respawn `inittab` entry is that the script to be called should include code enabling it to run continuously. If you create a script that performs a monitor function and exits when finished, `init` will assume that the program is constantly dying and continuously try to restart the process. On most systems, if this happens, you will start receiving messages in the system logs warning you that the process is *'respawning too fast'*. `Init` will then disable the respawn of the job for a period of time since it recognizes that there is some type of issue with the configured entry. The issue could either be that the configured job runs and exits normally, whereas respawned jobs should run continuously, or simply that the syntax of the `inittab` line is incorrect.

Chapter 34: Automatic RCS

RCS (Revision Control System) is a set of programs used for source code version control. It it heavily used by programmers to maintain source files and track source code changes. The script in this chapter[1] was created in an effort to control configuration files on a system without having to perform the manual check-in and check-out process used with RCS. This is done by replacing your system editor with this script, which in turn calls your editor with the appropriate RCS commands.

The script demonstrates a few useful techniques: It grabs command-line parameters, it calls the script through a link, and finally it demonstrates the use of the check-in and check-out commands in RCS. There are many more features and options available in RCS, but they are mostly outside the scope of this discussion.

This script isn't intended to be specifically called as an add-on utility; it is intended as a replacement for the original editor for your environment. I wrote it for use with vi, although other editors could be replaced in the same manner. You would first rename the original vi or vim binary in /usr/bin to something like /usr/bin/vim-rcs. When you move this script to its new location, you should replace the original /usr/bin/vi (or vim) with your script. This is so that when you call vi/vim, you will be running our script instead. The $VI variable refers to the new location of the original vi/vim binary, so the script knows where you moved it. This works even when calling vi (now the script) with a wildcard such as '*', because the shell will expand the wildcard before executing the call.

```
#!/bin/sh
CI=/usr/bin/ci
CO=/usr/bin/co
TEST=/usr/bin/test
```

---

1   Submitted by Brian Grell.

```
BASENAME=/bin/basename
ME=`$BASENAME $0`
DIRNAME=/usr/bin/dirname
```

We start out with some configurable system variables. The file locations defined with these variables may vary from installation to installation, so you'll need to make the appropriate changes for your site. Also note that you need to have RCS installed on your system, since it may not be installed by default.

The ME variable is assigned the name with which the script was invoked. If you named this script vi so that it would replace the vi binary, ME would be set to vi. This is done by using basename to remove any leading path used to call the script. We will come back to this variable and the way that it is used a bit later. For now, note that when installing the script on your system, you will also need to create a soft link in a directory in your PATH variable called vir that points to the script.

```
ALLTHEFILES=$@
```

When a script is run, environment variables are set that don't directly relate to the script itself, since they are part of the shell executing the script and its environment. One example is the variable '$@', which is set to the values of all the positional parameters (starting from 1) that were passed to the script. (As we have seen, positional parameter 0 is assigned the name of the script.) To be a little more explicit, consider this example where a script is called like so:

runme a b c d

In this example, the value of $0 would be runme, $1 would be a, $2 would be b, and so on. $@ would be set to the combination of all of the positional parameters: a b c d.

The reason we need to use this here in our script is because you might want to call your editor with a wild card, such as filename*, or you might want to call the editor to edit a list of files. The variable ALLTHEFILES is set for this purpose.

```
VI=/usr/bin/vim-rcs
for file in $ALLTHEFILES
do
  # Get some basic info about the file
  PATH=`$DIRNAME $file`
  FILENAME=`$BASENAME $file`
```

Here we start the main loop that iterates through the list of files passed to the script. First we determine the path and filename of the current file.

```
$TEST -f "$PATH/RCS/$FILENAME,v" -o -f "$PATH/$FILENAME,v" && \
  $CO -l $file
  $VI $file
```

Now the script should determine whether the file has already been checked in under RCS. If that is the case, we check it out. Then we edit the file as usual.

```
if [ "$ME" = "vir" ]
then
  $TEST ! -f "$PATH/RCS/$FILENAME,v" -o ! -f "$PATH/$FILENAME,v" \
    && $CI -i $file
else
  $TEST -f "$PATH/RCS/$FILENAME,v" -o -f "$PATH/$FILENAME,v" && \
    $CI -u $file
  fi
done
```

After each file has been edited, we want to see how the script was called in order to determine whether it needs to be checked back in. Recall that a soft link to the script was created when the script was installed. If the script was called with this `vir` soft link instead of with a `vi`/`vim` command, which we can find out by examining `$ME`, then the assumption is that even if the file was not under RCS control before, it needs to be checked in so that it will be available in the future. The script checks to see if the RCS-controlled version of the file exists. If the controlled version does not exist, it checks the file into RCS with the initial checkin (`-i`) switch, otherwise it just checks it in as normal.

You can see that by determining how the script was invoked (using the soft link or using the name of the file), you avoid having to force all of the files you edit into RCS. Chapter 13 contains further discussion of the technique of using the syntax of the invocation to select a script's behavior.

You could upgrade this script by defining directories for which it is assumed that all files inside those directories should be checked into RCS even if they weren't originally. (The `/etc` directory would be a good candidate for this treatment.) Files residing in other directories would be edited as usual, without any version control.

Chapter 35: Colorful /proc

Reporting

The proc file system is found on many UNIX and Linux variants and gives a virtual view into the running system. The proc file system is traditionally attached to the /proc mount point, but proc is not really a file system and mostly contains "files" of zero size. Even though these objects look as if they are empty when they are listed, they actually contain quite a lot of information about the running system. When viewed, they show system information from the kernel's perspective: their contents are based on system resources and characteristics, such as memory, cpu, kernel, and network utilization.

There are several kinds of files in the /proc directory tree on a Linux machine. The first type is a series of directories that have numbers as names, each containing a group of files that hold specific information about the running system. Each numbered directory corresponds to a running process ID. The files in these directories relate to the command that was invoked, the execution environment, parameters passed to the command, memory usage, and other valuable pieces of process information. The other file types and directories found in /proc contain items such as current resource usage, system settings, hardware information, and network usage.

The man page for proc contains far more detail, but users have to realize that implementations of the proc file system on different operating systems are by no means identical. I have worked on older versions of Solaris whose /proc only contained numbered directories for running processes, and those directories held files that were different from their Linux counterparts. With this state of affairs, you are certain to profit from exploring the documentation for your specific system.

The script we are about to explore had its origins in a utility that creates a brief system status report. The script returned a single line of key performance indicators; the information was derived from files located in /proc directories. It displayed all the process performance values for each system being monitored on a few lines all contained in a single window, using colors to indicate load level, memory and swap usage (green for normal usage and red for high). The main purpose of this tool was to permit a quick visual check of whether certain machines were overloaded.

Our code extends the functionality of the original script from providing just one line of output per system to displaying a more comprehensive report about the processes running on a single machine. The code itself is not very complex but it does demonstrate some of the /proc system usage data. You will also learn how to add color to your output.

```
#!/bin/sh
def_colors () {
# Attributes
  normal='\033[0m'; bold='\033[1m'; dim='\033[2m'; under='\033[4m'
  italic='\033[3m'; noitalic='\033[23m'; blink='\033[5m';
  reverse='\033[7m'; conceal='\033[8m' nobold='\033[22m';
  nounder='\033[24m'; noblink='\033[25m'
  # Foreground
  black='\033[30m'; red='\033[31m'; green='\033[32m'; yellow='\033[33m'
  blue='\033[34m'; magenta='\033[35m'; cyan='\033[36m'; white='\033[37m'
  # Background
  bblack='\033[40m'; bred='\033[41m'
  bgreen='\033[42m'; byellow='\033[43m'
  bblue='\033[44m'; bmagenta='\033[45m'
  bcyan='\033[46m'; bwhite='\033[47m'
}
def_colors
```

The first function sets up the colors that the script will use. These are standard ANSI color definitions. Each of the definitions begins with the string '\033'. This is the plain text ASCII code for an '*escape*' character. The numerical notation used here is easier to read in text form than the actual escape character. (The escape character happens to be '^[' and if you want to type it in, you would need to use your editor's mechanism for handling this character, for example pressing CTRL-v and then ESC in vi. This will give you the character displayed as '^['.) One thing to note is that these color definitions may not work on all terminal types. I have had no problems with using these values in a simple xterm window.

I did not use all of the colors or attributes defined in the function, but I included them for the sake of completeness. This function would be an excellent addition to a standard library, which we discussed in Chapter 2.

```
clear
hostname=`cat /proc/sys/kernel/hostname`
echo
echo -e "System Report for $white$hostname$normal on `date`"
echo
```

Now that the colors are defined, the script clears the display and then obtains the name of the machine from the /proc/hostname file. Then it displays a header for the report.

There are a few noteworthy items in the command that displays header line: First, echo is used with the -e switch, which translates escaped three-digit number sequences contained in text into the corresponding ASCII character; in our case, it translates the ANSI escape character sequence into the escape character. There are other escape values that can be used to represent other special characters, such as the carriage return, horizontal tab, and backspace.

The second item is the hostname variable, which is surrounded by variables that control color output. The first variable changes the output from the default color to white. Once the hostname variable's value has been presented, the color is reset back to default. Changes to the text color can be accomplished together with, and at the same time as, modifications of the foreground and background color. Other attributes, such as blinking text can be changed as well by using the appropriate variable.

ANSI graphics were common on old dial-up bulletin board systems prior to the availability of widespread Internet access. We should note that when the blink attribute is used, the blink function does use network resources when displaying in remote terminals. The bandwidth used is probably minimal, but you should be aware of it. The blink attribute poses more of an issue when it is used over a serial connection with a modem.

```
processor=`grep 'model name' /proc/cpuinfo | cut -d: -f2 | cut -c2-`
nisdomain=`cat /proc/sys/kernel/domainname`

cache=`grep 'cache size' /proc/cpuinfo | awk '{print $4,$5}'`
bogomips=`grep 'bogomips' /proc/cpuinfo | awk '{print $3}'`
vendor=`grep 'vendor_id' /proc/cpuinfo`

echo -e "Hostname:      $white$hostname$normal   NIS Domain:
$white$nisdomain$normal"
```

```
if [ "`echo $vendor | grep -i intel`" ]
then
  cpu_color=$blue
elif [ "`echo $vendor | grep -i amd`" ]
then
  cpu_color=$green
fi

echo -e "Processor:      $cpu_color$processor$normal"
echo -e "           Running at $white$bogomips$normal bogomips with\
  $white$cache$normal cache"
echo
```

The next section of code grabs more data from various files in /proc to get a few more items of information, such as processor type and NIS domain name. The script then determines if the processor is manufactured by Intel or AMD and changes the output color depending on the vendor before printing this portion of the report to the screen.

```
ostype=`cat /proc/sys/kernel/ostype`
osrelease=`cat /proc/sys/kernel/osrelease`
rev=`cat /proc/sys/kernel/version | awk '{print $1}'`
da_date=`cat /proc/sys/kernel/version | cut -d\  -f2-`
upsec=`awk '{print $1}' /proc/uptime`
uptime=`echo "scale=2;$upsec/86400" | bc`

echo -e "OS Type: $white$ostype$normal    Kernel:\
  $white$osrelease$normal"
echo -e "         Kernel Compile $white$rev$normal on\
  $white$da_date$normal"
echo -e "Uptime:         $magenta$uptime$normal days"
```

Now the script gathers information about the operating system and kernel, including their versions and release numbers. It also obtains the system uptime and outputs colorized text reporting the results.

```
set `grep MemTotal /proc/meminfo`
tot_mem=$2 ; tot_mem_unit=$3
set `grep MemFree /proc/meminfo`
```

```
free_mem=$2 ; fre_mem_unit=$3
perc_mem_used=$((100-(100*free_mem/tot_mem)))
set `grep SwapTotal /proc/meminfo`
tot_swap=$2 ; tot_swap_unit=$3
set `grep SwapFree /proc/meminfo`
free_swap=$2 ; fre_swap_unit=$3
perc_swap_used=$((100-(100*free_swap/tot_swap)))
```

These lines gather system memory and swap information and calculate the proportion of these system resources currently used by the running processes. One interesting bit is the use of the set command: It uses the result of grepping through /proc/meminfo to assign values to positional parameters. This is a convenient way of assigning each item in a space-separated sequence of items to its own variable.

```
if [ $perc_mem_used -lt 80 ]
then
  mem_color=$green
elif [ $perc_mem_used -ge 80 -a $perc_mem_used -lt 90 ]
then
  mem_color=$yellow
else
  mem_color=$red
fi
if [ $perc_swap_used -lt 80 ]
then
  swap_color=$green
elif [ $perc_swap_used -ge 80 -a $perc_swap_used -lt 90 ]
then
  swap_color=$yellow
else
  swap_color=$red
fi

echo -e "Memory:  $white$tot_mem$normal $tot_mem_unit Free:
     $white$free_mem$normal $fre_mem_unit      %Used:
     $mem_color$perc_mem_used$normal"
```

```
echo -e "Swap:    $white$tot_swap$normal $tot_swap_unit      Free:
    $white$free_swap$normal $fre_swap_unit   %Used:
    $swap_color$perc_swap_used$normal"
echo
```

Once the script has calculated percentages, the color of the output is set depending on the usage value that is being reported. Messages reporting usage levels of less than 80 percent appear in green, values between 80 and 90 percent appear in yellow, and 90 percent utilization or greater appears in red. I have chosen the percentages somewhat arbitrarily. One improvement to the script would be to replace the percentage values with variables which are initialized using either a command-line switch or a configuration file.

```
set `cat /proc/loadavg`
one_min=$1
five_min=$2
fifteen_min=$3
echo -n "Load Average:"
for ave in $one_min $five_min $fifteen_min
do
  int_ave=`echo $ave | cut -d. -f1`
  if [ $int_ave -lt 1 ]
  then
    echo -en "    $green$ave$normal"
  elif [ $int_ave -ge 1 -a $int_ave -lt 5 ]
  then
    echo -en "    $yellow$ave$normal"
  else
    echo -en "    $red$ave$normal"
  fi
done
echo
```

In addition to memory and swap utilization, the script determines the system load averages, again using the `set` command to assign values to the positional variables. The `/proc/loadavg` file contains a single line of space-separated fields, where the first three fields are the 1-minute, 5-minute, and 15-minute load averages of the running system. When the output of the file is applied to the `set` command, the first three fields become the values of the positional parameter variables `$1`, `$2`, and `$3`. Once these values have been obtained, the script then adjusts the color of the text. A load average below 1 will be reported in green, between 1 and 5 is reported in yellow, and any value 5 or greater is reported in red. Keep in mind that the colors for the load averages are assumed to be for single CPU systems.

```
running=0; sleeping=0 stopped=0; zombie=0
for pid in /proc/[1-9]*
do
  procs=$((procs+1))
  stat=`awk '{print $3}' $pid/stat`
  case $stat in
    R)   running=$((running+1));;
    S)   sleeping=$((sleeping+1));;
    T)   stopped=$((stopped+1));;
    Z)   zombie=$((zombie+1));;
  esac
done
echo -n "Process Count: "
echo -e "$white$procs$normal total $white$running$normal running\
  $white$sleeping$normal sleeping $white$stopped$normal stopped\
  $white$zombie$normal zombie"
echo
```

The final operation counts the running processes and determines their states. Once the total number of processes is calculated, the script displays the process count. It also gives a breakdown of processes by status type, telling the user how many processes are running, sleeping, stopped, or zombified.

```
System Report for casper on Thu Aug  4 21:33:19 PDT 2005


Hostname:        casper   NIS Domain: (none)
Processor:       Intel(R) Pentium(R) 4 CPU 1.80GHz
                 Running at 3555.32 bogomips with 256 KB cache

OS Type:         Linux   Kernel: 2.6.10-gentoo-r7
                 Kernel Compile #2 on Thu Feb 24 14:38:44 PST 2005
Uptime:          163.70 days
```

```
Memory:  514836 kB      Free:   183744 kB      %Used:  65
Swap:    506036 kB      Free:   491324 kB      %Used:  3


Load Average:    0.04    0.11    0.05
Process Count:   140 total 1 running 139 sleeping 0 stopped 0 zombie
```

This is a sample report that the script generates while running. I have used a boldface font wherever the report is supposed to appear in a special color. It is more informative with colorized output, although it is already a useful utility for capturing a snapshot of the system state and displaying everything on one screen.

It is possible to retrieve most of the information in the files located in the /proc directory tree using other methods. Programs such as hostname, netstat, top, ps, uptime, and others get their data from /proc. In some cases, those programs are easier to use because they condense information and present it in a more readable form. In other cases, getting the data directly from the files residing in /proc is easier or faster. This is the situation with our script: There is no data to format and there is no unneeded functionality that may impact performance.

The part that gets the load average provides a good illustration of the benefit, since this data can be found by running the uptime, w or top commands. The output of these commands contains uptime data as well as load information.

```
8:33PM up 33 mins, 4 users, load average: 0.00, 0.22, 0.38
9:13PM up 430 days, 0:09, 2 users, load average: 0.01, 0.13, 0.10
```

It is fairly simple to extract the load averages from this output with awk, but obtaining load averages directly as demonstrated in our script, without determining the uptime as well, is a bit more economical on system resources.

Another use of the /proc file system is that you can influence the running system by modifying the files located in /proc. A simple example is the system name found in /proc/sys/kernel/hostname: by redirecting a new name into this file, you would end up overwriting the previous entry, thus changing the system name. You can view the change by using the uname -n command. The change is permanent only until your next reboot, as the system configuration files still hold the original name of the system.

Other system attributes can be modified in the same way, such as RAID rebuild rates and the way the system handles swap or power management settings. One pitfall you might encounter is that the power to modify system settings is dangerous. You might cause the system to hang or even to crash. It would be wise to perform extensive testing on noncritical machines before implementing environment-wide modifications.

Chapter 36: Password Aging

Notification

With security concerns reigning supreme, it is wise to keep a tight leash on your user accounts. Unfortunately, it can be difficult to control password aging in an environment with many users. It's definitely preferable to have user passwords set to automatically expire; however, if the account goes unused for a long period of time, even though the password on an account is expired, the account will still be active. There are instances where an account can still be accessed without the password being updated. Also, if a user logs in to their account infrequently they may not know that their account is about to expire. Even when a user does use his or her account regularly, the expiration warning message may go unnoticed among the other items that typically scroll across the screen in the message of the day.

Requiring users to change their passwords after it has aged a certain number of days use is a common practice. The logic behind it is reasonable enough in that if a password is stolen or found out, it would only be useful for a limited amount of time. Another result that comes out of this practice is that users will tend to change their password in a way that is least impactive to their work so they don't have to learn a new password. A method might be to leave the main password in place but change only one or two characters such as a numeric digit so the password is only incremented but still basically the same.

A better solution might be to require strong passwords as defined by a policy in the environment and then periodically run a utility such as John the Ripper[1] against the encrypted passwords to ferret out any insecure ones. Implementing this solution combined with password aging might be even better albeit annoying to your user base.

---

1   http://www.openwall.com/john/

The following script watches over the `/etc/shadow` file to determine how long it's been since the users have changed their passwords. The `shadow` file contains, among other things, account information such as encrypted user passwords and the day when the password was last changed. When the expiration date of an account approaches, our script starts annoying the user with a canned email message letting them know that they need to change their password and that the account will be locked if they don't. The script could easily be modified to support other notification methods.

Some NIS and HP-UX environments don't use `shadow` files to hold encrypted passwords and account aging information. The users' encrypted passwords are held in the second field of the world-readable password file. If you think that this isn't the best method to maintain security, you are correct. Also, without the shadow file, there is no information tracking the age of a password. In Chapter 37, I will demonstrate another script that can be used to create and maintain a pseudo–shadow file on such systems.

```
#!/bin/sh
HOME=/usr/local/pass_aging
```

First off, we have to set a bunch of environment variables. Originally, these were set in a separate file accessed from our script. This makes configuration a bit more convenient, but in order to simplify this demonstration, I included the initialization of the variables in the script.

```
VALID_DAYS=90
```

This is the number of days that the user's password is valid before the account will be locked. The value could also be set dynamically by pulling the fifth field from the `/etc/shadow` file if the account has been configured appropriately. However, I have found that accounts on a system often are created by many different people and the fields in the `/etc/shadow` file are not always filled in correctly to include appropriate account expiration settings.

```
ENVIRONMENT="Scripting"
```

The ENVIRONMENT variable is used to customize the notifications with some meaningful information about the affected accounts. For example, you can assign 'Accounting' or 'Development' to the ENVIRONMENT variable. A notification might then read "Your Development account is about to expire..."

```
ADMIN_EMAIL=root
DEBUG_EMAIL=
```

These are the email addresses used for administrative notification. The reports of account password aging are sent to the admin email address. The second email address is used for testing.

Since this script has the potential for disrupting your environment by modifying `passwd` and `shadow` files, it would be wise to perform a lot of testing prior to running it. However, when the debug email variable is non-null, the shadow file will *not* be updated and users will *not* be notified. The notifications that would have been sent to the users will instead be sent to the debug email address. This may generate a lot of mail to that address, but this setting prevents potentially major problems and it is worth using it.

```
shad=/usr/local/pass_aging/bin/shadow_copy
pswd=/usr/local/pass_aging/bin/passwd_copy
```

Here is where the `passwd` and `shadow` files are configured to be used with this script. It would be wise to make backup copies of the real files. These definitions are useful in that you can configure the script to work with NIS since those files don't generally live in `/etc`.

```
exclude="$HOME/config/exclude_list"
```

The exclude file is a flat file containing a list of user names not to be modified by the script. In some environments, there may be userless accounts (such as `apache` or `sendmail`) that are associated with applications) which would break if the accounts were suddenly locked. You could improve this script by using a file associating userless accounts with the email addresses for the users responsible for those accounts. This would allow a notification to be sent to the account owner when expiration is approaching. It would also separate the management of this type of account from the general exclude list.

```
ED=ed.script
max=$VALID_DAYS
notify=$(($max-14))
OUTFILE=$HOME/aging
NOTEOUT=$HOME/notes
WARNOUT=$HOME/warnings
REPORT=$HOME/report
ARCHIVE=$HOME/archive
BIN="$HOME/bin"
```

A few more variables to set up some paths, file names, and various other items in our script. The ED variable defines the file that will contain editing changes to be made to the shadow file. The max variable represents the number of days a password is permitted to exist without change. The `notify` variable is used to start notifying users that their account is about to expire. The notifications start two weeks (14 days) prior to expiration. The remaining variable assignments specify files that will all contain parts of the final aging report that is sent to the administrator. Nothing too fancy here.

```
if [ "`id -un`" != "root" ]; then
   echo "This script must be run as root - exiting" >&2
   exit 1
fi
```

Since this script is going to read and potentially modify the `shadow` file, it must be run as root. You have to ensure that this is the case when installing the script.

```
for file in $OUTFILE $WARNOUT $NOTEOUT $REPORT
do
   if [ -f $file ]
   then
     rm $file
   fi
done
```

Then we have to clean up any old transient report files that exist.

```
seconds_since_epoch=$((`date +%s`))
seconds_per_day=86400
days_since_epoch=$(($seconds_since_epoch/$seconds_per_day))
```

Next we determine the number of days that have passed since 1/1/1970. Password aging information in the /etc/shadow file is held in the third field of each account entry. This field contains an integer that expresses the date on which the password was last changed as a number of days since 1/1/1970. Subtracting this number from the current number of days elapsed since 1/1/1970 gives us the age of the password.

```
backdate=`date +%m%d%y%H%M`
cp -p $shad $ARCHIVE/shadow.$backdate
```

We now back up the `shadow` file for safety. We want to be able to return to the original file to start all over if necessary. Using a `cp -p` will also preserve the original modification time and permissions on the new copy of the file.

```
find $ARCHIVE -mtime +7 -exec rm {} \;
```

You should also clean the archive directory by removing old reports and backup `shadow` files more than 7 days old.

```
for user in `cut -d: -f1 $pswd`
do
```

Now here is where the real script begins. We start a loop that iterates through all the user names in the `passwd` file.

```
padding=""
user_length=`echo $user | awk '{print length}'`
padding_len=$((15-$user_length))
counter=1
while [ $counter -lt $padding_len ]
do
  padding="${padding} "
  counter=$(($counter+1))
done
```

To line up the text in the final report in columns and make it a little more readable, you might like to create some padding spaces based on the length of the user name to be reported. The code would also benefit from using `printf` to format the report appropriately instead of manually inserting spaces to line up the columns. The `printf` command is a print function that gives you a lot of control over how the output is formatted.

```
exp_days=`grep "^${user}:" $shad | cut -d: -f5`
pass_days=`grep "^${user}:" $shad | cut -d: -f3`
```

Next we populate some variables with the values from the current user's `shadow` entry. First is the number of days after which the user must change their password. The second is the number of days since January 1, 1970 that the password was last changed. These will be used to determine when an account should be expired.

```
#pass_word=`grep "^${user}:" $pswd | cut -d: -f2`
pass_word=`grep "^${user}:" $shad | cut -d: -f2`
```

Depending on whether the encrypted password is located in the `passwd` or `shadow` file, you have to use one of these two lines. In our implementation, the second (uncommented) line is used: it gets its data from the `shadow` file. You probably think the script could just check for the existence of the `shadow` file; in case it isn't there, it should default to the passwd file. This would work in most, but not all, situations. I have worked on some machines that have both files but only use the /etc/passwd. I have also seen systems that will normally use the /etc/passwd file unless an /etc/shadow exists. In that case, the shadow file will be used. For your purposes, this script will need to be customized to fit your environment.

```
if [ "$pass_word" = "*" ]
then
  pass_word="\*"
fi
```

You also need to check for a special case: if the encrypted password consists of a single '*', you have to escape it with a backslash '\'. If the asterisk isn't escaped, it would be evaluated later as a wild card denoting all filenames residing in the current working directory (the traditional meaning of '*'). Another method to get around this problem would be to set noglob in the shell environment, which turns off that type of evaluation.

```
if [ "$pass_word" = "" ]
then
    echo "$user $padding WARN:        $user has null password set, set
password or lock account" >> $WARNOUT
  fi
```

If the user account is incorrectly configured with a null password for some reason, the script creates a message explaining this state of affairs and appends it to the warning output file. The contents of this file will be added to the final report at a later stage.

```
exempt=`grep "^${user}$" $exclude`
if [ "$exempt" = "" ]
then
```

Then we determine whether the current user is one of those exempted from password expiration by checking the exclude file. If the user is not exempt from password expiration, the script continues on to the core of the program.

```
  if [ "$pass_days" != "" -a "$exp_days" != "" ]
  then
```

Before proceeding further we have to make sure that the user's password has an expiration date set for it. If you have not set an expiration date yet, the 'else' clause that follows will create a notification for the final report.

```
days_since_change=$(($days_since_epoch-$pass_days))
if [ $days_since_change -lt $notify ]
then
```

This is the beginning of the core of the script. First we determine how many days have passed since the password was last changed. Then we evaluate this number to determine if the user should start receiving notifications that their account is about to be disabled.

```
first_char=`echo $pass_word | cut -c1`
if [ "$first_char" = "*" ]
then
    echo "$user $padding $days_since_change    Already locked"\
        >> $OUTFILE
else
    echo "$user $padding $days_since_change    OK" >> $OUTFILE
fi
```

If the password is still young, no action needs to be taken against the account. However, we should check to see if the account has already been locked, and if so, append a notice to the report. A locked account is indicated by the first character of the password: an asterisk. When the script locks an account, it changes the encrypted password string of that user to a string of the form:

```
*CLOSED_${the_date}*.
```

```
    elif [ $days_since_change -ge $notify -a $days_since_change -le
$max ]
    then
        exp=$(($max-$days_since_change))
```

This checks whether the password is still valid, but the user notification period has begun. If so, we determine how many days it will be before the account is locked. (The length of the notification period is configurable; recall that at the beginning of the script I set it to start 14 days prior to the password expiring.)

```
    if [ "$DEBUG_EMAIL" != "" ]
    then
        echo "$user $padding $days_since_change    Expires in $exp
days ; Would have sent mail ; sent mail to $DEBUG_EMAIL" >> $OUTFILE
    else
```

```
        echo "$user $padding $days_since_change      Expires in $exp
days ; sending mail" >> $OUTFILE
        fi
```

We then report warning notifications to the output file and to the debugging email address, provided it has been configured.

```
        $BIN/send_email $user $days_since_change about_to_expire
    else
```

Finally, we notify the user that the password will expire in the determined number of days. Please also recall that if the DEBUG_EMAIL variable is *not* null, notifications will only be sent to the debug address specified in the configuration section. Only when this variable is null will notifications be sent to the specified user. This is handled in the send_email script called above; it also checks whether the debug email address has been set. At a first glance it may seem that the notifications should always be sent to the user, but this is not the case. The send_email script is not included here and should be simple enough to implement.

```
    first_char=`echo $pass_word | cut -c1`
    the_date=`date +%y%m%d`
    CLOSED="*CLOSED_${the_date}*"
```

In the remaining case the password has expired and the account needs to be locked. We first set some variables in preparation of changing the user's password to a CLOSED string showing the date on which the user account was locked, as described earlier.

```
    if [ "$first_char" = "*" ]
    then
      echo "$user $padding $days_since_change      Already locked"\
        >> $OUTFILE
    else
```

If the account has already been locked, this line reports the fact to the output file. (The logic for account checking could be reorganized so that the same checks wouldn't have to be done multiple times; here I have broken down the cases as shown for easier understanding, at the cost of some repeated code).

```
      if [ -f $HOME/$ED ]
      then
        rm $HOME/$ED
```

```
        fi
```

To lock the account, we will construct and run an `ed` script that modifies the password or shadow file. First we remove any existing `ed` scripts created from previous runs.

```
if [ "$DEBUG_EMAIL" != "" ]
then
  echo "$user $padding $days_since_change     \
    Would have locked account ; sent mail to\
    $DEBUG_EMAIL" >> $OUTFILE
else
```

Once again, if the debug email address has been set, we only append a report that the account is expired to the output file.

```
echo "$user $padding $days_since_change    Locking account\
    *CLOSED_${the_date}*" >> $OUTFILE
```

Otherwise, we append the notification that the user account is now being locked to the output file.

```
pass_word=`echo $pass_word | sed -e s/\\\./\\\\\\\\\./g`
pass_word=`echo $pass_word | sed -e s/\\\*/\\\\\\\\\*/g`
pass_word=`echo $pass_word | sed -e s/\\\$/\\\\\\\\\$/g`
pass_word=`echo $pass_word | sed -e s/\\\\\//\\\\\\\\\\\//g`
```

The `ed` script contains instructions to substitute the user's encrypted password with the CLOSED string. When we construct this code, we have to escape all occurrences of special characters '.', '/', '$', and '*' in the encrypted password string with a backslash, thus: '\.' or '\$'. See Chapter 24 and 25 for more information on escaping special characters.

```
pass_word=`echo $pass_word | sed -e\
    's/\(.*\)\(.\)\(.\)$/\1/'`
```

We now have to cut off the last two characters of the modified password string. These are extraneous and were introduced by the preceding transformations. The '$' character, which is a valid character in an encrypted password string also denotes the special end of line character in a string. This is the nature of strings on a UNIX or Linux system. Since all of the '$' characters of the encrypted string were replaced with '\$', the replacement action also included the end of line character that is now escaped and shouldn't be included in the encrypted string: both the trailing \ and $ characters need to be removed. This form of the sed command is explained in more detail in Chapter 24.

```
echo "/$user:$pass_word/s/$pass_word/$CLOSED" > $HOME/$ED
echo "w"                                >> $HOME/$ED
echo "q"                                >> $HOME/$ED
```

Now we create the ed script that will replace the encrypted password string with the CLOSED string.

```
    # ed -s $pswd < $HOME/$ED > /dev/null
    ed -s $shad < $HOME/$ED > /dev/null
fi
```

To run the ed script, use one of these two lines, depending on whether your password entries live in the passwd or shadow file. The same ed script can be used to replace the encrypted password within the passwd or shadow file, whichever applies. As you can see, my example uses the shadow file. More information on how to modify files using ed can be found in Chapter 25.

```
    if [ "$DEBUG_EMAIL" = "" ]
    then
        $BIN/send_email $user $days_since_change account_locked
    fi
  fi
fi
```

Now, we send an email notification to the account stating that it has been locked. Once again, if the debug email is set, the message will go to that address and not to the real user.

```
  else
    echo "$user $padding WARN:      $user password not set to expire.
Fix shadow entry" >> $WARNOUT
  fi
else
  echo "$user $padding Note:      $user is exempt from password\
    expiring" >> $NOTEOUT
fi
```

```
done
```

The next 'else' matches the line far above in the loop where the check was performed to see whether the user account is exempt from expiration. If that test fails, we append a message about the non-expiring account to the output file for the final report. This completes the main loop.

```
for file in $WARNOUT $OUTFILE $NOTEOUT
do
  if [ -f $file ]
  then
    sort -rn +1 $file >> $REPORT
    rm $file
  fi
done
```

The script then collects all notification output files and sorts each of them by the age of the passwords. Then all transient files are removed. The final report will list any warnings in order of importance; for example, users without a password will appear first.

```
cat $REPORT | mail -s "$ENVIRONMENT password aging report" $ADMIN_EMAIL
mv $REPORT $ARCHIVE/report.$backdate
```

Finally, the report is sent to the administrator and archived for later reference. Here is a sample of the output from a final report.

```
fred          122 Already locked
rbpeters      105 Locking account *CLOSED_041124*
yabbadmin     14  OK
xfs           14  OK
webalizer     14  OK
vinmaster     14  OK
vcsa          14  OK
uucp           9  OK
```

Chapter 37: Pseudo–Shadow File

There are some environments that do not use a shadow file for maintaining passwords. These environments keep encrypted passwords in either a local passwd file or one that is handled through NIS. I have seen this mode of operation in several versions of HP-UX and NIS. I believe that NIS can support using a shadow file, but not all NIS clients have this capability.

Now, whether or not this is a good idea is irrelevant for my purposes here. This script, which is intended to be run daily, creates and maintains a pseudo–shadow file to track the age of user passwords and their change history. The script does not, however, remove the encrypted password from the already existing passwd file.

I intended this contrived shadow file generator to be run in conjunction with the password aging script in Chapter 36. The script in that chapter relies on information contained in a shadow file in order to determine the date of the last password change.

```
#!/bin/ksh
HOME=/usr/local/pass_aging
ARCHIVE=$HOME/archive
BIN="$HOME/bin"
DEBUG=duh
shad=/usr/local/pass_aging/bin/shadow_nis
pswd=/var/yp/src/passwd
PERL=/usr/bin/perl
```

```
ED=ed.script
```

The first section of the script sets up several environment variables to be used later. The variables had originally been taken from a separate configuration file, but for the sake of simplicity I have included them at the beginning of the script.

The only interesting variables being set here are the debug flag and the variables storing the locations of the `passwd` and `shadow` files. The DEBUG variable just needs to be set to anything non-null in order to generate some debugging output while the script is running, so that you can see what it is doing when you are testing.

The `shad` variable holds the location of the `shadow` file. Since the `shadow` file is a regular file that the system itself doesn't actually use, you can call it anything you want. The `pswd` file definition is the real master `passwd` file that the machine relies on. This script only ever has read access to that file, so there is no danger in possibly modifying the live file even when testing. If your level of anxiety is high, you could copy the original and run the script against the copy.

```
seconds_since_epoch=`$PERL -e 'print time'`
seconds_per_day=$((60*60*24))
days_since_epoch=$(($seconds_since_epoch/$seconds_per_day))
```

We determine the number of days since 1/1/1970, the start of the UNIX epoch. The number in the third field of a `shadow` file entry represents the date that the password for that account was last changed, expressed as a number of days since the beginning of the epoch. This value can be determined in a number of ways. Please refer to Chapter 3 for more discussion on this topic.

```
if [ ! -f $shad ]
then
   test "$DEBUG" != "" && echo DEBUG: $shad does not exist, creating
   cat $pswd | awk -v days=$days_since_epoch -F: \
     '{print $1 ":" $2 ":" days ":0:90:7:::"}' > $shad
fi
```

If this is the first time the script is run and there is no existing `shadow` file, the script will create one based on the specified `password` file. Since the age of the password was probably not tracked before the first time this script is run, the script assumes that '*today*' is the day that the password was last changed and enters that value in the new `shadow` file. This gives users the benefit of the doubt.

```
backdate=`date +%m%d%y%H%M`
```

```
test "$DEBUG" != "" && echo DEBUG: Backing up $shad to
$ARCHIVE/nis_shadow.$backdate
cp -p $shad $ARCHIVE/nis_shadow.$backdate
find $ARCHIVE -mtime +7 -exec rm {} \;
```

Even though this file isn't used by any system process, we want to back it up in order to be able to retrace our steps in case something goes wrong. I have used saved files many times to restore account information without having to use a system backup. We also want to be able to remove the older files in the backup directory.

```
if [ -f $HOME/bin/$ED ]
then
    test "$DEBUG" != "" && echo DEBUG: Cleaning up old ed.script
    rm $HOME/bin/$ED
fi
```

Like the script in Chapter 36, this script will construct and run an ed script. The ed script technique allows us to edit the shadow file in place when there are changes that need to be made. This is discussed in more detail in Chapter 25. First we have to remove any previously created ed script files that may be lying around.

```
for user in `cut -d: -f1 $pswd`
do
```

Now we're in the core of the program. The loop iterates through the current passwd file and updates the corresponding entries in the new shadow file.

```
    user_exist=`grep "^${user}:" $shad | cut -d: -f1`
    if [ "$user_exist" = "" ]
    then
        echo "$user:$cur_pass_word:$days_since_epoch:0:90:7:::" >> $shad
        test "$DEBUG" != "" && echo DEBUG: Missing $user, adding to $shad
    fi
```

First you have to determine whether the user's name appears in the shadow file. If he has a new account, he may not have been entered into it yet. If this is so, you have to create an entry in the shadow file.

```
    cur_pass_word=`grep "^${user}:" $pswd | cut -d: -f2`
    old_pass_word=`grep "^${user}:" $shad | cut -d: -f2`
```

```
pass_days=`grep "^${user}:" $shad | cut -d: -f3`
test "$DEBUG" != "" && echo DEBUG: \
   $user, $cur_pass_word, $old_pass_word, $pass_days
```

Now the script gathers the user's encrypted password from the `passwd` file and its age from the `shadow` file.

```
if [ "$old_pass_word" != "$cur_pass_word" ]
then
   test "$DEBUG" != "" && echo DEBUG: $user password has changed,\
      updating $shad
```

The `shadow` file is only updated when this script is run. If the password saved in the `shadow` file isn't the same as the current one in the `passwd` file, some updates need to be made to the `shadow` file.

```
old_pass_word=`echo $old_pass_word | sed -e s/\\\./\\\\\\\\./g`
old_pass_word=`echo $old_pass_word | sed -e s/\\\*/\\\\\\\\*/g`
old_pass_word=`echo $old_pass_word | sed -e s/\\\$/\\\\\\\\$/g`
old_pass_word=`echo $old_pass_word | sed -e s/\\\\\\//\\\\\\\\\\\\//g`

cur_pass_word=`echo $cur_pass_word | sed -e s/\\\./\\\\\\\\./g`
cur_pass_word=`echo $cur_pass_word | sed -e s/\\\*/\\\\\\\\*/g`
cur_pass_word=`echo $cur_pass_word | sed -e s/\\\$/\\\\\\\\$/g`
cur_pass_word=`echo $cur_pass_word | sed -e s/\\\\\\//\\\\\\\\\\\\//g`
```

Now we have to make sure that the encrypted passwords are handled correctly. These passwords contain special characters '.', '/', '*', and '$' that need to be escaped with a preceding backslash where they appear in the `ed` script. This operation will ensure that the correct password string is entered in the `shadow` file.

These `sed` commands look pretty ugly, but that's because a lot of escape slashes have to be evaluated and in turn the following escape slash needs to itself be escaped. For more coverage of `sed` commands for updating encrypted password strings, refer to Chapter 36.

```
old_pass_word=`echo $old_pass_word | sed 's/\(.*\)\(.\)\(.\)$/\1/'`
cur_pass_word=`echo $cur_pass_word | sed 's/\(.*\)\(.\)\(.\)$/\1/'`
```

With all the characters being replaced, there is one character that gets escaped, but should not be part of the final password string. The special '$' sign character which is the 'end of line' character for all strings on UNIX and Linux systems that is normally not visible. When all the special characters were escaped in the previous `sed` commands, this trailing `\$` is now visible at the end of the string. It wasn't really part of the original encrypted password, so the last two characters ('`\$`') need to be removed from the strings. This use of `sed` is discussed in more detail in Chapter 24.

```
    test "$DEBUG" != "" && echo DEBUG: Creating ed file to change\
        $old_pass_word:$pass_days to $cur_pass_word:$days_since_epoch
    echo "g/$user:$old_pass_word/s/$old_pass_word:\
        $pass_days/$cur_pass_word:$days_since_epoch/g" \
        >> $HOME/bin/$ED
  else
    test "$DEBUG" != "" && echo DEBUG: No changes for $user
    continue
  fi
done
```

Now we create an instruction in the `ed` script that will replace the old encrypted password and its '*days since last change*' value with the new encrypted password and the current '*days since epoch*' value. We do this by taking the new values from the current `passwd` file. One such instruction is appended to the `ed` script using the double greater-than signs ('`>>`') for each user account, and then all `shadow` entry updates are made at once by running the `ed` script.

```
# Complete and process the file with the ed.script
echo "w"                          >> $HOME/bin/$ED
echo "q"                          >> $HOME/bin/$ED
test "$DEBUG" != "" && echo DEBUG: Running ed.script for $user on $shad
ed -s $shad < $HOME/bin/$ED > /dev/null
```

Now that the loop is complete for all the users, you should add the final two lines to the `ed` script and process the shadow file with all its changes.

There is one refinement you might want to make: Once the modifications are complete, you could check the line counts of the `passwd` and `shadow` files to see whether they match. If they don't match, it is possible that an account has been removed and the account is not present in the `passwd` file; the entry is still visible in the `shadow` file, though. The script should then remove the old user names from the `shadow` file to keep both files synchronized.

Chapter 38: Linux Gold

System Build

Building a system manually can be fun. Building many systems manually is tedious and prone to error, especially when all systems should be built in exactly the same way. For this reason, Kickstart by Red Hat, Jumpstart by Sun, and other utilities were created to automate a network-based system build that is based on preset parameters. These utilities work well when you are building new systems on a regular basis. The downside of this method is that a client is required to be on the network and it needs to have access to the server in order to do a system build. Also, a build server needs to be set up and maintained, but if you are only building a moderate number of systems, it may not be worth the extra effort to set up a build server.

This build script has a small image size and can be run from a bootable CD. The CD boots, and then automatically calls a script which partitions and formats the hard disk. The script then proceeds to install a pre-configured OS image to the system hard disk. This method has the advantage that there are no network or build server requirements. The newly built system can also have site-specific configurations which may not be part of a standard installation. The script also has the added advantage that it can install applications that may not be in a proprietary format, such as an RPM.

The process I used was to find a Linux live distribution on a single boot CD which was designed to be customizable. The one I chose was the 'Roll your own Linux Rescue or Setup CD'.[1] There are now many distributions like this including live DVD images for larger installations, but at the time this one seemed to be the best choice.

The way this distribution works is that it is installed on a hard disk on a running system, from which you can customize the final CD image. The gold image file and this

---

1   http://www.phenix.bnl.gov/~purschke/RescueCD

script are placed into the distribution directory tree, and the final modification is to change the live CD startup script to call our build script. The last task is to run the script that came with the distribution to create the final .iso file, which you would then burn to a CD. The resulting CD automatically boots and runs this install script, prepares the hard drive, and installs the customized gold image.

The process of building a master gold system is basically manual. Once the template system is built, fully customized, and tuned to your environment, an image file should be created from that disk. The gold system will then mount an NFS server (at /mnt/nfs) with sufficient space for the image and run the following command to create the image file.

```
tar cvfz /mnt/nfs/wholedisk.tar.gz / --exclude /proc/* \
  --exclude /mnt/nfs/*
```

This command creates a compressed tar file of the whole disk on the running gold system. It does exclude the contents of the /proc and /mnt/nfs directories because they are specific to the gold system, and you can't use the contents if they are propagated to subsequent builds.

Most of the build script is for preparing the hard disk to accept the final image created from the gold system. The process determines the hard drive geometry parameters and bases the partitioning on those values, since the disk model and manufacturer are likely to vary from system to system. Once the disk has been prepared, the script creates the file systems and un-archives the gold image.

```
#!/bin/sh
bytes_per_cyl=`sfdisk -l /dev/hda | grep Units | awk '{print $5}'`
tracks_per_cyl=`sfdisk -l /dev/hda | grep Disk | awk '{print $5}'`
sectors_per_track=`sfdisk -l /dev/hda | grep Disk | awk '{print $7}'`
sectors_per_cyl=$(($tracks_per_cyl*$sectors_per_track))
bytes_per_sector=$(($bytes_per_cyl/$sectors_per_cyl))
cyl_count=`sfdisk -l /dev/hda | grep Disk | awk '{print $3}'`
usable_cyl=$(($cyl_count-4))
disk_in_sectors=$((($sectors_per_cyl*$usable_cyl)-$sectors_per_track))
mem_in_bytes=`cat /proc/meminfo | egrep "MemTotal:|Mem:" |\
  awk '{print $2}'`
swap_in_bytes=$(($mem_in_bytes*2))
```

First we assign a bunch of variables that determine and store the architecture parameters of the hard disk; they will be used to create the input file for sfdisk, which is a Linux partition table manipulator. Also, they determine the amount of memory on the system and then use double the memory value for the swap partition. It is safe to calculate swap memory as double the amount of base memory. The value in /proc/cpuinfo that contains the total amount of memory on a system may vary depending on the live CD image that is being used. To deal with this case, the egrep command checks for two of the possible values. If you choose a different live CD, you may want to validate that these are valid.

```
sector_calc () {
size=$1
slice_in_sectors=$(($size/$bytes_per_sector))
slice_in_cyl=$(($slice_in_sectors/$sectors_per_cyl))
slice_rem=$(($size%$bytes_per_sector))
if [ $slice_rem -ne 0 ]
then
  slice_in_cyl=$(($slice_in_cyl+1))
  slice_in_sectors=$((($slice_in_cyl*$sectors_per_cyl)-
$sectors_per_track))
else
  slice_in_sectors=$((($slice_in_cyl*$sectors_per_cyl)-
$sectors_per_track))
fi
}
```

The input file that is sent to sfdisk specifies the size of each partition in sectors. This function takes its input in bytes and converts the number of bytes into sectors. This is used to calculate the size of each file system in sectors. It also determines whether the file system fits evenly on cylinder boundaries. If not, the function rounds up the value to the next cylinder.

```
sector_calc $swap_in_bytes
swap_in_sectors=$slice_in_sectors

sector_calc 250000000
root_in_sectors=$slice_in_sectors

sector_calc 30000000
boot_in_sectors=$slice_in_sectors
```

```
sector_calc 1000000000
var_in_sectors=$slice_in_sectors

sector_calc 512000000
home_in_sectors=$slice_in_sectors

sector_calc 512000000
tmp_in_sectors=$slice_in_sectors
```

Now the script determines the size in sectors for each of the file systems that will be on the final build by sending the file system size values to the `sector_calc` function. There are a lot of file systems that were part of this build, but it would be trivial to modify the code to remove unnecessary ones or to add your own file systems to match your gold build.

```
rest_of_disk_in_sectors=$(($disk_in_sectors-$swap_in_sectors-\
    $boot_in_sectors-$root_in_sectors-$var_in_sectors-$home_in_sectors-\
    $tmp_in_sectors))
usr_in_sectors=$(($rest_of_disk_in_sectors/2/$sectors_per_cyl*\
    $sectors_per_cyl))
usrlocal_in_sectors=$usr_in_sectors
```

The last two file systems split in half whatever is left over after the other file systems are allocated. This was done in my environment because we used these two partitions more heavily than the rest and wanted to evenly distribute the remainder of the space. Their sector calculations are slightly different because they are based on the size of the whole disk minus the other file systems.

```
PARTTAB=/tmp/parts.out
double_sectors_per_track=$((2*$sectors_per_track))

cat > $PARTTAB <<SOMETAG
# partition table of /dev/hda
unit: sectors
```

We need to define and write the partition table file that will be used to format the hard disk of the new system. We begin by reproducing the partitioning output from `sfdisk -d` `/dev/hda`. That command dumps the partition table in a format that can be used as input to subsequently partition another disk. You would want to do this on your gold system to make sure the script output and the gold partition table match while accounting for any hard drive architecture variations

The interesting scripting technique here is the use of the `cat` command to enter text in a free format. Here `cat` takes input from the code up to the tag SOMETAG and then redirects that output to the output file specified by $PARTTAB. This technique is called a here-document. The previous version of this code had each of the lines of text individually redirected to the output file. This technique makes the code less cluttered and easier to read; you can find more details about this in Chapter 28.

```
/dev/hda1   :\
 start=$sectors_per_track,size=$boot_in_sectors,Id=83,bootable
/dev/hda2   : start=$(($sectors_per_track+$boot_in_sectors)),size=$\
(($disk_in_sectors-$boot_in_sectors)),Id=5
/dev/hda3   : start=0,size=0,Id=0
/dev/hda4   : start=0,size=0,Id=0
/dev/hda5   : start=$(($double_sectors_per_track+$boot_in_sectors)),\
size=$usr_in_sectors,Id=83
/dev/hda6   : start=$\
(($double_sectors_per_track+$boot_in_sectors+$usr_in_sectors)),\
size=$usrlocal_in_sectors,Id=83
/dev/hda7   : start=$\
(($double_sectors_per_track+$boot_in_sectors+\
$usr_in_sectors+$usrlocal_in_sectors)),size=$var_in_sectors,Id=83
/dev/hda8   : start=$\
(($double_sectors_per_track+$boot_in_sectors+\
$usr_in_sectors+$usrlocal_in_sectors+$var_in_sectors)),\
size=$home_in_sectors,Id=83
/dev/hda9   : start=$\
(($double_sectors_per_track+$boot_in_sectors+\
$usr_in_sectors+$usrlocal_in_sectors+$var_in_sectors+\
$home_in_sectors)),size=$tmp_in_sectors,Id=83
/dev/hda10 : start=$\
(($double_sectors_per_track+$boot_in_sectors+\
$usr_in_sectors+$usrlocal_in_sectors+$var_in_sectors+\
$home_in_sectors+$tmp_in_sectors)),size=$swap_in_sectors,Id=82
/dev/hda11 : start=$\
```

```
(($double_sectors_per_track+$boot_in_sectors+\
$usr_in_sectors+$usrlocal_in_sectors+$var_in_sectors+\
$home_in_sectors+$tmp_in_sectors+$swap_in_sectors)),\
size=$root_in_sectors,Id=83
SOMETAG
```

The above code may be somewhat daunting to read and comprehend because of the formatting and the length of each line. With a bit of close examination, you'll see it isn't quite as complex as it might seem at first. Each line is simply a partition definition. They are all part of the cat output that is being written to the file that will build the file system structure on the hard disk. Each line is of the form:

/dev/partition : start={starting sector},size={in sectors},Id={partition type},[bootable]

The start (start=) and size (size=) calculations are very long and may get a little confusing. If you read these lines in order, starting at /dev/hda5, you'll see that the calculation just increments the start position of the file system by the size of the previous file system.

```
sfdisk -f /dev/hda < $PARTTAB
```

Finally you are able to install the newly created partition table to the disk.

```
for slice in 1 5 6 7 8 9 11
do
   echo Making file system on slice $slice...
   mke2fs /dev/hda$slice
done
```

Now you can create all ext2 file systems on disk. Of course, you may want to use other file system types.

```
mkdir -p /tmp/root
mount /dev/hda11 /tmp/root

for dir in boot usr var home tmp
do
   mkdir -p /tmp/root/$dir
done
```

We create a mount point in /tmp for accessing the hard drive and mount the root partition to it. Note that when this script is running, the /tmp directory is part of a ramdisk from the live CD. Once the root partition has been mounted, the script creates all other drive mount points on the physical disk .

```
mount /dev/hda1 /tmp/root/boot
mount /dev/hda5 /tmp/root/usr
if [ ! -d /tmp/root/usr/local ]
then
  mkdir /tmp/root/usr/local
fi
mount /dev/hda6 /tmp/root/usr/local
mount /dev/hda7 /tmp/root/var
mount /dev/hda8 /tmp/root/home
mount /dev/hda9 /tmp/root/tmp
```

Since there is some dependency between the file systems, the mounting process needs to happen in the proper order: the lowest-level partitions should be mounted first.

```
cd /tmp/root
tar xvfzp /usr/wholedisk.tar.gz
cd /
```

Here is where the prepared disk is populated. We un-archive the whole disk image file onto the newly formated hard drive. All the files should land in the correct file system, since the file system has been partitioned in exactly the same way as the original gold system.

```
mkswap /dev/hda10
chroot /tmp/root lilo -C /etc/lilo.conf
```

Once that is complete, you need to create the swap partition and install the boot loader. The chroot command is used to run the lilo boot loader installation based on the hard drive /root directory, and not from the root of the CD. Of course if you choose to use grub instead of lilo, this command will need to be modified.

```
for slice in 6 1 5 7 8 9 11
do
  umount /dev/hda$slice
done
```

```
echo Done!
```

We have reached the end of the installation process. The script un-mounts all partitions in the proper order. Partition 6 should be unmounted first, since `/usr/local` is attached to `/usr`, and partition 11 last, since it is `/root`. Now when the newly built system is rebooted, it should be an exact duplicate of your original gold system except for any hard drive size differences. Now all that is left to do is to make system-specific changes, such as entering your IP address and a system name, and then you can connect the finished system to the network.

Chapter 39: System

Snapshots

Disk snapshots are a way of taking backups of files and directories at given time intervals. Accessing the specific snapshot interval, you can go back in time and find the version of a file from its specific snapshot backup. This script backs up a list of directories that is configurable within the script to another location on either the same disk or to a separate disk all together. The disk space requirement for this type of backup is at least the same amount of space as the files you are backing up plus the incremental space increases of any changes you may make to those files.

The way the script works is that you first take a copy of the original source directories and back them up as the first snapshot. Any subsequent snapshot backups use hard links for any files that have *not* changed, while copying any files that have. A hard link is somewhat different than a soft link. While both allow multiple points of access to a single file, a soft link is just a pointer to the original file. A hard link is a secondary or tertiary file that points to the same data as the original. Once a hard link is established, there is no distinction between it and the original file except for name and path. The benefit in this situation is that you have the same file (since it was not modified) in multiple snapshot locations, but it is not taking up any extra disk space. This is all performed with the rsync command.

If you have a directory tree that contains an archive of something like digital photos where there isn't much change in the files, you will only need the room to backup the space that is being taken by the photos. This would be the minimum amount of space required. If you have a directory that contains a lot of source code that regularly gets modified, the space required will be the same as the original example plus the space required to contain all the changed files. The amount of change that occurs in the files you back up will determine the amount of space required.

This script is a heavily modified form of one that I found on the Internet.[1] The main difference with this script and the original is that the original saved backup sets based on the schedule that the job was run whereas this one saves many snapshot types, decreasing in granularity as they increase in age.

For example, with the original script, if you create a `cron` job for an hourly snapshot, it would run every hour, make a complete backup of the specified directories in the first hour and then backup any changes to that original backup for each subsequent hour following. Also, the current `HOURLY.0` directory is moved up one hour to `HOURLY.1` along with any older snapshot and the new snapshot is created as `HOURLY.0`. If you then wanted to create a daily snapshot of the same directories as the hourly backups, you'd have to schedule another `cron` job that would run once a day. The downside of this method is that each backup type (hourly, daily etc) will take up another 100% of the originally backed up disk space plus any changes.

This version of the script should be configured and then scheduled as a `cron` task to run hourly much the same as the original. In the destination directory specified, it creates snapshot directories in the form of `HOURLY.0`, `HOURLY.1`, ... `HOURLY.23`, .. `DAILY.0`, `DAILY.1` etc. The main difference here is that the script automatically takes the oldest hourly snapshot and rolls it to the current daily. The daily snapshots roll to weeklies, then monthlies and finally yearlies. This is all done while only consuming the original space from the source files plus any changes.

In the snapshot destination directories are the locations where the configured source directories to be backed up are rooted. In other words, if you are backing up `/etc` and `/usr/local/bin`, there will be an `HOURLY.0/etc` and `HOURLY.0/usr/local/bin` directory containing your backed up files.

The default script behavior is as follows:

- Hourly snapshots occur every time the job is run. Presumably this will be an hourly scheduled job.

- Daily snapshots are created from the oldest hourly snapshot rolled to the newest daily every time the job is run *and* it is 1am.

- Weekly snapshots are created from the oldest daily snapshot rolled to the newest weekly every time the job is run, it is 1am and Monday.

---

1   The original author of the script is Mike Rubel. He goes into great detail about how his script works and any updates that have been made. That information can be found at:
    http://www.mikerubel.org/computers/rsync_snapshots/index.html

- Monthly snapshots are created from the oldest weekly snapshot rolled to the newest monthly every time the job is run, it is 1am and the 1st of the month.

- Yearly snapshots are created from the oldest monthly snapshot rolled to the newest yearly every time the job is run, it is 1am and the 1st of the year.

With this method, you only need one job to keep snapshots for a long period of time and don't take the extra disk space with multiple jobs. One thing that I noticed about running this script on my system was that the snapshot destination directories didn't keep their creation date when moved. When they were moved, they would get a new modified date from the time that the move happened. This is noted on the web page from the original script as well as some hints for workarounds. What I found is that this is the case for at least `ext2` file systems. I converted my `ext2` file system to `ext3` using the `tune2fs` command which can be done hot, and the problem was resolved.

```sh
#!/bin/sh
SEPARATE_MOUNT=1
SYNCDIR="/root /etc /home /var/www /usr/local /var/spool/cron \
         /var/mail /var/named /var/lib/squirrelmail"
MOUNT_DEVICE=/dev/hdb1
SNAPSHOT_RW=/snapshot
DEST=/$SNAPSHOT_RW
```

The first part of the script sets some configuration variables. The `SEPARATE_MOUNT` variable is specified when you are saving your backups to a separate physical disk. A value of 1 will use a different disk and 0 will not. It's a good idea to keep your backups on a separate disk, but it's not always feasible. The `MOUNT_DEVICE` value is the disk device that you are going to use. This is only required if you are going to use a separate mount. The `SNAPSHOT_RW` value is the mount point that will be used to mount the separate device if you are using one. The `DEST` directory is the destination directory that all the snapshots will be written to.

```sh
MONTHLY_STAMP=`date +%e`
WEEKLY_STAMP=`date +%u`
DAILY_STAMP=`date +%k`
HOURLY_STAMP=`date +%k`
MONTHLY=11
WEEKLY=3
DAILY=6
HOURLY=23
```

```
BACKUPS="MONTHLY WEEKLY DAILY HOURLY"
```

This next group of variables set the values that will be tested against for determining whether to roll a specific snapshot up to the next oldest group. Also, they set the number of snapshots to keep for each type as well as defining the types of snapshots. The BACKUPS variable is the list of backup types that you will be looping through. The order of this variable is important and should be listed from least to most granular.

```
ID=`which id`
ECHO=`which echo`
MOUNT=`which mount`
UMOUNT=`which umount`
FUSER=/sbin/fuser
RM=`which rm`
BC=`which bc`
MV=`which mv`
TOUCH=`which touch`
RSYNC=`which rsync`
DATE=`date +%m.%Y`
```

This group of variables define the binaries that will be used in the script. Most of these could be removed and the actual binary could be used in the code except fuser which wouldn't be in the path of a cron job.

```
if [ `$ID -u` != 0 ]
then
    $ECHO "Sorry, must be root. Exiting..."
    exit 1
fi
```

Since this script is backing up system files as well as potentially mounting and dismounting separate disks, we need to make sure we're running as root. Otherwise exit and echo a warning message.

```
if [ $SEPARATE_MOUNT -ne 0 ]
then
    mounted=`mount | grep $SNAPSHOT_RW`
    if [ "$mounted" != "" ]
    then
```

```
$FUSER -k $SNAPSHOT_RW
$UMOUNT $SNAPSHOT_RW
if [ $? -ne 0 ]
then
  $ECHO "snapshot: could not umount $SNAPSHOT_RW"
  exit 1
fi
fi
```

If you are using a separate disk device, check to see if it is already mounted. If it is, use the `fuser` command to kill any processes that are active on that device and then dismount the disk. If the dismount is not successful, `echo` a warning stating the same and exit.

```
/sbin/fsck -y $MOUNT_DEVICE
if [ $? -ne 0 ]
then
  $ECHO "snapshot: had problems fsck\'ing $SNAPSHOT_RW"
  exit 1
fi
```

Now that the disk is dismounted, perform a file system check on it using `fsck`. Since we are dismounting and remounting the disk every hour, the file system likes to make sure it is clean. If we didn't perform the `fsck` here, eventually we would start receiving messages stating that the device has been mounted too many times without an `fsck`. Also corruption of the file system can occur in this state which happened to my system before I added this check.

```
$MOUNT -o rw $MOUNT_DEVICE $SNAPSHOT_RW
if [ $? -ne 0 ]
then
  $ECHO "snapshot: could not mount $SNAPSHOT_RW"
  exit 1
fi
fi
```

Once the file system checks out, you can then mount the disk in a read-write mode. If the mount is unsuccessful, issue a warning.

```
if [ ! -d $DEST ]
then
  mkdir -p $DEST
fi
```

Now check to see if the destination directory exists. If it doesn't, then create it.

```
for BU in $BACKUPS
do
  eval max_count=\$$BU  # Maximum to keep
  eval stamp=\$${BU}_STAMP  # The timestamp for that type
```

This is where we prepare to roll up the previous snapshots to the next least granular. This starts a loop through all the backup types and determines the maximum number that should be kept. Perform this for each snapshot type (hourly, daily etc). An example would be to roll the DAILY.7 backup to the WEEKLY.0.

The two eval lines here make this function for each snapshot type. The eval command evaluates the line once before it is evaluated for the script. Lets take the backup type ($BU) of MONTHLY as an example. First it sets the max_count variable to the value of $MONTHLY. Intuitively, it might appear that it would be using $BU instead. Because of the eval, it was using the value of $BU to set the name of the variable that we want the value from. In this case it was $MONTHLY. This is a method of using a variable as a variable name or what might be called indirect variables. More on this technique can be found in Chapter 7.

```
  oldest_one=`echo $max_count+1 | $BC`
  if [ -d $DEST/${BU}.0 ]
  then
```

First determine the oldest possible snapshot of a particular type and check for the existence of any of that type.

```
    current_oldest=`ls -td $DEST/${BU}* | tail -1 \
                 | cut -d. -f2`
  fi
```

If there are previous snapshots of that type, determine which one is the oldest to roll up. This may not be the highest number that you are keeping.

```
  if [ -d $DEST/$BU.$oldest_one -a $HOURLY_STAMP -eq 1 -a \
```

```
        $stamp -eq 1 -a "$PREV_BU" = "" ]
then
    $RM -rf $DEST/$BU.$oldest_one
fi
```

This test condition seems somewhat complex. What it is really doing is this. If the oldest possible snapshot exists and it is 1am and this snapshot type is set to its date to roll up and this is the first time through the loop, then remove the oldest possible snapshot. This is so you can clean up the oldest possible snapshot type on your system. The script will only remove the oldest snapshot on the system because the PREV_BU variable is set when the loop for rolling up the old snapshots completes its first iteration. This is so you won't remove the oldest of each type of snapshot, just the oldest one of them all.

```
if [ $HOURLY_STAMP -eq 1 -a "$PREV_BU" != "" -a ! -d \
      $DEST/$PREV_BU.0 -a ! -d $DEST/$PREV_BU.1 ] || [ \
      $HOURLY_STAMP -eq 1 -a $stamp -eq 1 -a \
      "$PREV_BU" != "" -a $DEST/$PREV_BU.0 ]
then
    if [ "$current_oldest" != "" ]
    then
```

Prepare to roll up the oldest backup of this snapshot type to next least granular type .0 backup if necessary. An example would be to move the DAILY.4 snapshot to the WEEKLY.0 snapshot.

```
        if [ -d $DEST/$PREV_BU.0 ]
        then
            $RM -rf $DEST/$PREV_BU.0
        fi
        $MV $DEST/$BU.$current_oldest $DEST/$PREV_BU.0
    fi
fi
```

Check again for any pre-existing snapshot .0 backup that would get in the way of moving the oldest of this type up to the next least granular type. If it does find one, remove it. This check should never find a directory to remove, but it is a safety net. Once that is complete, move the oldest snapshot of this type ($current_oldest) to the .0 snapshot of the next least granular.

```
if [ $HOURLY_STAMP -eq 1 -a $stamp -eq 1 ] || \
```

```
     [ $HOURLY_STAMP -eq 1 -a "$BU" = "DAILY" ] || \
     [ "$BU" = "HOURLY" ]
then
   while [ $max_count -ge 0 ]
   do
      count_plus=`echo $max_count+1 | $BC`
      if [ -d $DEST/$BU.$max_count ]
      then
```

Now that the oldest snapshot of this type has been moved out of the way, determine if you should roll up all the rest. This should always be done for hourly snapshots. The other types of snapshots should only have this done if their time stamp criteria is met.

```
      if [ -d $DEST/$BU.$count_plus ]
      then
         $RM -rf $DEST/$BU.$count_plus
      fi
      $MV $DEST/$BU.$max_count $DEST/$BU.$count_plus
   fi
   max_count=`echo $max_count-1 | $BC`
   done
fi
```

Now determine if you have more snapshots of a type that you want to keep than you have configured. If you do, then you should remove the oldest one. If not, then just move the oldest one up an iteration. This loop iterates through all the snapshots of a particular type from the oldest to the newest and moves them up one. For clarity, if you have daily snapshots 0, 1 and 2. You would first move 2 to 3, then 1 to 2 and finally 0 to 1.

```
   PREV_BU=$BU
done
```

The PREV_BU variable as previously discussed, needs to be set so the next time this loop iterates, it knows what the next least granular type is. This is why the order for the $BU variable is important.

```
for dir in $SYNCDIR
do
   final_location=`dirname $dir`
```

```
    mkdir -p $DEST/HOURLY.0/$final_location
    $RSYNC                                                      \
        -a --delete \
        --link-dest=$DEST/HOURLY.1/$final_location \
        $dir $DEST/HOURLY.0/$final_location
done
```

This loop is where the real magic happens. The `rsync` command copies from each of the source locations into the latest `.0` snapshot. It also creates the hard links for any unchanged file to the next oldest hourly `.1` snapshot while simply copying any files that have been changed since the last `rsync` was performed.

```
if [ $? -ne 0 ]
then
  $ECHO "$RSYNC error, sync did not complete \
        correctly, aborting"
  exit 1
fi
```

Determine if the `rsync` completed successfully. Since this is the heart of the script, you want to validate that it had no issues.

```
if [ $SEPARATE_MOUNT -ne 0 ]
then
  $MOUNT -o remount,ro $MOUNT_DEVICE $SNAPSHOT_RW
  if [ $? -ne 0 ]
  then
    $ECHO "snapshot: could not remount $SNAPSHOT_RW readonly"
    exit 1
  fi
fi
```

The last item that the script does is remount the separate disk device as a read-only file system. The idea here is that you want access to the files you are backing up, but you don't want to run the risk of having the backups removed accidentally. This only happens if you are saving your snapshots to a separate disk.

```
if [ -d $DEST/hourly.0 ]
then
```

```
    $CP -al $DEST/hourly.0 $DEST/hourly.1
fi
```

One final note about this script. This bit of code can replace the section where the `rsync` is performed above by the `cp` command in the event you don't have the required version available. The extended `rsync` options are a bit more clean though. These four lines should not be included in this script and are only here for example. They are part of the original script this one is based on and can be found at the link above.

Another modification that could be done to this script for enhancement would be to use the remote capabilities of `rsync`. This would allow you to save your snapshots to a totally separate machine.

Chapter 40: Removing Large

Files and Log Rolling

his chapter gives a few tips relating to moving or removing files that are
consuming large amounts of disk space. In some cases, you may have a file
system that's filling up because a process adds copious amounts of entries to a log file.
When you run into a large log file which is found to be the primary cause of a full file
system, your first inclination may be to remove the file to reclaim space. However, this
may not work as you might intend.

Before I go into why, let me first talk a little about files and their structure. The file
name is the visible representation of an inode that allows you to access the data in the file.
The inode contains all the important information about a file such as its ownership,
permissions, modification times, and other items of interest. An inode also holds
information about the location of the data on the hard disk. A file name is a user-friendly
way of accessing an inode, which is represented by a number. You can determine the
inode number of any file by running the command ls -i *filename*.

Here is an example of a full directory:

```
$ ls -i
 474322 3715152.pdf       214111 rsync.tar.gz
 474633 770tref.pdf       215939 yum-2.0.5-1.fd.fr.noarch.rpm
 215944 openbox-3.1-1.i386.rpm
```

Note that in each case the inode number precedes each of the five files listed here. As just mentioned, part of the data contained in an inode is a pointer to the data on the physical disk. If the file has been opened by a process for writing, the process writes to this location on the hard disk.

The potential problem with removing a large file to clean up disk space is that if a user or an administrator removes the file, the inode may still be kept open by a process that is writing the data and the disk space will not be returned to the system. The operating system won't realize it should release the disk space for reuse until the process closes the file. At that time the disk space will definitely be reclaimed.

One way of finding out if a process is keeping a file open is to use the `fuser` command. This command will display a list of process IDs that are accessing a given file. Another utility that you can use to find this information is the `lsof` command which is specifically designed to list open files and the processes that are accessing them. Once you know the processes that are using the file, you can stop them before deleting the file. However, you may not be able (or want) to do this. The other problem with needing to stop a process that is holding a file open lies with the site limitations against stopping the offending application. The potential is that the process or application that is holding the file open might be production critical and will impact business needs if it is halted.

Another way to clean up the space used by a file is to zero out the file by redirecting `/dev/null` into the file. This trims the file down to zero bytes, while leaving the file itself in place. The file remains open and accessible to any process that might be using it. However, the operating system will release the disk space in a timely fashion. Keep in mind that some processes may keep a file open for writing for a very long time.

```
$ ls -l
total 113172
-rw-rw-r--  1 rbpeters rbpeters  1057862     Jun  7 18:21 3715152.log
-rw-rw-r--  1 rbpeters rbpeters   449184     Jun  7 18:21 770tref.log
-rw-rw-r--  1 rbpeters rbpeters 1104249096  Jun  7 21:22 really_big.log
```

Here is a sample of a directory listing, including an offending log file that is consuming large amounts of disk space. We have a choice of several possible commands that will zero out the file.

```
$ >really_big.log
```

The command above is one, `cp /dev/null really_big.log` is another, and `echo > really_big.log` is yet another. All of these commands overwrite a large file with nothing.

```
$ ls -l
total 1484
-rw-rw-r-- 1 rbpeters rbpeters  1057862   Jun  7 18:21 3715152.log
-rw-rw-r-- 1 rbpeters rbpeters   449184   Jun  7 18:21 770tref.log
-rw-rw-r-- 1 rbpeters rbpeters        0   Jun  7 21:25 really_big.log
```

This is the resulting directory listing after the file has been zeroed out.

This procedure can be used to rotate log files. For example, you may have an application for which you would like to keep one week's worth of log information. You would then rotate it to an older version to keep up to one month. After a month, you would delete the file. One solution includes the `logrotate` command which can be found on multiple Linux distributions.

Here I present a simple script that copies the existing log file to a backup with a version number and then zeroes out the file. During the time when the script is being run, any existing processes that are writing to the file will still be able to access it.

```
#!/bin/sh
LOGFILE=./my.log
if [ ! -f $LOGFILE ]
then
  echo "Nothing to do... exiting."
else
```

The code first defines the file in question and then checks whether it exists. If it does exist, execution continues.

```
  cp -p $LOGFILE ${LOGFILE}.0
  > $LOGFILE
fi
```

We've already seen the use of the re-direct (>) to zero a file. The main addition to this idea here is the `cp -p` command. This command preserves the original file's ownership and time-stamp for the new copy. Thus, the new copy maintains the attributes of the original file and it appears as if the file had been moved. This is also a useful technique when making modifications to scripts, configuration files, or any other file for which preserving the original file's attributes would be valuable.

Chapter 41: Core Finder

In a production environment, it is a good idea to know whether your applications are dumping core often. It is also considered good housekeeping to know about your core files so that your hard disk won't be filling up with unnecessary files. This small script tracks down and cleans up core files. The script was intended to be run as an hourly cron job, although you could change the schedule to fit your needs. The job also has its priority lowered using the nice command so that it won't interfere with the performance of regular processes on the machine. The notifications I've received from this script have characterized chronic issues with applications on more than one occasion. Without the script, I would have never seen the patterns.

This script steps through each of the locally mounted file systems and finds all core files. It determines the applications that created the core files and moves the core files to a central location for later examination. The script also logs its actions and cleans up old saved files.

```sh
#!/bin/sh
HOWOLD=30
FSLIST="/ /boot"
UNAME=`uname -n`
DATE=`date +%m%d%I%M`
DATADIR="/usr/local/data/cores"
LOGFILE="$DATADIR/cor_report"
```

First we have to set up some straightforward variables. The HOWOLD variable is used as the maximum age, in days, for saved core files. Any files older than this will be removed.

The FSLIST variable contains the list of file systems that will be checked for core files. The list will vary from system to system. The FSLIST variable could also be set dynamically by using the df command to determine the locally mounted file systems. The command might look something like this: FSLIST=`df -l | grep '^/dev' | awk '{print $6}'`, which gathers the lines starting with /dev and then prints the field containing the file system name.

The last few variables contain the name of the system that the script is running on, the current date, the directory to which the core files will be saved, and the name of the log file.

```
if [ ! -d $DATADIR ]
then
  mkdir -p $DATADIR
fi
```

Now we determine whether the data directory exists. This is the directory where the core files will be saved. If it doesn't exist, you have to create it. The -p option to mkdir adds any omitted parent directories to the path of the directory being created.

```
find $DATADIR -name \*\.core\.\* -mtime +$HOWOLD -exec rm {} \;
```

Then you need to find all previously saved core files that don't need to be kept around anymore and remove them.

```
for file in `find $FSLIST -mount -type f -name core -print`
do
  if [ -s $file ]
  then
    coretype=`file $file | cut -d\' -f2`
    mv $file $DATADIR/$UNAME.core.$coretype.$DATE
    echo "$coretype $UNAME $DATADIR/$UNAME.core.$coretype.$DATE" | tee
-a $LOGFILE | mailx -s "core_finder: $coretype core file found on
$UNAME" sysadmins
  else
    rm $file
  fi
done
```

Here is the main loop of the script. It finds all the new core files created since the last time the script was run. If a core file is zero bytes in size, we should just remove it. If it is larger than zero bytes, we use the file command to determine the application that created the core file. Then the core file is saved in the archive directory, and its name is changed to include the type of core and the date when the file was found. Then we add an entry to the log file noting the action that was taken, and send an email notice to the administrators.

Chapter 42: Network Adapter

Fail-over

The purpose of this script is to provide network redundancy. It monitors the network accessibility of the local machine for issues. When there is a problem detected with a primary network interface, it reverts its configuration to a backup interface. We are assuming a network architecture where two network interfaces cards (NICs) are installed in the machine that runs the script. It is also assumed that there are network connections running to both interfaces which are configured in the same the same fashion (subnet/vlan, speed, duplex, and so on). Each interface should be physically connected to a different network switches for the sake of redundancy.

The goal is that if the primary network hardware fails for any reason, the system will recognize the lack of connectivity and switch the network settings over to a backup interface. This script probably wouldn't be be very useful in a small environment, as redundant network hardware can get expensive. However, it is a good tool for use in an environment where high availability and redundancy are key.

This script performs very well: In testing, I was logged into the system through the network and after executing some commands validating connection, I disconnected the primary interface cable. The fail over of the interface occurred in less than 10 seconds and my command line session carried on as if nothing had happened.

Depending on when the interface failure occurs, the maximum time for a fail over to complete would probably be about 15 seconds. The script first checks network availability, sleeps for 10 seconds, wakes up and checks again, and continuously repeats this process. The shortest amount of time that the script could take to recognize and execute a fail over is probably less than 5 seconds. I would imagine that most systems can take that amount of interruption without much impact.

```
#!/bin/sh
LOG=/var/log/messages
PRIMARY=eth0
SECONDARY=eth1
ME=`uname -n`
```

Like many scripts in this book, the configuration of variables happens in the script itself. It would probably make for cleaner code to save the configuration information in a separate file, which can then be sourced from the script. If this were done, you could change the values without interfering with the code .

This first group of configuration variables sets up the log file where log entries for any potential network failures will be entered. The primary and secondary interface names are also defined. These names will change depending on your hardware and operating system. For instance, network interfaces on most Linux machines have names like eth0 or eth1. Other UNIX variants might use names such as iprb0 or en1. We also determine the system name so that fail over messages can indicate the machine that had the problem.

```
IP=`grep $ME /etc/hosts | grep -v '^#' | awk '{print $1}'`
NETMASK=255.255.255.0
BROADCAST="`echo $IP | cut -d\. -f1-3`.255"
```

The next section sets the networking information. These are the settings that will be switched when a failure occurs. The networking information will also be specific to your implementation. You will need to determine your IP address appropriately. The address could be located in quite a few places: possibly the local hosts file (as shown here) or the NIS or DNS information locations. The IP address could also have been set manually. The subnet mask and broadcast address are also system-specific.

```
PINGLIST="Replace with a space-separated list of IP addresses"
PING_COUNT=2
SLEEPTIME=10
MAILLIST=sysadmins
```

The next set of configuration variables determines the way the script monitors for network availability. The PINGLIST variable holds a list of IP addresses situated in a route architecturally beyond the switches to which the redundant interfaces are attached. All PINGLIST addresses should refer to systems that are always running such as core network routers. The variable can specify any number of IP addresses. Having a single address doesn't give enough redundancy, whereas two or three do. I used three router addresses outside our local subnet.

The PING_COUNT and SLEEPTIME variables describe the number of pings to use for each of the addresses in the PINGLIST and the amount of time to sleep between network checks.

```
if [ "`uname | grep -i hp`" != "" ]
then
  ping_switch="-n"
elif [ "`uname | grep -i linux`" != "" ]
then
  ping_switch="-c"
fi
```

The ping utility has operating system–dependent command-line switches that are used when sending specific numbers of ping packets to a system. This check determines the OS of the system the script is running on. It then sets a variable containing the appropriate ping switch.

```
NICS=`netstat -i | awk '{print $1}' | \
  egrep -vi "Kernel|Iface|Name|lo" | sort -u`
NIC_COUNT=`netstat -i | awk '{print $1}' | \
  egrep -v "Kernel|Iface|Name|lo" | sort -u | wc -l`
```

Now we have to determine the currently active network interfaces. The script needs to know which interface is the primary interface prior to entering the main loop. This is so that it will be able to switch interfaces in the correct direction. The commands may need to be validated on your specific operating system. There may also be other values that you'll want to filter out with the egrep command. For instance, on my FreeBSD box, there is a point-to-point interface that I wouldn't want involved, and I'd filter it out here.

```
if [ $NIC_COUNT -gt 1 ]
then
  for nic in $NICS
  do
    current=`ifconfig $nic | grep $IP`
    if [ "$current" != "" ]
    then
      CURRENT_NIC=$nic
    fi
  done
```

```
else
  CURRENT_NIC=$NICS
fi
```

Now we have the list of currently active interfaces on the system. If there is only one interface, we of course assume it to be the primary interface. If there are more interfaces, we loop through all the active ones to find the interface with the specified primary IP address and make it the current interface.

```
if [ "$CURRENT_NIC" = "$SECONDARY" ]
then
  SECONDARY=$PRIMARY
  PRIMARY=$CURRENT_NIC
fi
```

If the initial active primary interface is the specified SECONDARY interface, you have to reverse the variables so that the script won't switch interfaces in the wrong direction.

```
while :
do
  sleep $SLEEPTIME
  answer=""
```

This starts the main loop for checking the availability of the network. It starts by sleeping for the configured amount of time and then initializing the variable for the ping response.

```
  for node in $PINGLIST
  do
    if ping $node $ping_switch $PING_COUNT > /dev/null 2>&1
    then
      answer="${answer}alive"
    else
      answer="${answer}"
    fi
  done
```

The core of the script can be found in this loop. It iterates through each of the IP addresses in the PINGLIST variable and sends two pings to each of them. The answer is based on the return code of the ping. If a ping fails, the return code of the ping will be nonzero. If the ping is successful, the `answer` variable will have '*alive*' appended to it. Under normal conditions, if all routers addresses are replying, the `answer` variable will be in the form of "alivealivealive" (if you have, say, three addresses in the `PINGLIST`).

```
if [ "$answer" != "" ]
then
    echo network is working...
        continue
```

If the answer from the pings is non-null, we break out of the loop since the network is available. Thus, all IP addresses present in the `PINGLIST` variable must fail to respond for a fail over to occur. This allows us to avoid moving the network settings unnecessarily in the event of one IP address in the `PINGLIST` being slow to respond or down when the network is in fact available through the primary interface.

```
else
    logger -i -t nic_switch -f $LOG "Ping failed on $PINGLIST"
    logger -i -t nic_switch -f $LOG "Possible nic or switch \
        failure. Moving $IP from $PRIMARY to $SECONDARY"
```

If all pings fail, you should use the `logger` program to put an entry in the `LOG` file. Logger is a shell interface to `syslog`. Using `syslog` to track the fail over in this way is simpler than creating your own formatted entry to the log file.

```
ifconfig $PRIMARY down
ifconfig $SECONDARY $IP netmask $NETMASK broadcast $BROADCAST
ifconfig $SECONDARY up
```

Now we perform the actual interface swap. First we need to take down the primary interface. Then we have to configure the secondary interface. Depending on your operating system, the final command to bring up the newly configured interface may not be required. With Linux, configuring the interface is enough to bring it on line, whereas Solaris requires the separate command to this.

In Solaris, the interface remains visible with the `ifconfig` command after it is brought down. To remove the entry, we have to perform an '`ifconfig INTERFACE unplumb`'. The same command used with the `plumb` option accomplishes the opposite. FreeBSD will work with the same command options, although this has only been provided for Solaris compatibility. The native `ifconfig` options for FreeBSD are `create` and `destroy`.

```
echo "`date +%b\ %d\ %T` $ME nic_switch[$$]: Possible nic or \
```

```
        switch failure. Moving $IP from $PRIMARY to $SECONDARY" | \
        mail -s "Nic failover performed on $ME" $MAILLIST
```

We now need to send out an email notification that the primary interface had an issue and was switched over to an alternate NIC. An additional check here to verify that the network is available would probably be wise. This way, if both interfaces are down, mail won't start filling the mail queue.

```
        place_holder=$PRIMARY
        PRIMARY=$SECONDARY
        SECONDARY=$place_holder
    fi
done
```

Now that the interfaces have been switched, the script will swap the values of the PRIMARY and SECONDARY variables so any subsequent fail overs will be performed in the right direction.

Appendix A: Test Switches

 One of the fundamental elements of programming is the ability to compare: you test for certain conditions to be able to make decisions. The test command can be used to evaluate many items such as variables, strings, and numbers among others. This appendix is another reference that I like to keep close at hand since I haven't memorized all of the parameters. I often use these switches for checking files and strings and this is a simple quick reference for easy lookup. Note that the **test** column refers to the system command test such as `/usr/bin/test`. The **bash** and **ksh** columns refer to the built-in test command for those shells.

Switch	test	bash	ksh	Definition
-a FILE	•	✓	✓	FILE simply exists.
-b FILE	✓	✓	✓	FILE exists and it is a block special file such as a disk device in `/dev`.
-c FILE	✓	✓	✓	FILE exists and it is a character special file such as a tty device in `/dev`.
-d FILE	✓	✓	✓	FILE exists and it is a standard directory.
-e FILE	✓	✓	✓	FILE simply exists.
-f FILE	✓	✓	✓	FILE exists and it is a standard file such as a flat file.
-g FILE	✓	✓	✓	FILE exists and it is set-group-ID. This is the file permission that changes the users effective group on execution of the file.
-G FILE	✓	✓	✓	FILE exists and its group ownership is the effective group ID of the user.
-h FILE	✓	✓	✓	FILE exists and it is a symbolic link. This is the same as -L.

Switch	test	bash	ksh	Definition
-k FILE	✓	✓	✓	FILE exists and it has the sticky bit set. This means that only the owner of the file or the owner of the directory may remove the file.
-l STRING	✓	•	•	Length of STRING is compared to a numeric value such as: `/usr/bin/test -l string -gt 5 && echo`
-L FILE	✓	✓	✓	FILE exists and it is a symbolic link. This is the same as -h.
-n STRING	✓	✓	✓	STRING has non-zero length.
-N FILE	•	✓	✓	FILE exists and has been modified since it was last read.
-o OPTION	•	✓	✓	True if shell OPTION is enabled such as `set -x`.
-O FILE	✓	✓	✓	FILE exists and its ownership is determined by the effective user ID.
-p FILE	✓	✓	✓	FILE exists and it is a named pipe (or FIFO).
-r FILE	✓	✓	✓	FILE exists and it is readable.
-s FILE	✓	✓	✓	FILE exists and its size is greater than zero bytes.
-S FILE	✓	✓	✓	FILE exists and it is a socket.
-t [FD]	✓	✓	✓	FD (file descriptor) is opened on a terminal. This is `stdout` by default.
-u FILE	✓	✓	✓	FILE exists and it has the set-user-ID bit is set.
-w FILE	✓	✓	✓	FILE exists and it is writable.
-x FILE	✓	✓	✓	FILE exists and it is executable.
-z STRING	✓	✓	✓	STRING has a length of zero.

Table C-1: Test Switches

Appendix B: Special Parameters

Shell special parameters are variables internal to the shell. These variables reference various items such as the parameters passed to a script or function, process ids, and return codes. It is not possible to assign a value to them since they can only be referenced.

This appendix is a compilation of the parameters available in bash, ksh, pdksh and Bourne sh. All of these variables are accessible in each of the shells mentioned except for $_ which is not available in the Bourne shell. I have referred to these variables many times while I code with a book lying open in front of me and I found that this section comes in handy.

It isn't necessarily obvious from the man page that you would need to pre-pend the variables with a '$' sign to reference these variables. For instance, to find the value of the return code of the previous command, you would use a command like this:

```
echo $?
```

or

```
RETURN_CODE=$? ; echo $RETURN_CODE
```

Parameter	Definition
*	*Complete list of all positional parameters starting at 1. If double quoted, becomes a single word delimited by the first character of the IFS value.*
@	*Complete list of all positional parameters starting at 1. If double quoted, becomes individual words for each positional parameter.*
#	*The number of positional parameters in decimal.*
?	*The return code from the last foregrounded job. If the job is killed by a signal, the return code is 128 plus the value of the signal. Example: Standard kill is signal 15*

Parameter	Definition
	which would result in a return code of 143.
-	*(dash) All of the flags sent to the shell or provided by the set command.*
$	*The process ID of this shell. If in a sub-shell, this expands to the value of the current shell, not the sub-shell.*
!	*The process ID of the most recently backgrounded command.*
_	*(underscore) Expands to the last argument of the previous command.*
0	*Expands to the name of the shell or shell script.*
1...9	*The positional parameters provided to the shell, function or script. Values larger than 9 can be accessed with ${number}.*

Table B-1: Shell Internal Special Parameters

Appendix C: Other Shell

Scripting Resources

Manual Pages

When you are working on a Linux or UNIX system, the resources you will nearly always have at hand are your system man pages. This means that a copious amount of free and detailed information regarding your specific system is available and man pages are highly recommended. With that said, man pages are not always known to be intuitively understandable or easy to read but they are usually accurate. In all, I would advise you to take the rough with the smooth.

I would also recommend looking at similar man pages from different system types to gain differing views of the same utility. For example, I have noted that the `proc` man page on one version of Linux is not as complete as that of another Linux version, although the more complete version is still applicable to the other. Another example is the `date` man page on Linux that contains many formatting options where a Solaris man page does not, even though the formatting syntax still functions on Solaris. If you have a variety of systems available to you, it is worth the comparison.

Books

Scripting Books

Here are a few books, all of which I have on my bookshelf although some of mine aren't the current revision. This first group relates to the nuts and bolts of shell scripting in that they teach you how to script and use various shell types. The first two I have used for many years (older editions) and have found them highly valuable.

Olczak, Anatole. *The Korn Shell User and Programming Manual*. Addison-Wesley, 1997.

Kochan, Stephen and Patrick Wood. *UNIX Shell Programming Third Edition*. Sams, 2003

Burtch, Ken O. *Linux Shell Scripting with Bash*. Sams, 2004.

Supplementary Books

This group is my tier two book recommendation list. They are not necessarily related to shell scripting directly but they are an excellent resource for enhancing your scripting capabilities. I have used all of them from time to time when coding shell scripts.

Dougherty, Dale and Arnold Robbins. *sed & awk 2nd Edition*. O'Reilly, 1997.

Mccarthy, Martin. *The Procmail Companion*. Addison-Wesley, 2001.

Libes, Don. *Exploring Expect*. O'Reilly, 1994.

Friedl, Jeffrey E. F. *Mastering Regular Expressions*. O'Reilly, 2002.

Frisch, Æleen. *Essential System Administration Third Edition*. O'Reilly, 2002.

Nemeth, Evi, Garth Snyder, Scott Seebass and Trent R. Hein. *UNIX System Administration Handbook Third Edition*. Prentice Hall, 2000.

Taylor, Dave. *Wicked Cool Shell Scripts*. No Starch Press, 2004.

Shell Resources

The following sites are the primary sources of shell scripting wisdom. They contain various levels of information including documentation, man pages, FAQs, and download instructions.

The Bash shell site: http://www.gnu.org/software/bash/bash.html.

The Korn shell site: http://www.kornshell.com/

The Pdksh shell Site: http://web.cs.mun.ca/~michael/pdksh/

Online Resources

There are endless resources on the Internet relating to shell scripting. Carefully selected search criteria is only a search engine away. The following resources represent a selection of what I have used over the years.

Advanced Bash Scripting Guide: (http://www.tldp.org/LDP/abs/html/). This is a complete how-to shell scripting guide that starts out from the beginning and assumes no previous expertise, and then works up to advanced scripting.

Introduction to the Bourne Shell by its inventor:
(http://www.softlab.ece.ntua.gr/facilities/documentation/unix/docs/sh.txt). I've not found
an official Bourne shell site but this is a good start. There are also plenty of other Bourne
shell programming guides available.

Heiners Shelldorado – your UNIX shell scripting resource.
(http://www.shelldorado.com). This site is an excellent resource for all sorts of shell-
related topics. There are articles, best practices, tutorials, tips, scripts and more.

SysAdmin Magazine. (http://www.samag.com). This publication does not focus
specifically on shell-scripting and is mainly focused on system administration, but it
usually has some excellent shell-programming articles discussing useful procedures or
problem solutions.

LiveFire Labs (http://www.livefirelabs.com) is a hands-on UNIX training company.
On their site they have an email list you can sign up for that will send you the UNIX tip,
trick or shell script of the week.

Usenet comp.unix.shell group. Though not a web site, this resource is one of the best
that I have found relating to shell scripting. It is a news discussion group that focuses on
everything to do with shells. There are incredibly talented people hanging out in this
Usenet group willing to answer your shell related questions. There is also a vast amount
of history that can be searched and an FAQ maintained by its members.

Printed in the United States
88141LV00004B/8/A